LEOPARDI

and the

THEORY

of

POETRY

∽

by

G. SINGH

∽

UNIVERSITY OF KENTUCKY PRESS

Copyright © 1964 by the University of Kentucky Press
Manufactured in the United States of America
Library of Congress Catalog Card
No. 64-14001

TO

Geoffrey Tillotson

IN ADMIRATION AND GRATITUDE

Preface

As its title indicates fairly clearly, this book does not deal exclusively with Leopardi's theory of poetry as such, but also with its relation or its similarity with other theories or views of poetry, with its background and sources, with its influence and implications as well as with its evaluation in the light of what has been written on the subject since Leopardi's death in 1837. The word theory itself has been used in a sense somewhat different from the usual—in a sense, that is to say, that neither implies nor presupposes an organic and coherent system conceived in philosophical or quasi-philosophical terms. Again, the phrase theory of poetry, while it is used for the most part to mean views concerning the art and nature of poetry as poetry, does, since poetry is a part of literature, include the theory of literature and literary criticism as well. For indeed after a certain point the distinction between the theory of poetry or literature and literary criticism itself, both in its essence and actual application, tends inevitably to disappear— which is, of course, as it should be.

Comparison between Leopardi and other critics and theorists of poetry—especially Wordsworth, Coleridge, and Housman, whom Leopardi does peculiarly resemble—has been resorted to as a useful expedient as well as an effective means for determining the range, depth, and subtlety of Leopardi's meaning and all its multiple implications. This does not, of course, mean that this sort of approach by means of comparison and contrast between Leopardi and others with an altogether different background, tradition, and training is the only approach that has been adopted in these pages; nor that it has altogether supplanted another equally sound and valid approach, namely, that of studying the critical thought of a given writer in its proper historical setting and tracing and analyzing all its real or conjectural sources, as much, if not sometimes actually even more than, what that thought is *per se*. The book, in fact, tends to combine these two approaches—combine them consciously and as a matter of principle—as often as it is possible to do so within the space available.

However, it is Leopardi's thought in itself—whether his own original thought or the thought of others that he has characteristically made his own—that counts in this book far more than anything else. For even where the source is definitely clear and irrefutable, what mainly interests a student of Leopardi's theory of poetry is not so much what its source is, though that too is of capital importance, as it is the reason why he borrowed, or even unconsciously echoed, the ideas of a given writer. Many writers—perhaps most—while consciously or unconsciously, and especially unconsciously, imitating others do not but imitate themselves. There is, then, another thing that makes a radical difference. Leopardi's achievement in the field of creative writing is simply so formidable that his pronouncements on the very art and process of creating are bound to command more respect and more confidence, and therefore they prove more effective and more persuasive, than those of a mere theorist or philosopher of poetry who has no practical experience of what he is talking about. In other words one cannot shirk the conclusion—and in this case, as in so many others, the exceptions merely prove and strengthen the rule—that the greater the artist, the more valuable his criticism and his views on the art he practices are bound to be. Hence, for example, the same opinions expressed by Leopardi in *Zibaldone* and elsewhere, as have been expressed by much less creatively gifted and inspired poets like Monti and Tommaseo, possess a greater value and mean something quite profounder and subtler and carry a greater conviction behind them in his hands than in the hands of the latter. As to what originality and imitation in this connection mean Leopardi himself enlightens us with the following thought of his: "Both the poet and the philosopher can be original while dealing with one and the same truth. For not only to different individuals, but even to the same individual . . . the same truths appear in different forms on different occasions . . . so that the individual, unless he has great powers of penetration and attention and an exceptionally good memory, would hardly be able to recognize those truths to be the same as he has already seen and considered. Thus a philosopher as well as a poet, while dealing with the same truth, can differentiate himself and be original, not only in regard to others, but even in regard to himself."[1] Not the intrinsic originality of a thought or a concept in itself, but the original which means, among other things, the personal and individual way of making it relevant to the entire framework of one's thinking and dialectics, is what really matters in the case of ideas that a poet may choose to express outside his poetry.

One reason why Leopardi's thought is often put together along with the thought of a modern or contemporary writer or critic, and examined and analyzed in relation to that thought is to show the almost incredible modernity of Leopardi's ideas—modernity in virtue of which he has been considered by the consensus of critical opinion, both in Italy and abroad, to be the most pioneering, the most liberal-minded, and the most original of all the poetic theorists of the nineteenth century, and, indeed, so far as Italy is concerned, of all times.

I am grateful to Carlo Dionisotti, Professor of Italian, Bedford College, London University, J. H. Whitfield, Professor of Italian, Birmingham University, and René Wellek, Professor of Comparative Literature, Yale University, for their reading of the manuscript and for making some extremely valuable suggestions. This book also owes a special debt to the numerous discussions, conversations and consultations that it has been my privilege to have with such distinguished Italian critics as Sergio Solmi, Professor Mario Fubini, and the late Professor Francesco Flora. Whatever else the defects and loopholes of this book may be due to, they certainly cannot be ascribed to a lack of mature and authoritative guidance—a guidance that has proved very useful even when there was on certain points a divergence of opinion between them and me. I also wish to record my deepest thanks to Professor Ettore Mazzali and Miss Raffaella Solmi, of whose generous help in so many things and at so many stages of my work I have availed myself quite frequently. The charmingly modest way Miss Solmi wears her learning and her sound understanding of the spirit of Leopardi's work may itself be taken as a lesson in practical criticism—especially when one has to deal with a figure like Leopardi, in respect of whom nobody, I suppose, could be too learned.

It is my pleasure to record another kind of debt to my personal friends—Kenneth G. Laycock and Dr. Martin S. Allwood. Whenever there was any hitch clogging the evolution or expression of certain thoughts, any problem that seemed too complicated to induce right thinking or any thinking at all, a friendly and casual chat with them, whether they were conscious of its effect on me or not—and in all likelihood they were not—swiftly cleared the path of the argument and gave me back my hold on things that I seemed for the nonce to have lost. Another personal friend—Miss Ritva Tuutti—and still another—Thomas Evans—helped me in a more material way: the former, together with Miss Laura Ferruta, in preparing the index and in checking the notes, and the latter, together with Anna Postiglione, in going through the proofs. To all these friends, therefore, I am very sincerely grateful.

And in so far as this book may make any claim to manifesting even in the scantiest degree the spirit of criticism, the claim has to be related to the critical stimulus as well as critical discipline, "the curb as well as the spur," to borrow Longinus' famous expression, that a study of the writings of Dr. F. R. Leavis, on the one hand, and Professor Geoffrey Tillotson, on the other, infallibly provides. To both of these critics therefore I am deeply and particularly grateful.

Milan, June 1963   G. SINGH

Contents

Contents

CHAPTER ONE

Leopardi's Critical Method and Principles

∽

No POET in the history of Italian literature occupied himself with the theory of poetry so much as Leopardi; and, indeed, "few men have given so much hard thought to the matter."[1] As a poetic theorist, he not only compares well with Goethe, Wordsworth, and Coleridge on the one hand, and Edgar Allan Poe and Baudelaire on the other, but in virtue of his classical learning and philological scholarship, which he brought to bear on certain aspects of the literary and poetic theory, especially the linguistic and stylistic aspects, he easily surpasses them all. Moreover, the range of the literary and philosophical reference within which his critical mind worked was not limited to ancient thought and literature; it embraced modern literature and modern thought as well. Besides French and Italian literatures, which he had thoroughly mastered, he was also fairly well acquainted with the major literary works in English, German, and Spanish. Hence for his "incomparable literary education" alone, leaving aside the still more important fact that he was "the greatest Italian writer of modern times,"[2] Leopardi's views on the art of poetry as well as on individual authors and works deserve our serious consideration. Indeed, *Operette Morali*, "Discorso di un italiano intorno alla poesia romantica," *Epistolario*, and, above all, *Zibaldone* constitute a body of criticism as remarkable for its depth and soundness as for its range and variety.

In *Zibaldone* and elsewhere not only is Leopardi uninterested in expounding any systematic philosophy of art or poetry, but he does not even pretend to throw any new light on the revaluation of any particular author or question in literary history. His main interest is to register impressions and reactions in the course of his loving study of both ancient and modern literary masterpieces and to ponder on their implications. Having little or no use for a priori rules and formulas, Leopardi considered each work of art to be itself furnishing, to a discerning mind, the very basis and criteria, according to which it ought to be judged. Invented by "poor grammarians," rules serve to produce not art but artifice; and while art "conserves the variety and delight of nature, artifice, which is the food of reason, is monotonous and it is merely the product of 'dry' curiosity."[3] Hence his condemnation of literary academies like the Della Crusca as being detrimental to the progress of arts. All great poets among the Greeks, for instance, had written before Aristotle, as all the Latin poets before or at the same time as Horace. As against academies and systems of rules and formulas, Leopardi favors the possession or cultivation of good taste both among

the individuals and the nations.[4] Homer, who wrote
before any rules were formed, did not dream, says
Leopardi, that from what was so fresh and original
in his work, rules and formulas would be derived that
would prevent others from following his own example,
i.e., from being "true, irregular, great, and original
like him."[5] Hence Leopardi's attitude to preestab-
lished rules and canons governing creative arts, and
even the very science or art of criticism, and his
desire to assert the autonomy of both creative activity
and the critical function is more or less the same as
that of Coleridge, though he had never heard the
latter's name. "Could a rule be given from *without*,"
said Coleridge, "poetry would cease to be poetry,
and sink into a mechanical art."[6] Instead of assessing
the literary worth of a work merely in terms of the
degree to which it measures up to certain preconceived notions or standards derived from past models,
one should, Leopardi emphasized, try to enter into
the very spirit of a given work, both in so far as it is
different from and in so far as it is similar to other
masterpieces. And this one can do not so much by
analyzing the milieu or the personality of the artist,
as by recreating and reexperiencing the spirit and
meaning of that work of art within the bounds of
one's own imagination, sensibility, and culture, or by
transferring it into ourselves.[7] For all his respect for
the ancient classics, and especially for Homer, "the
father and the perpetual principle of all the poets of
the world,"[8] Leopardi never fails to stress the link
between the reader's or the critic's inner world of

sensibility and experience (both of life and of other works of art and poetry), and his ability to judge a particular work of art. It is in this sense that one can say of Leopardi that he combines the sense of tradition with the spirit of modernity. And tradition does not mean blind subservience or uncritical acceptance of the classics, any more than modernity means a cloak for inane extravagances or innovations, indulged for their own sakes. One proof of Leopardi's critical liberalism and independence of judgment is the fact that in turning to ancient critics, literary historians, and theorists he does not always follow the footsteps of Plato and Aristotle, but quotes minor poets, historians, and orators as well.

Leopardi's theory of poetry, like all theories of poetry more or less, is based on certain fundamental assumptions regarding the role of memory, imagination, sentiments, and sensibility as well as the nature and function of poetry itself. It is inseparably bound up with his particular view of life, with what may be called his philosophical system, which has its roots in eighteenth-century French thought and literature. "All great poetry," says T. S. Eliot, "gives the illusion of a view of life. When we enter into the world of Homer, or Sophocles, or Virgil, or Dante or Shakespear, we incline to believe that we are apprehending something that can be expressed intellectually; for every precise emotion tends towards intellectual formation."[9] Not only in Leopardi's poetry, but even in Leopardi's theory of poetry we have something like

[4]

this illusion. His never-failing sense of the fundamental unity between art and life happily prevented him from divorcing the aesthetic pleasure or emotion from the moral and intellectual aspects of poetry, from divorcing form from content, and contemplating them in isolation.

Some, Fubini for one, have found Leopardi's union of the aesthetic with the moral a weakness in his theory. In Leopardi, Fubini tells us, "an aesthetic problem is transformed . . . into a moral problem: the primitive spontaneity of true poetry, which Leopardi exalts, and whose unique model he sees in his Greeks, is mistaken by him for every other form of spontaneous life which reason falsifies and mortifies."[10] The vital humanity of Leopardi's attitude to poetry lies mainly in this: that he identified poetry with every spontaneous form and manifestation of life.[11] In other words, there is, in this attitude, something at once more human and more philosophical than one usually finds in a purely literary or critical attitude. Defining the function of a philosopher, which in his view cannot altogether be separated from that of a literary critic or a poet,[12] Leopardi notes:

Naturally and of necessity [a philosopher] looks for a thread in his consideration of things. It is impossible for him to be content with isolated notions and truths. If he had contented himself with these, his philosophy would have been the most trivial and the most wretched, and would not have yielded any result. The aim of philosophy (in the widest sense of the term) is to discover the causes of truths. These causes are to be found only in the interrelationships among these truths, and they are to be found by means of generalization. Do we not know that the faculty of generalization alone constitutes the thinker? Do we not admit that philosophy consists of speculation on these relationships?[13]

It is in relating the specific problems of literary criticism and poetic theory to the general problems of life, in deriving from the criticism of life not only the material for his poetry, but also the values and criteria by which that poetry ought to be judged, that Leopardi's merit as a philosophic critic or theorist of poetry lies. His absorbing concern is not with the form or technique of poetry, though one of the paramount qualities of his own poetry is its formal and prosodic excellence, nor even with style in the abstract sense, though his own style (both prose and poetry) is uniformly superb, but with poetry in its purest essence. But instead of defining this essence in metaphorical terms—such as "the breath and finer spirit of all knowledge . . . the impassioned expression which is in the countenance of all science" (Wordsworth), or "the identity of all other knowledges, the blossom of all other systems of thought . . . the perfect and consummate surface and bloom of all things" (Shelley) —terms and definitions which, for all their rhapsodical charm, leave the essence of poetry as much in the vague as ever, Leopardi tries to approach this essence not in order to discover what it is *per se,* but in order to identify and characterize the qualities common to all great poetry, and, as far as possible, to try to account for them. Hence, whatever amount of interdependence there might be between Leopardi's poetry and his theory of poetry, it does not constitute exactly the same sort of relationship as one finds between, say Shelley's poetry and his *Defence of Poetry.* Of the latter, W. P. Ker says that "it is not itself poetry and Shelley would not have us think so. But it is one mode in which he expresses a theory which is expressed poetically in *Prometheus* and *Adonais.* The prose meaning of the *Defence* is the poetical meaning of Asia and Urania."[14] Now this cannot be said of the meaning of the *Canti* and the general critical import of Leopardi's poetic theory, which consists, for the most part, of factually plain and prosaic observations concerning the art of poetry treated almost as a science. The content of Leopardi's poetic theory is largely intellectual rather than emotional, and it is constructive only in so far as it is analytical. Behind each and everything he condemns or exalts there is always the specific prose-reason why he does so; and it is his own critical sensibility, rather than any a priori rules or standards, which molds his judgments and reactions. Appreciation and criticism, evaluation and analysis are not two processes divided into tight compartments, as unfortunately they sometimes are, but two complementary aspects of the same process in Leopardi's poetic and critical theory. And the language he employs is mostly a language consisting of direct and factual remarks, and, as far as possible, shunning rather than, like Goethe or the English romantics, indulging in mystical and emotive observations.

If, however, Leopardi does sometimes use the

metaphorical language while talking of poetry, it is not so much in order to adorn or mystify, as to clarify and drive home a particular truth. For instance, while differentiating between poetic vocabulary and scientific vocabulary, he observes:

It is the duty of poets and writers (who create *belles lettres*) to cover as far as possible the nudity of things, just as it is the duty of scientists and philosophers to reveal it. Hence, precise words suit the latter, and they are extremely unsuitable for the former. . . . To a scientist the more precise and more expressive of an idea in all its nudity the words are, the more convenient they are. On the contrary, to a poet and to a man of letters the more vague and the more expressive of uncertain ideas and of a large number of ideas the words are, the better.[15]

The metaphorical phrase, "to cover the nudity of things," makes the poet's thought and its various implications more clear and impressive than an analytically factual statement would have done, since the subject happens to be such a subtle and abstruse one as not so much the difference but the distinction between the poet's language and the language of science. Moreover, the phrase "the nudity of things" does in itself embody a very rich and very typical concept of Leopardi's. It does not mean the same thing as, for example, Tasso's phrase "the naked material" in "Discorso dell'arte poetica," material, as Tasso himself explains, "which has not yet received any quality from a poet's or an orator's artifice." For Leopardi, on the other hand, the phrase means the reality of things as they are in themselves—a reality that is not simply less beautiful than poetic illusions, but also more restricted in its scope and relevance than it would be if charged with the pathos and power of illusions, which confer on it almost a symbolic value. Similarly, to take another example, Leopardi's statement that an inexperienced person has always a more or less poetic character, and that he becomes prosaic with experience,[16] sums up the opposition between worldly experience and poetic character, but not between experience and poetry, because the songs of experience are as legitimately poetry as the songs of innocence.

For all his concern with going to the very root of the problem, and for all his endowment as a thinker, which was certainly richer than that of a Wordsworth or a Shelley, Leopardi rarely strayed into the realm of metaphysical abstractions or metaphorical rhetoric while discussing poetry. To his life-long study of poetry and his own experience as a poet, Leopardi added a long and close study of philology. This enabled him to compare the poetic validity of one word with that of another, the vocabulary of one poet or epoch with the vocabulary of another, and sometimes to distinguish between the nuances of meaning and poetic character of the same word in the same author occurring in different works or even in the different contexts of the same work. The poet's art, for Leopardi, lies not so much in the invention of new things, or in communicating original ideas or truths, as in the manipulations of words in such a way as to be able to create a new effect, a new melody, a new style. Extremely dubious of the

novelty of subject-matter or content as being a very
useful or important factor in poetry, Leopardi emphasizes that poetry should move us by means of those
very objects that we already knew before we started
reading poetry, and should delight us through those
very causes and circumstances, which are already
familiar to us. The poet's art consists in choosing

the most beautiful things among the known things, in
newly and harmoniously . . . arranging the known things
and adapting them to the capacity of the majority, newly
clothing, adorning and embellishing them by means of
the harmony of verse, metaphors, and every other splendor
of style, in conferring light and nobility upon the unknown and ignoble things, in giving novelty to what is
commonplace, in changing, as if by some magical incanta-
tion, the aspect of anything he happens to be dealing
with; in taking, for instance, persons from nature and
making them talk naturally, but nonetheless in such a way
that the reader, while recognizing in that language the
very language he is used to hear from such persons in
real life in similar circumstances, may at the same time
find it new and incomparably more beautiful than the
ordinary language on account of the poetic ornaments,
the new style, in a word, the new form and body which
the poet has given it.[17]

This reads like a condensed but more lucid account
of practically all the major arguments that parade
through Wordsworth's celebrated *Preface* as well as
through Coleridge's equally celebrated critical examination thereof.

Similarly Leopardi's account of the nature and
function of poetic imagination is far more simple and
straightforward, without being less elucidating, than,

say, sometimes that of Coleridge himself. "That synthetic and magical power," says Coleridge, "to which
I would exclusively appropriate the name of imagination . . . reveals itself in the balance or reconciliation
of opposite or discordant qualities . . . the sense of
novelty and freshness with old and familiar objects;
a more than usual state of emotion with more than
usual order; judgment ever awake and steady self-
possession with enthusiasm and feeling profound or
vehement."[18] And the chief gifts of imagination are
"the sense of musical delight . . . together with the
power of reducing multitude into unity of effect, and
modifying a series of thoughts by some one predominant thought or feeling."[19] In comparison, Leopardi, regarding imagination as "the most fertile and
most marvellous inventor of the most hidden relationships and harmonies,"[20] points out that a man endowed
with such imagination ". . . sees such connections,
passes on from one proposition to another so rapidly,
understands the link between them so vividly and so
easily, accumulates so many syllogisms in one moment,
and all so well-connected, so well-ordinated and so
clearly conceived that in one leap he covers the
distance of many centuries."[21] As to the inventive
power of imagination, Leopardi goes even further
than Coleridge, in so far as he regards it as not only
the fountainhead of sentiments, passions, and poetry,
but of reason itself. It is imagination that makes
"great philosophers and the discoverers of great
truths," imagination from which, when "differently
applied, differently modified, and differently deter-

mined by diverse circumstances and habits, came the poems of Homer and Dante, and the mathematical principles of the natural philosophy of Newton."[22]

Thus Leopardi's critical as well as interpretative pronouncements have both the edge and concreteness of a particular truth or statement and the depth and universality of what is called a generalization. In this he may be compared with Samuel Johnson, for neither he nor Johnson thought of literary criticism as being something essentially different from the general criticism of life. Leopardi's theory of poetry itself is constantly buttressed by a solid hold on the realities of human nature on the one hand, and by a full awareness of the specific problems and difficulties of practical literary criticism on the other. It is only by disassociating Leopardi's poetic theory from the general critical awareness that almost invariably informs it that one can come to the partial view of that theory as being, to quote Mario Fubini, "rather an ideal of art than a concept of art, rather a moving celebration of poetry than a satisfactory definition of the aesthetic activity."[23] As to the definition of the so-called aesthetic activity and its absence from Leopardi's theory and criticism of poetry, one can dismiss the charge by reminding oneself of F. R. Leavis's highly apt statement that "as so often, the term 'aesthetic' signals a lack of grip."[24] If while theorizing about the nature and effect of poetry, Leopardi is at times capable of soaring into what Santayana calls the "realm of essence" and of arriving at that "intuition of pure Being as well as the sense

[12]

of existence" without which, as Sir Herbert Read so rightly points out, "the highest poetry is inconceivable,"[25] it is mainly on account of his taking a habitual recourse to hard analytical reflection, backed up as it almost invariably is by a keen and alert sensibility and subtle perception. That is why his poetic theory convinces and enlightens us far more than all the excogitations of the aesthetic critics and philosophers; that is why "a critical page of Leopardi's is much more firm than one of De Sanctis' . . . the richness of critical terms in Leopardi (not in the formal or extrinsic sense, but in the sense of feeling and understanding) is superior to that of De Sanctis."[26]

In one of his *Operette Morali*, "Il Parini ovvero della gloria," written when Leopardi was only 26, one can trace the structure of Leopardi's major critical assumptions, in virtue of which he may be regarded as a critic who was strikingly ahead of his times. He represents, indeed, what T. S. Eliot called, apropos of Remy de Gourmont, "the critical consciousness of a generation," the literary generation in Italy from 1820 to 1837. While discussing the precariousness of posthumous literary glory, and the preference which in ancient times great writers and poets displayed for great actions rather than literary fame, Leopardi (or his mouthpiece the eighteenth-century poet Parini) tells us, echoing Buffon, that it is the force of style that may be regarded as the enduring warrant of literary fame, at least with posterity, thereby showing his tendency, which would grow stronger with years, to consider the literary merit of a given work as being very largely, if not exclusively, dependent rather on its formal and stylistic qualities than on anything else. And in order both for the reader and the critic to fully appreciate these qualities, it is necessary to recreate a work, as it were, within oneself "almost as perfectly as the author of that work himself did it."[27] Thus criticism is considered from the very outset as not merely an act of analyzing, inquiring, and evaluating, but also one of creating. There are, however, certain pitfalls to which this subjective or personal method of criticism may sometimes be exposed. For one thing it may be unduly influenced, or even dictated "rather by blindly embraced habits than by one's own judgment"; for to be able to criticize a work of literature "with complete liberty of judgment and with no care whatsoever of others' authority" is not within the reach of the majority of readers, who even with the help of the enlightened guidance and authority are more likely to be delighted "by the gross and patent beauties than by the subtle and delicate ones, by what is bold (and prominent) than by what is subdued and bashful, by the appearance than by the substance of things; and ordinarily by what is mediocre rather than by what is best."[28]

But if, on the one hand, Leopardi pleads for, or at least approves of, a direct approach to literary works on the part of the common reader, with an open mind and with an independence of judgment he warns, on the other hand, against the fallacy of judging literary works not so much on the basis of their qualities in themselves, as on the effect they produce

on the reader. A due balance between the consideration of what the work in itself is and of what effect
it produces on a certain reader, which itself may very
largely depend on the literary sensibility and the
general character and culture of that person, is according to Leopardi the *sine qua non* of what may
be called creative criticism. Another prerequisite is
the reader's ever active and vigilant passivity, so to
say, his inward disposition to "follow the minimum
impulse of what is being read, feel vividly every light
touch" and thus create in oneself "thousands of move-
ments and images, wandering at times in the sweetest
delirium, almost transported beyond oneself."[29]

Leopardi goes on to demonstrate that the very
basis of poetry is illusions—illusions which are naturally more rife and more efficacious in youth than in
old age. And just as the creative faculty generally
declines with the loss of youth, so also does the
critical faculty itself to some extent. It is not merely
that, to paraphrase T. S. Eliot, one outgrows the
majority of poems as one outgrows the majority of
human passions,[30] but also that one's capacity for the
"suspension of disbelief" and (what is even harder)
for belief itself or the capability of being "strongly
moved by what is imaginatively grand and beautiful"[31]—which is the most indispensable condition
involved in all critical activity—perceptibly declines.
Preferring as a rule, however, "the excessive to the
moderate, the pretty and superb to the simple and
the natural, as regards modes and ornaments, and
false beauties to the true ones," the young are gen-

erally incapable of appreciating the "mature and accomplished virtue of literary works."[32] A true critic, therefore, is obviously one who combines in himself the maturity of judgment with the emotional vigor and liveliness of youth.

Even though young, it was by dint of long systematic study and reflection that Leopardi had come to achieve this degree of critical consciousness. Having spent all his boyhood and early youth in his father's library in an intensive study of the literary—and not merely literary—works both of classical antiquity and modern times, Leopardi had acquired that academic discipline and intellectual maturity, which are, generally speaking, the basis of critical thought. In fact his study was not that of one who is merely a scholar or an erudite; from the very earliest stage of his scholarly career—in itself precocious—one notes in him the presence of a certain critical vein which determined his reactions to everything he read or wrote about. In one of Leopardi's earliest writings, "Discorso sopra Mosco," written when the poet was hardly 18, one already discerns the power of critical discrimination, coupled with an independence of judgment that enabled him to attribute a certain idyllic poem to Stobaeus, instead of as the universally prevalent opinion of his day did, to Moschus. Behind this ability to sift the evidence, which, in such cases, is bound to be internal rather than external, and to come to a more satisfactory and more convincing conclusion than the one hitherto prevalent, there lies not merely the power of reasoning, but also, and above all, the poetic sensibility in the judging critic himself —a sensibility that helps him distinguish between the characteristic merits of Moschus and Theocritus, and to indicate his own cautious preference. "In Theocritus," says the young Leopardi, "one likes the negligence, in Moschus the delicacy. Theocritus has more carefully hidden the art with which he has depicted nature. Moschus has let it come out a little, but in a way so that it attracts rather than annoys, makes us relish, without being satiated, and by showing only one part, and by hiding the rest, makes us desire to see the whole"; as regards his own preference, Leopardi characteristically remarks: "I dare not prefer Moschus to Theocritus, who has inimitable beauties, and who is, among the ancients, the poet *par excellence* of the shepherds and meadows; but I have no difficulty in saying that to some of his *Idylls,* in which there dominates that austere style, which puts before our eyes the countrymen with all their rusticity, I prefer the graceful and finished poems of Moschus."[33] This is not merely the expression of a personal whim or liking, but the statement of well-pondered and well-balanced opinion that has in it all the elements and evidence of a degree of critical evaluation quite surprising in a boy of 18.

Leopardi's early bent for philological and literary research was itself an aid, as far as it went, to the development of his critical and reflective powers. In this research Leopardi did not merely confine himself to the compilation of data and to the sifting of factual external evidence, but he was also led to exercise his own faculty for reflection and discrimination. In "Discorso sopra la Batracomiomachia," written in 1815, while examining all the scholarly evidence and the various authorities' efforts to determine the authorship of *La Batracomiomachia,* Leopardi sometimes makes pungent fun—a fun and pungency worthy of A. E. Housman—of those who on the basis of a very slender evidence, accompanied by a very specious piece of reasoning, jump to a conclusion which neither commonsense nor the scholarly conscience can ever approve. For instance, apropos of Alexander Pope's argument in favor of the view that the work might be attributed to Homer, because "a great author can sometimes amuse himself by composing a jocose work, [because] even the most sublime spirits are not averse to fun, [because] the talent for fun ordinarily accompanies beautiful imagination," Leopardi justly observes that all this is very true, "but it only proves that Homer *could* write a jocose poem, not that he is in fact the author of *La Batracomiomachia.*"[34] Sometimes the evidence brought in to establish Homer's authorship is more amusing than convincing. "Stefano Bergler," says Leopardi, for instance, "counts as far as eight words in *La Batracomiomachia,* which do not seem to have been in use in Homer's time, who never used them in *Iliad* or in *Odyssey,* although he had often occasion to do so."[35] Thus though himself an erudite philologist, Leopardi knew how to preserve one's critical sense, which alone can duly interpret the facts and data which philological scholarship lays in one's hands.

The same critical spirit, coupled with common-sense and equipped with erudition, Leopardi manifests in another early work of his—"Discorso sopra la vita e le opere di M. Cornelio Frontone." More than his first-hand knowledge of the material in question, which is itself impressive for its wide range and depth, it is Leopardi's masterly grasp of the problems that arise, and the extremely sound and pertinent notions that he puts forward, which renders this work so interesting. Here one can find Leopardi's theory of style and language delineated in a more than rudimentary form—a theory that Leopardi would reaffirm, later, in *Zibaldone* in a more elaborate and more detailed way. Describing Frontone's zeal for the purity of language, Leopardi tells us what is almost as true of himself: "He was most zealous about the purity of language; he pondered long over single words, examined at bottom the propriety of terms, weighed the particular value of every synonym, and did not disdain the office of a grammarian, since he was persuaded that it is not enough to think, that one must also talk, that the Orator cannot do without words any more than he can do without things, that if not helped by terms, thought languishes, and that at the back of the corruption of the fable [subject-matter] lies the very corruption of eloquence itself."[36] A veritable master and philosopher of style, Frontone was not desirous "of the unheard and the marvellous; he preserved his style exempt from exaggeration, excessive exquisiteness, affected sublimity; in a word he escaped with every possible care from the excess of artifice."[37]   Through such observations Leopardi both underlines his preference for a particular style, and defines what his own ideal of style is. He also gives proof of his deep involvement, from a very early age, in the problem of style, a problem whose subtlety and complexity he realizes just as fully as he realizes its importance. "The force and the use of the word *style*," says Leopardi, "are obscure and almost fluctuating, not only in the case of the majority of people, but in the case of the most cautious and most learned," in so far as it is not easy to discern, as one must, "the qualities of the form of style from the quality of the material or of the words and the fable."[38]

Whatever, therefore, be the intrinsic or historical value of Leopardi's juvenile writings of philological character as such, they constitute an indisputable proof of the level of critical awareness that his mind had reached at such an early age, and that governed his whole attitude to all he read or wrote. "No modern poet," Cardarelli justly observes, "seems to be so philologically armed and such a master of his proper means as Leopardi."[39] With such an arduous training and background behind him, whatever Leopardi was going to say henceforward about poetry and literary criticism must at least have one infallible quality about it, that, whether it was basically right or wrong, it was the voice of a man who knew what he was talking about, and whose most casual observation was directly or indirectly the fruit of close study and earnest thought.

CHAPTER TWO

The Attack upon the Romantics:
Leopardi's Early Theory

∽

LEOPARDI'S ESSAY "Discorso di un Italiano intorno
alla Poesia Romantica," written in 1818, and published
for the first time in 1906 in *Scritti Vari Inediti,* was a
critical response, couched in deliberately polemical
terms, to Cavaliere Lodovico Di Breme's *Osservazioni
sulla Poesia Moderna,* published in *Spettatore italiano,*
1-15 January 1818. As regards the nature of its genesis
and the spirit of enlightened zeal mingled with critical
sanity and argumentative power which Leopardi man-
ifested in the defence as well as the exposition of the
cause not so much of classical poetry as of poetry in
general, this essay bears no insignificant resemblance
with Shelley's *Defence of Poetry,* which was written
in reply to Peacock's *Four Ages of Poetry.* Both, besides being models of creative polemics, are also
illuminating accounts of what their authors considered
to be the essential nature and function of poetry
itself, not merely the difference between classical and
romantic poetry. In many respects, therefore, this
essay adumbrates Leopardi's theory of poetry as such
and is an indication of the remarkably parallel or

allied developments in him both as a poet and as a theorist and critic of poetry.

One thing that must be made clear at the very outset is that what Leopardi condemned as romantic has very little to do, in spite of his reference to English and German poetry, with those attitudes, assumptions, and features which characterized English poetry at the beginning of the nineteenth century. Similarly, though he extolled ancient classical poetry, what Leopardi criticized in modern poetry in general, and not simply that of his own country, was altogether different from those qualities which constitute at once the greatness and the modernity of poetry written in the first quarter of the nineteenth century, and which Leopardi's own poetry so well represents. This clearly shows that there was in Leopardi's own scale of values and criteria no clear-cut and well-defined distinction between romantic and classical, that his avowed allegiance to classicism[1] meant nothing more and nothing less than his sticking to the norms and principles of all good verse-writing since the days of Homer, just as his attack on the romantics amounted to little more than an exposure of such faults and weaknesses as would be considered detrimental to classical poetry and romantic alike.

"The romantics," says Leopardi, "try to divert poetry, as much as possible, from the commerce with the sense, through which it is born and would live so long as it is poetry, and to connect it with the intellect, to drag it from the visible to the invisible, from the things to the ideas, and to transform what is material,

fantastic, and corporal in it, into something metaphysical, rational, and spiritual."[2] Granted that the
poetic fervor of the ancient poets, as Di Breme says,
came chiefly from ignorance, Leopardi would not,
however, approve of the logical deduction that since
men have now learnt so much and are therefore no
longer susceptible to the pretensions of poetry, poetry
must neither pretend nor lie, but must always go
behind reason and reach after truth. It is the domain
of reason, thought, and truth, as distinguished from
and even opposed to that of imagination, illusion, and
fable or myth, that Leopardi considers to be utterly
unwholesome for the growth of true poetry. Though
his own poetry is seldom free from thought, and
sometimes thought at the deepest level, in theory
Leopardi is as much in favor of the "life of sensations
rather than that of thought" as Keats himself. Even
if "logical intuition" and "fabulous prestige," as Lodovico Di Breme put it, are incompatible today, and
even though our imagination is weaker than that of
the ancients, it does not mean that the essential nature
and material of poetry has changed. The romantic
poets themselves, by their very use of the Nordic or
Oriental mythologies instead of the Greek mythology,
which, inconsistently enough, they find unsuitable
for treatment in modern poetry, show in practice
what they deny in theory, that the primary appeal
of poetry in the modern age is, as it always has been,
to imagination, and not to intellect or reason.

The principal function of poetry is to beguile or
convince imagination, rather than intellect. Leopardi

distinguishes between the intellectual and the imaginative deceit; the former is that of a philosopher who is convinced and who also succeeds sometimes in convincing others regarding the validity of what is inherently false; the latter is that of the poet. While defining the nature of this poetic deceit or illusion Leopardi at the age of 20 sums up what Coleridge in the maturity of his critical powers described as "the willing suspension of disbelief": "the intellect, in the course of the imaginative ecstasy or delirium, knows perfectly well that it is raving and believes always and every time as much in what is the least false as in what is the falsest, as much in the Angels of Milton and in the allegorical substances of Voltaire as in the Gods of Homer, as much in the spectres of Bürger and the fairies of Southey as in the hell of Virgil . . . because in fact we know that a poet, be he in everything a Christian, a philosopher, or a modern, will never deceive the intellect, just as, whether he shows himself to be a pagan or an idiot or an ancient, he will always deceive the imagination, every time he pretends to be a true poet."[3] All that a poet has to do is to choose "within the limits of verisimilitude such illusions as seem best to him and as are the most pleasant to us and the most suitable for the purpose of poetry, which is to imitate nature and to delight."[4] This Aristotelian gloss on the nature of poetry, mingled with the Renaissance ideal of its function which is to delight, is an evidence of Leopardi's whole-hearted concurrence with the traditional line of poetics.

Nor does Leopardi agree with Lodovico Di Breme,

according to whom the material of poetry must of necessity be drawn from contemporary customs, beliefs, and religion. In doing this Leopardi not only anticipates most of Matthew Arnold's arguments on the subject, but also adumbrates and justifies, as it were, the very nature of the subjects and titles he would choose for his own poetry. Whether a poem is modern or not, that is, whether or not it makes any appeal to modern readers by representing their sensibility and outlook, does not depend on the nature of the subject chosen, nor even on the contemporaneity of the material used, but on how, through his very treatment of the subject and by means of the language employed (which too need not be too self-consciously imitative of the current idiom—and here most modern poet-critics may differ from Leopardi), the poet succeeds in communicating his own essential individuality. As regards the subject-matter, if not the language, we have in our own times the example of T. S. Eliot, whose *Murder in the Cathedral,* by no means a subject drawn from contemporary history, appeals as much to our sense of modernity, as a poem or a play with such a typically contemporary subject and material as *The Waste Land* or *The Cocktail Party.* But the greatest proof of how Leopardi was right and Di Breme and the school he represented wrong is Leopardi's own *Canti,* in which, by sometimes using old historical themes, he achieves the same poetic results as in those poems where the themes have a contemporary relevance. "It is necessary," Leopardi insists, "that we adapt ourselves to nature, and not nature to us, and that in any case poetry should not change, as the moderns would have it do, but in its principal character remain, like nature itself, immutable."[5] This is not simply a matter of poetic creed or taste in Leopardi, but something based on a sound psychological principle, on "our incontestable inclination to the primitive, to the naturally pure and spotless," on "those two capital dispositions of our spirit, the love of naturalness and the hatred of affectation"—a principle which is all the more pronounced in persons endowed with artistic taste. By "primitive" Leopardi means something more than what one generally understands in a historical context. Partly under the influence of Rousseau's thought, but largely in the light of his own experience of childhood and what it came to mean to him in his recollection as a grownup, together with his literary-cum-historical consideration of the role and the quality of imagination in the works of the ancient poets, like Homer, and in those of the moderns, the word "primitive" stood for something fresh and unpolluted by civilization, intellectual progress, and metaphysical speculation. It is, as Flora justly points out, "an efficacious metaphor, not a temporal qualification." In poetic style, which itself stands for something more than the merely formal, linguistic, or prosodic quality of a poem, the word "primitive" comes to signify "candid simplicity" as, in terms of human psychology, it could very well signify "uncorrupted nature" and innocence. Hence, even though we may no longer live in a primitive age, there is something similar in

our childhood, and consequently the poetic value of
what is primitive in the historical or chronological
sense of the term comes to be merged with the poetic
value of childhood itself. And the principal tendency
of childhood, as according to Leopardi it is of poetry
itself, is that it not only tends to apprehend things and
their significance with the help of imagination rather
than with that of reason or understanding, but it also
tends to be attracted to the appearance of the things
rather than to what they are in reality. It is not the
poet's, but the philosopher's business, says Leopardi,
to consider what is useful and true; the poet's main concern is with the delightful, and significantly enough,
with what is delightful above all to the imagination.
That is why a poet can derive his inspiration and
material as much from the false as from the true,
since what he is looking for is not the truth but the
semblance of truth.

One of the cardinal and ever-recurrent points in
Leopardi's theory of poetry is the contrast between
truth and illusion, or between poetic truth and scientific or factual truth. The foremost quality of
imagination, according to Leopardi, consists in its
liberty, and it is in the nature of scientific truth to
kill this liberty. For the imagination to produce in us
the same effects as it once produced in the ancients
(and even in us during our childhood), it is necessary
to defend it against the tyranny of the intellect, which,
in the realm of poetry, stands for the corruption of
taste in the poets as well as in the readers of poetry.
It is as a consequence of this corruption—a corruption

to which the romantics contributed, says Leopardi, both by their choice of the subjects and by their treatment—that many readers of poetry are hardly capable of perceiving "the delicate keys of nature; they require great shocks and blows such as the romantic poets are in the habit of giving in order to be moved and awakened . . . ; on their imagination a half-dead lamp among the columns of a big Gothic church painted by the poet produces greater effect than the moon on a lake or in a wood."[6] In terms of his own choosing and in a context that too has a particular relevance and significance of its own, what Leopardi says is virtually the same truth as the one William Wordsworth declared when he said that "the human mind is capable of being excited without the application of gross and violent stimulants; and he must have a very faint perception of its beauty and dignity who does not know that."[7] Not that Leopardi thinks that one set of objects or one species of poetic material is necessarily superior to another so far as its creative utility is concerned; what he does, how-ever, think and regret is that imagination should have reached such a stage of torpor that in order to awaken it one needs such shocks and blows as are often administered by the romantics. If Leopardi had known Wordsworth's thought and poetry, which he did not, he would not have been so sweeping in his condemnation of the English and German romantics as the worse perpetrators of this tendency to habituate the mind to such shocks and stimulants. Among the English romantic poets he knew the works of Byron and Southey and among the German those of Goethe, and it may fairly well be conceded that there are certain elements in their work, which would, to some extent, justify his charge. But so far as Wordsworth is concerned, not only is his poetry completely immune from these gross and violent shocks, but his prefaces themselves are one strong consistent campaign, in the sphere of literary polemics and criticism of his age, against these things—a campaign in the service of which Wordsworth uses, interestingly enough, more or less precisely the same terms and arguments as Leopardi to describe the passivity to which imagination, long and habitually subject as it has been to gross stimulants and shocks, inevitably becomes a prey. "For a multitude of causes," says Wordsworth, "unknown to former times, are now acting with a combined force to blunt the discriminating powers of the mind, and, unfitting it for all voluntary exertion, to reduce it almost to a savage torpor."[8]

Another charge laid by Leopardi against the romantics is that they confound novelty of themes and ideas with poetic originality, as is evident from their unqualified and uncritical support of the themes from contemporary life, instead of the time-honored themes celebrated in ancient classical literature. Analyzing the novelty of romantic poetry to consist not so much in the objects as in the manner of imitating them, Leopardi gives his own opinion on poetic originality when he notes that poetry is more efficacious "when imitation is rare and the object imitated is common."[9] It is the ancient poets who, according to Leopardi, represent an ideal combination of the rarity of imitation and the familiarity of the objects imitated—rarity and familiarity that have both inevitably suffered on account of the passage of time and with the increasing dependence of poetry on the imitation of art rather than of nature. In so far as the originality of poetic images is concerned, this too results from the manner of describing or observing the object, rather than from the object itself. And this is as it should be, in as much as the poet "ordinarily does not and cannot portray the whole figure, but uses a few strokes of his brush," and hence for the imagination to be able to fill out or grasp the rest it is necessary that the object in question be a familiar object. The basic error of the romantics is that they confound the originality of subjects or the novelty of objects as such with the novelty of imitation. For, the novelty that belongs to the subject-matter is an easier (and therefore the more sought after), but not necessarily a superior or even a genuine kind of novelty, than the novelty or efficacy that the poet discovers and makes others discover in what is familiar, common, and simple.

The sphere of poetry is vast enough to include the common and ordinary objects of life as well as those uncommon, unfamiliar, and novel. Not only that, but the central function of poetry is not so much to imitate the world and nature of everyday experience, but to rediscover it, penetrating through what is so commonly familiar to us about it into what is seldom seen or realized and yet is no less an integral part of it. It is not enough, says Leopardi, that a poet should imitate nature; it is also necessary that he should discover it, not merely "by sharpening the eyes in order to perceive what, even though it is present all around us, we are not used to see, impeded as we are in this by custom"—and here Leopardi's thought touches Wordsworth's and, what is more, goes beyond it—but by "removing the objects that hide it . . . and by cleaning it of the mud of civilization and human corruption."[10] In Leopardi's pleas for the imitation of nature—an imitation that clearly amounts to discovery and has the core of an almost mystical interpretation within itself, raising it far above the level of the so-called realism in art—we have the confirmation and at the same time the assertion of the fundamental kinship between ancient and modern poetry, in so far as its scope and function are concerned. It is in connection with the imitation of nature that Leopardi makes the psychologically profound statement that "the most ordinary things, especially when they are also very common, appeal to our thought and imagination much more strongly when they are imitated (in art) than when they are presented in their real form . . . [that] while reading poetry one is better disposed to feel the efficacy of things than when the things are physically present."[11]

Rejecting Di Breme's distinction that the ancient poets make an appeal to our imagination and the modern (especially the romantic) to our heart, Leopardi observes that Homer, whom, like Pope, he calls "almost another nature," is as much a master of sentiment as of poetic imagination, even though he is generally considered to be among the least sentimental poets of classical antiquity. The only difference between a sentimental poet like Homer and a romantic poet is that while the latter is consciously and deliberately sentimental, as is evident from his endeavor to produce at all costs the effect of the pathetic, the former is so by chance and in a natural and unselfconscious manner. In other words, the same sensibility is at the back of poetry, whether it makes its appeal to the heart or the imagination (if, indeed, any poetry does so exclusively to one of the two). It is in virtue of the possession of this sensibility not only that one can create poetry, but also that one can judge and appreciate it. It was doubted by the ancients and one doubts it even today, says Leopardi, that the majority of people can competently judge poetry. For, most people have a kind of sensibility that is better fitted for the appreciation of comedies, satires, and works generally matter of fact than for that of poetry properly so-called. This sensibility Leopardi calls "the most impure and most unnatural," consisting as it does of nothing more than "a medley or a string of remembrances of stories, maxims, sayings, and proverbs read or heard" and consequently, when memory fails, sensibility likewise fails. The sort of sensibility one needs for the creation and the appreciation of poetry, Leopardi writes in one of the most poetic and yet most critically significant passages of his prose, is the one which is "intimate and spontaneous, very modest, rather shy and wayward, pure, sweet and sublime, at once superhuman and childlike, mother of great delights and great sorrows, dear and painful like love, ineffable and inexplicable, donated by nature only to a few persons, in whom, when it is not vitiated and corrupted, when it is not ill-treated, suppressed and trampled on, since it is so tender, when it is not suffocated and destroyed, when, at last it can fully conquer the most ferocious and most powerful adversaries—a task in which one but rarely succeeds—and, besides, when it is not unaccompanied by other noble and distinguished qualities, produces things that last, and that are worthy of lasting, in man's memory."[12] This sensibility is the most potent source of poetic inspiration, the essential prerequisite of all poetry, ancient or modern, something in which Homer's own poetry is so incomparably rich. It is this sensibility that we have in mind when we think of a poet as one who is so born, and who cannot otherwise so become in spite of "all science and civilization."

Whatever an artist undertakes to do ought to be informed by this sensibility; for, self-conscious art and diligence, when divorced from it, tend to imitate nature with little or no naturalness, and for Leopardi one does not and cannot imitate nature unless one does so in a natural way. It is this sensibility that enables Dante, whom Leopardi calls "the second Homer," to do with just one or two strokes of his pen what Ovid, with all his elaborate art and efforts, can hardly ever do. The chief difference between ancient poets and modern romantics is that while the former imitate and reproduce in words the effects of their sensibility in a natural way, the latter try to do the same thing in an unnatural way, that is to say, in a self-conscious and deliberate way. The ancient poet wrote, says Leopardi, not like "one who contemplates, turns around, sounds, searches, squeezes, and penetrates the heart, but like one who receives the very dictate of the heart itself," so that in his poetry what we hear talking is not "the man skilled in the qualities, affections, and vicissitudes, however obscure and secret, of our spirit, nor the scientist, nor the philosopher, nor even the poet, but the poet's heart itself, not the man acquainted with the sensibility, but the sensibility itself personified."

And just as Leopardi opposes naturalness, which ought to be preserved in all artistic imitation, to affections, which should be eliminated as far as possible, so he opposes sensibility to sentimentality. The ancient poets were masters of sensibility; the modern romantic poets, on the other hand, excel in sentimentality, which they often mistake for sensibility. In distinguishing between poetic sensibility and sentimentality the young Leopardi, in some respects, anticipates the very essence of what Ruskin meant by "pathetic fallacy," or what T. S. Eliot meant when he says that poetry is not a turning loose of emotion, but an escape from emotion, not the expression of personality, but an escape from personality. The deliberate search for the pathetic in the romantics—a search that has no semblance of being something "casual, careless and spontaneous"—and their firm determination to turn

out a sentimental passage is obviously in contrast with
the self-governing and self-controlling habit of sensibility, in virtue of which, however deeply one might
feel and live within oneself a certain object or situation, one does not lose sight of its objective identity.
This is what Leopardi means by true sensibility,
which distinguishes a real poet from "the romantics
and other sentimental crowds."

The relation between sensibility and naturalness
or sincerity raises the question of the degree of
compatibility between science and poetry. Much science (or knowledge), says Leopardi, "takes away
naturalness from us and the capacity to imitate nature,
not like a philosopher but like a poet as the ancients
did, and we consequently everywhere display what
we know . . . so that we write treatises in verse, in
which it is not the things that talk but we, not nature
but science. . . ."[13] This, of course, does not mean
that a modern poet should write as if he were completely ignorant; nor does it mean that he should not
exploit in his poetry his own knowledge of himself
and his surroundings. But he should make use of
this knowledge in such a way that it may not altogether kill those illusions without which there cannot
be any poetry. Leopardi draws a very subtle distinction between "making use of the knowledge of
ourselves" and "showing as if we knew ourselves,"
the former being beneficial, the latter detrimental to
the spirit of poetry. This distinction is charged with
further meaning when we are told that we must learn
from the ancients, not how to write poetry by avoiding

or suppressing all that we know, but how, while knowing ourselves and the universe around us, we can still create poetry and still keep ourselves open to the power and influence of illusions. "One really needs," says Leopardi, "a profound study of those [ancient] poets who made such use of the lesser amount of knowledge they possessed, a use without which the greater degree of knowledge and science in the hands of the modern poets is useless."[14] As regards the question of relationship between knowledge and learning on the one hand and poetry on the other, Leopardi himself affords an illuminating illustration. One of the most widely learned poets of all times, and perhaps the most learned of his own throughout Europe, Leopardi made an admirably discreet use of his learning and knowledge, without letting it kill altogether the spirit of poetic illusion. And perhaps nowhere is the sense and the spirit of poetic illusion more manifest than in those very poems where he is out to lament its death or enfeeblement in modern times in face of what Thomas Hardy called "the plethoric growth of knowledge" and the irresistible encroachments into the field of poetry of what Leopardi himself calls "il vero acerbo."[15]

The question of knowledge and truth in relation to poetry raises another question, which Leopardi discusses briefly in this essay; namely, the question of what constitutes poetic truth and what is its bearing on the element of verisimilitude in poetic art as an imitation of nature. While the aim of poetry is to delight, this delight, in so far as it issues from the imitations of what is real and true, depends "not only on the qualities of the objects imitated but also, and especially and essentially, on the feeling of wonder born out of seeing those objects almost transported to where one could not imagine them to be and represented by means of things which, it seemed, could not represent them, so that an infinite number of objects which in nature [or reality] do not delight us at all do so very much when imitated by a poet or painter and those which already delighted us in their reality do so all the more."[16] The Aristotelian definition of art as an imitation of nature Leopardi accepts as a general principle; but what really matters is not so much his acceptance of this definition as it is his interpretation of it and especially of the term "imitation." This altered view of a time-honored principle on Leopardi's part is an evidence of his true critical individuality. "The romantics think," he says, "that the excellence of imitation should be estimated only according to its nearness to truth, so much so that while searching for the truth, they almost forget to imitate, because the truth cannot be an imitation of itself."[17] Such an imitation is not only easy, it is even trivial. Everyone imitates every day in this manner without being able to attain to that sense of wonder which is the very essence of artistic imitation. The principle of verisimilitude in artistic imitation is not to be confounded with a mechanical or photographic reproduction of the object imitated. As an example of this sort of imitation, to be found in plenty in the romantic poets, Leopardi refers to their attempt to imitate the trampling of the horses by means of the words "trap, trap, trap" and the sound of the bells by using such meaningless words as "tin, tin, tin." Leopardi himself, it may be pointed out in passing, succeeds well in conveying to us the sound of the evening bells borne by the wind in one of the most beautiful verses he ever wrote: "Viene il vento recando il suon dell'ora / Dalla torre del borgo" ("Le Ricordanze").

If factual imitation or mechanical reproduction is not quite the same thing as what Leopardi means by artistic imitation, neither is invention exactly the same. It was known to our ancestors, writes Leopardi, and it is no less known to children that, generally speaking, it is far easier and much less marvelous to invent than to imitate. For, the principal ingredient in our sense of wonder is based on the feeling of resemblance between the thing imitated and its artistic version—a feeling that has no place in the case of something invented, something which cannot well be compared or contrasted with what we already knew or what already existed.

Later on, we shall come back to the subject of imitation in Leopardi's theory of poetry in the light of his maturer experience as a poet and critic, as it is embodied in *Zibaldone*. For the moment it may be noted how in the essay against the romantics Leopardi has succeeded, at the very early age of 18, in summing up and in defining to himself not only the major fundamental problems of literary criticism as well as of poetic theory but also his own attitude to them—an attitude that would go to modify as certainly as it would in turn be modified by Leopardi's own development as a poet and as a theorist of poetry.

CHAPTER THREE

The Myth of Antiquity in Leopardi's Theory of Poetry

∽

THE CONTRAST between the ancient and the modern that serves as a cornerstone to much of Leopardi's thinking on the nature and meaning of poetry originates from Leopardi's conviction regarding not only the indisputable supremacy of ancient poetry, especially that of Homer, over modern poetry, but also the ideal character of the historic conditions under which ancient poetry was written—conditions which cannot be repeated. Almost invariably did Leopardi judge and compare modern poetry with ancient poetry, and with Homer—the "prince of poetry," "the father and the perpetual prince of all the poets of the world"—and found it, on the whole, inferior. "From Homer onwards," we are told, "everything has been perfected, but not poetry."[1] It is a kind of unique perfection in the art of poetry that Leopardi associated with the name of Homer and with ancient poetry in general, a perfection that he considered to be the final goal and criterion of all poetry. This criterion led him to analyze the very conditions of man's mind and social and historical environment that made the achievement of such poetry possible. In the creation of this myth there entered all the loving labors of Leopardi's youth and manhood as a scholar —labors undertaken in no pedantic spirit, but with a view to enriching his culture, sensibility, and critical judgment. These, in turn, helped him see classical antiquity with the eyes of a modern and to look upon its literature as well as the literature of modern times in the spirit of pure criticism, or rather in the spirit of criticism directed upon the work of art in its essence and purity as art and as nothing else. His exclusive interest in the intrinsic character of poetic excellence enabled him, in spite of his overt preference for classical poetry as a whole, to see ancient poetry "not as consecrated by time," to borrow T. S. Eliot's words, "but to see it beyond time; to see the best work of our time and the best work of twenty-five hundred years ago with the same eyes."[2]

While adducing the reasons for the inferiority of modern poetry as a whole to ancient classical poetry, Leopardi analyzed the adverse effects of the growth of science and other kinds of knowledge on poetic imagination and sensibility—effects which he summed up as "the aging of our spirit," "the loss and weakening of the illusions."[3] In a way, Leopardi regards only the ancients as poets and the moderns as merely thinkers and philosophers. And this is chiefly so because in ancient times the unity between nature and art was still preserved—a unity that has been irrevocably lost in modern times. A happy period it was, says Leopardi, "when the poet, while seeing everything in fresh, virgin, and intact nature with his own eyes without endeavoring to create novelties, because everything was new, and while creating, without knowing it, the rules of heart with that carelessness of which all the force of talent and study can hardly give us an idea, sang divine and eternally lasting things."[4] Far from merely preaching up the ancients—the phrase is W. P. Ker's—Leopardi went to the roots of the difference between ancient and modern poetry, analyzing its cultural, historical, and psychological aspects. In this attempt Leopardi's thought sometimes runs fairly parallel to that of Vico and Rousseau, whose works he knew. It also sometimes parallels that of T. L. Peacock, whom he had never read. The main difference, however, between Leopardi's condemnation of the modern age and Peacock's is that the latter challenged not merely the fitness of modern age for the creation of great poetry, but the very value of poetry itself in a scientific and utilitarian age. Leopardi, on the contrary, never challenged the value and *raison d'être* of poetry in the modern world at all. What he did, however, doubt, like Peacock, is the possibility of writing great poetry in an age which has been practically deprived of all its illusions. And according to Leopardi, few can be great—and in art and poetry, perhaps none—unless dominated by illusions. It is by deliberately cherishing or embracing illusions and not by discarding them that a poet can really have—paradoxical though it may seem to say so—any insight into the nature of reality in the philosophical sense of the term. Plato, says Ralph Waldo Emerson, "has a strong solving sense to reconcile his poetry with the appearances of the world,"[5] and, in more recent times, Yeats has more or less confirmed the same truth when he observed: "In my heart I thought that only beautiful things should be painted, and only ancient things and the stuff of dreams were beautiful."[6]

Leopardi's concern with antiquity was not a literary fad; it was rooted in his awareness of the irremediable conflict between science and poetry, between poetry and civilization. It was an awareness that was more or less shared by practically all the poets and critics of the nineteenth century. In fact this feeling of contrast between science and poetry lies at the very core of the romantic attitude to life and poetry. In Keats's "Lamia" and "Sleep and Poetry" as well as in Hazlitt's essays, for instance, we have the direct or indirect expression of the inner conviction, later on summed up by Macaulay, that "as civilization advances, poetry almost necessarily declines."[7] It is the same conviction that is at the back of Matthew Arnold's deploring "the modern situation in its true *blankness, barrenness* and *poetrylessness*"[8] or Newman's statement that "as time goes on, and we number and sort and measure things, as we gain views, we advance towards philosophy and truth, but we recede from poetry."[9] But while these critics of the *Zeitgeist* and its impact on the creation of poetry unanimously recognized the contrast between poetry and civilization, a contrast accentuated by the inarrestible march of science and reason and consequently by an orienta-

tion to the universe around oneself altogether different
from the one which the Homeric man was used to,
no one, with the possible exception of Vico, tried to
interpret and analyze it in terms not only of the
historical cause and effect, but also of the essential
nature of science and poetry and of their interrelationship (where and to what extent this relationship
exists) so profoundly and so exhaustively as Leopardi.
Moreover, whereas poets and critics like Gray, Keats,
Hazlitt, Peacock, Matthew Arnold, and Macaulay,
when they talked of the unpoetic nature of the modern
age, chiefly meant their own age, it is the whole
historical epoch, which is generally termed modern,
as distinguished from the Middle Ages, that was
unpoetic for Leopardi—unpoetic, that is to say, in
comparison with the primitive ages or the Homeric
and post-Homeric ages. That in coming to such a
conclusion Leopardi did not sufficiently take into
account the richness and originality of the great
Renaissance literature, to which the English Elizabethans and his own countrymen Petrarch and
Michaelangelo contributed so much, is not indeed a
consequence of Leopardi's ignorance of this literature
or his particular prejudice against it, but a corollary
of his own definition of a great poetry, which ought
almost always to be essentially lyrical and which
derives its main strength and inspiration from the
poet's implicit faith in illusions and their complete
hold on his heart and imagination. Obviously, therefore, the ancient times were, in this sense, more
propitious for the writing of poetry than the modern

[44]

times, in which the scientific-cum-rational spirit has all but administered a death-blow to man's illusions. These illusions are not so much a matter of individual poetic faith, so that any poet at any time and in any period can create them and cling to them if he so chooses, as they are inherent and indistinguishable parts of the total consciousness of a whole age or period. Leopardi, therefore, would not have agreed with a poet like William Blake, according to whom it is possible for an individual poet, no matter in what age he lives, to cast aside the shackles with which science, or what Leopardi calls "the cognition of the bitter truth" has succeeded in chaining the wings of imagination. "I come," says Blake:

I come in Self-annihilation & the grandeur of Inspiration,
*   *   *   *   *   *   *   *   *   *
To cast off Bacon, Lock & Newton from Albion's covering,
To cast off his filthy garments & clothe him with
                                                Imagination,
To cast aside from Poetry all that is not Inspiration.[10]

For Leopardi, a poet, however original and resourceful he might be, could not simply do it, in so far as the resuscitating of those illusions concerning his relationship with the physical world around him, his place in the universe, and his belief that this earth exists for his happiness, is concerned.

However, if scientific and rational knowledge have served to destroy most of our illusions in modern times, it does not, therefore, follow that Homer's times were entirely devoid of scientific or rational spirit. But while this spirit tends to kill and has, according to

Leopardi, practically killed all the poetic illusions in our day, in Homer's time it could not only coexist with those illusions in which the poet, along with his whole age more or less, believed but it also, in a way, sustained and corroborated those illusions. That is why the imagination of the ancients was not only more fertile and more powerful than ours, but it also governed their daily life and thinking much more than it does ours. In our case reason has definitely supplanted imagination, and a poet, however individual and creative he might be, cannot but be affected by this profound and radical change. Being, as Leopardi says, "in a habitual state of physical vigor normally superior to ours," the ancients disposed of a greater fund of enthusiasm for everything in life and for life itself than do the moderns. Their enthusiasm sometimes bordered on that state of divine delirium (and this was all the more so in the case of a creative artist) which in *Phaedrus* Plato considered as not only the principal source of all fine arts, but also among the greatest boons of mankind. Leopardi himself compared this enthusiasm with "a sweetest delirium," which is not only, as in Nietzsche and Baudelaire, a saving antidote against "ennui" but also a necessary condition for creative activity.[11] It is in virtue of passion and enthusiasm that the poet's imagination can "see the liveliest affinities between things" and "the connection between the most diverse things, discover the most abstruse and ingenuous similitudes," and compare "the objects of the most distinct species, for instance, the ideal with the most material, incorporate the most abstract thought, reduce everything to images and furthermore create the newest and the liveliest images conceivable."

Now, the superior measure in which the ancients (meaning, thereby, chiefly the Greeks) possessed both this sort of enthusiasm and imagination, as compared with the moderns, and the degree in which the illusions were to them not only a source of poetic inspiration but also a part of reality itself, far more so than it can be for a modern poet, is nowhere more evident than in their powers of myth-making and generalization. As a consequence, the ancients found the universe not "a universe of death"—the phrase is Wordsworth's—but something plainly sentient and palpitating with a perennial joy and vitality. "What a beautiful time it was," says Leopardi, referring to the ancient times, "when everything was lively according to human imagination, and humanly alive, that is to say inhabited by or consisting of beings equal to us! When one believed it to be almost certain that there lived in the most deserted forests the beautiful Hamadryads, fauns, sylvans, Pan, etc."[12] And, that is to say, "the sight of Proteus rising from the sea" was not a too uncommon or incredible sight, since both heart and intellect were prone to follow the lead of imagination.

The same enthusiasm, and the freshness of imagination and experience that was at the back of it, go to account for the ancients' power of generalization, which not only enabled them to discover and make their own the poetic truths, but even truths in the sphere of morals and metaphysics so that they have practically said, once and for all, all that is to be said. Leopardi quotes the following remark by Voltaire with implicit approval. "In metaphysics, in morals, the ancients have said everything. We either compare ourselves with them or we repeat them. All the modern books of this sort have done nothing but repeat them."[13]

Imagination of such a happily and spontaneously creative kind as this, which Leopardi considered to be the sole property of the ancients, has been irreparably undermined by the advance of scientific knowledge in our times; the great illusions are gone, giving place to the uninspiring and sorrowful knowledge of the things as they are in their humdrum prosaic reality. The imagination of the moderns is languid and brooding, deriving its poor sustenance "from the truths of philosophy and reason," rather than "from nature and from vague ideas, the natural property of the primitive imagination."[14] Having lost its hold on the sweet illusions of life, imagination is no longer the "deceiving elf" that it once used to be. A heart-felt commerce with the world of nature and with the resultant world of illusions—for nature is the mother and source of all illusions—has been rendered almost impossible by what Matthew Arnold called "the dialogue of the mind with itself."

The kind of imagination that the ancients possessed is nowadays to be found only in children, or, if at all, to some extent in those adults who are not very cultured or educated. Like Wordsworth, Leopardi laid great stress on childhood and the memories of childhood as an important source of poetic inspiration. Children, he says, "find everything even in nothing, the grown-ups nothing in everything,"[15] which is just another way of saying with Wordsworth that childhood has "more power than all the elements," or with Walter de la Mare that "between their [the children's] dream and their reality looms no impossible abyss."[16] Being the happiest period in man's life, childhood is also the richest and the surest source of those vague and indefinite images which are, for Leopardi, the very substance of poetry and which continue to wield a more or less conscious influence in man's later life. That is why a child "sees clearly and at once the truths and the reasons of those truths which the philosopher either does not see at all or sees in a very confused way."[17]

Belonging as they did to the infancy of the world, the ancients were therefore endowed, like children, with a more fertile and more vigorous imagination than the moderns. Their imagination worked more freely in proportion as it was less handicapped and circumscribed by reason and philosophical cognition of the nature of things than the imagination of the moderns. In fact, the sharp antagonism between reason and imagination that is so fundamental a characteristic of modern experience was not so deeply felt by an ancient poet. Not that the power of reasoning in the ancients was in itself inferior to our power of reasoning, but they made a more sparing use of it than do the moderns. For instance, in their understanding of external nature, they used imagination as much, if not more than, reason or intellect, so that together with their understanding of nature there was also inevitably linked up the rapt appreciation thereof. It was in consequence of this that they clothed the truths at which they arrived in myths and fables and generally proclaimed them in verses, not because they wanted to mystify the uninitiated or the common people, but because they believed that a truth, so clothed and so expressed, is likely to make greater appeal to the imagination than the truth expressed in terms of abstract logic and reasoning or in terms of mathematical formulas. And an appeal to the imagination counted with the ancients at least as much as an appeal to the heart or intellect. That is why even the ancient philosophers were, in a way, poets, and, like Plato, frequently availed themselves of poetic language and allegory. Seen with the eye of imagination, nature appeared to the ancients, as it can never appear to the analytical eye of a modern man, "composed, adjusted and ordinated to poetic effect."[18] Inspiring such a vision of nature and in turn inspired by it, the imagination of the ancients was itself like "those fields, fertile by nature, but never cultivated, which, when subjected to human industry, yield in the first few years two or three times more and produce a more vigorous and more lively crop than they can ever do in subsequent years, in spite of industry and culture."[19]

It is in the incomparable degree of freshness and fertility to be found in the ancients' imagination, which is itself to be largely accounted for by their infinitely closer contact with nature, that Leopardi found the main justification for his regarding the ancients' poetry and imagination as being immeasurably superior to that of the modern. This led him to the inevitable conclusion that, "strictly speaking, there were no poets if not the ancients, and now the only poets are the children or the youths, and the moderns who are called poets are nothing but philosophers."[20] Now, while using these terms of extreme simplification, based on a rather deliberately exaggerated antithesis between ancient and modern poetry, Leopardi might give us the impression of being so profoundly bewitched by the myth of antiquity that he cannot see the logic of any other point of view than his own. Now, while this is true up to a point, it is equally true that, within his own system of poetic values and principles, Leopardi goes a long way toward demonstrating that his convictions have all the force and consistency of logic behind them. The poetry of the ancients is predominantly the poetry of imagination, even though sentiment as such could not but play a very considerable part in it; on the other hand, the poetry of the moderns is predominantly the poetry of sentiment, inasmuch as the strength and efficacy of imagination have incalculably shrunk because of the advance of scientific knowledge, including the knowledge of the universe around us and of the place that man and his planet occupies in it. "The poetry of sentiment is uniquely and exclusively characteristic of this [modern] age, as the true and simple poetry of imagination was uniquely and exclusively characteristic of the Homeric age or of similar periods in other nations."[21]

The distinction between the poetry of imagination and the poetry of sentiment is in essence very similar to the distinction drawn, for example, by Matthew Arnold between the poetry of Dryden and Pope on the one hand and that of the Elizabethans or the Romantics, especially Wordsworth, on the other, and also to the one drawn, in our own times, by Robert Graves between Muse poetry and Apollonian poetry, which is itself reminiscent of the Nietzschean distinction between the Dionysian and the Apollonian in classical literature. "Apollonian poetry," says Graves, "is composed in the forepart of the mind: wittily, should the occasion serve, always reasonably, always on a preconceived plan, and derived from a close knowledge of rhetoric, prosody, Classical example, and contemporary fashion. . . . Muse poetry is composed at the back of the mind: an unaccountable product of a trance in which the emotions of love, fear, anger, or grief are profoundly engaged, though at the same time powerfully disciplined; in which intuitive thought reigns supralogically, and personal rhythm subdues metre to its purposes."[22] Leopardi regarded the poetry of the ancients as belonging indisputably to the category called Muse poetry, that of the moderns to the category of Apollonian poetry, with, of course, some exceptions in each case. And the reason why it is so is, according to Leopardi, the kind and quality of the imagination that the ancients possessed in the early dawn of civilization—an imagination free and creative of something not only poetically beautiful, but also something to which one could lend, as the ancients did lend, a whole-hearted emotional, and at times and to a certain extent, even intellectual credence, without having to suspend deliberately their faculty of belief or disbelief. It is not so with the moderns; the poetic myths and fables and illusions of the ancients, which constituted what Leopardi calls "the poetic [part or aspect] of nature" and which were for them something more than merely a myth or an illusion, have ceased to be poetic in proportion as they have come to be recognized for what they are really worth in a world predominantly governed by rational and scientific truth. While enlightening us about the various aspects and significance of nature, reason almost invariably tends to destroy the beauty and poetry of nature: "nature should like to be illuminated and not burnt by reason."[23]

The contrast between the ancients and the moderns, thus, presents itself in Leopardi's poetics as a contrast between reason and imagination as well as between the poetry of sentiment and the poetry of imagination. This contrast comes to affect Leopardi's conception of poetry and its very function. One paramount function of poetry being to lay bare the subtle and hidden relationships between the most diverse and dissimilar things or to reveal what Baudelaire was to call "correspondences," it is the kind of imagination possessed by the ancients rather than the enlightened but disillusioned kind held by the moderns that can best do so, that can best help poetry reveal "the intimacies, the secrets, the parts of the things, the remotest and the most segregated things."[24] It is imagination, and imagination alone, that can truly enrich our knowledge of things as they are in their hidden and imperceptible interrelationships, that can produce in us what Pater so happily described as "a quickened, multiplied consciousness." Reason can penetrate "to the essence of existing things or even of its own self."[25] But that "privileged world within a world" of physically non-existent, scientifically undemonstrable, and rationally unanalyzable and inexplicable relationships between the most dissimilar things as well as of illusions can be explored and mastered only with the help of imagination. One can say that imagination represents, as it generally always did in the case of the ancients, man and things as being greater and nobler than they really are, just as reason represents them in their prosaic exactness, thereby considerably impoverishing them.

Reason [says Leopardi] is harmful, it renders its user impotent, and the more one uses it, the more impotent one becomes; in proportion as the power of reason grows, that of him who exercises and possesses reason diminishes; and the more perfect the reason is, the more imperfect becomes the reasoning person. Reason renders all the objects to which it is applied small, vile, and insignificant; it annuls what is great and beautiful, and, so to speak, very existence itself; it is the true fount and mother of nothing, and the more it grows, the smaller things become; and the more powerful reason is in terms of intensity and expansion, the more the very being and essence of things is diminished and restricted and the more it approaches nothing.[26]

Associating reason with civilization, and both with modern times, Leopardi came to see nature, imagination, and antiquity as together forming an ideal pattern of social, historical, and cultural conditions within which great poetry can be and has been written. In so far as the ancients saw nature with the eye of imagination, more than with the eye of analytical reason, nature was for them something both lively and elevating, and not, as it very often is for the moderns, "a dead body."[27] Not that reason cannot help us understand the nature of things as they are; but the deeper the light of reason penetrates into the nature of an object, the smaller that object becomes: "The more it [reason] sees, the less it can see."[28] It is in the Leopardian sense of the imaginative approach to things, which necessarily renders them greater than they are, that Whitman stated in his preface to *Leaves of Grass:* "The greatest poet hardly knows pettiness or triviality. If he breathes into anything that was before thought small, it dilates with the grandeur and life of the universe." Hence, the ancient poets and writers seldom talked of man or nature except with a view to exalting or magnifying them. The modern poets, on the other hand, generally do nothing but belittle man and nature, for they see man, as Leopardi himself saw him in his poem "La Ginestra," pitiably dwarfed in the mighty context of an impersonal and unrecognizing universe, in which "not only man, but even / This globe, where man is nothing, / Is altogether unknown."

But that not even the ancients were "of imagination—all compact" is clearly demonstrated by the fact that both reason and imagination play an important part not only in their philosophy, but also in their myths, fables, and poetry. So a great philosopher as Plato was at the same time a poet, in so far as his use of language and his general approach and exposition of the nature of things are concerned. That is why, says Leopardi, one can say "that this quality [of being a perfect philosopher] is the rarest and the strangest quality that one can ever imagine, and that every ten centuries there is hardly one, if at all, who comes up endowed with such a quality." Describing how indispensable the collaboration between reason and imagination is,[29] Leopardi observes: "Reason needs imagination as well as the illusions that it destroys; just as truth needs falsehood; substance, appearance; the most perfect insensibility, the most lively sensibility; ice, fire; patience, impatience; impotence, the greatest power; the smallest, the greatest; geometry and algebra, poetry,"[30] in order to have any meaning at all. It is in their attitude to their mythology and poetic fables that the ancients are to be seen at their ablest in combining the offices of reason and imagination. If, as Leopardi says, "Homer did not, for certain, believe in what he imagined,"[31] much less did the people in Homer's times and later on believe in the mythologies and fables in their literal sense; and yet they not only felt delighted by their poetic form, but they were also impressed by their allegorical significance, which they accepted as far as it went. In other words, ancient mythology, or

rather the use of mythology in ancient times, does
not represent a contrast, but rather a harmony between
reason and imagination. The ancient poets knew
quite well that "imagination, except in the case of
children, has not, and need not have, a basis in
persuasion" and that though science "can greatly
weaken the imagination, it is still not incompatible
with it." What is, on the other hand, incompatible
with the lack of persuasion is sentiment, because
"sentiment, if it is not grounded in persuasion, is just
nothing."[32] In ancient Greek mythology, one finds
the combination of reason and imagination effected
by what Leopardi calls "amiable and natural illusions"
which serve to add sentiment to imagination, and
thus a certain degree of persuasion to the mythology
itself. In the use of mythology, too, the ancient poets
were both happier and wiser than the moderns. They
used myths, because

they wanted to explain and discover, and not mystify;
they tried to expound by means of sensible things those
things that cannot be perceived by the senses, and to
justify as best they could those very things which man
cannot understand, or which they themselves had not yet
been in a position to understand. The inventors of the
later mythologies, the Platonists, and especially people
in the early centuries of our era, decisively tried to look
for what is obscure in what is clear, to explain sensible
and intelligible things by means of things insensible and
unintelligible; they tried to justify things which were clear
and manifest by means of mysteries and secrets. The
early mythologies had no mysteries; on the other hand,
they were meant to explain clearly, to each and everyone,
the mysteries of nature; the later mythologies have been
invented in order to make us regard as mysterious and

superior to our intelligence that which we touch with our hands, that wherein, except for these mythologies, we should not have suspected to be any mystery at all.[33]

For the ancients, in virtue of the happy illusions and the fresh vision of the universe on which their imagination nourished itself without being obstructed or circumscribed by reason or scientific knowledge, mythologies were an important medium for interpreting their own experience to themselves and to others; for the moderns, whose imagination, no less than whose reason itself, is almost always, to borrow a phrase from Meredith, "hot for certainties" and much less capable of indulging in illusions than that of the ancients, mythologies cannot but have merely an ornamental function.

As regards also their treatment of pain and suffering in poetry, the ancient poets differed from the moderns and were, in a certain way, superior to them. For all their haunting awareness of the brevity of this life, and of the extreme uncertainty regarding any other, they did not sentimentalize pain or attribute any spiritual meaning to suffering. Instead of placing their hopes for happiness in another life, they sought to realize them in this very life and regarded misfortunes and calamities as mere "impediments and contrasts to that happiness, which did not seem to be a mere dream to the ancients as it seems to us—evils that could have been avoided and that have not been avoided."[34] Our attitude to suffering is not only more sentimental, but also more fatalistic than that of the ancients. Believing that suffering and pain have a certain spiritual meaning beyond our actual experience of it and that "some far off divine event" would bring some compensation for it in a future life, we resign ourselves to it and thus at least in part alleviate it. The ancients, on the contrary, were out to bear the full brunt of suffering or misfortune, without any consolation of a future reward. They did not, for instance, let their sense of Niobe's sorrow be influenced by or confounded with any sentiment of self-pity or tenderness. They faced it in all its tragic desperation and inevitableness as they faced, what Nietzsche in *The Birth of Tragedy* calls, a "non-teleological and godless" universe, "with highest affirmation, born of fullness and overfullness, a yea-saying without reserve to suffering's self, to guilt's self, to all that is questionable and strange in existence itself."

Thus, even though the ancients' attitude to as well as experience of suffering was more conducive to a genuinely tragic view of life, the general drift of their life and writings is, on the whole, cheerful rather than melancholy. It is only in the modern times that melancholy has come to be an inseparable ingredient in poetic sentiment.

No other poetry is proper to our times than melancholy poetry, no other tone of poetry than the melancholy tone, whatever might be the subject. . . . Among the ancients, everything was contrary. The natural tone that came out of their guitar was that of joy, of strength, of solemnity, etc. Their poetry was all joyously dressed, even when, in a certain way, the subject obliged it to be sad. What does it mean? Either the misfortunes of the ancients were less real than ours (and this is perhaps not true), or they knew or felt them less, which comes to mean the same thing, and to yield the same result, namely that the ancients were less unhappy than the moderns. And among the ancients, I also put, proportionately, Ariosto.[35]

For one thing this passage shows that Leopardi's demarcation between the ancient and the modern eras was flexible and fluctuated according to the argument he was discussing. Secondly, while referring to the modern age, he was, quite naturally, much influenced by his own age and his own interpretation of the *Zeitgeist*, which obviously influenced and in a certain way distorted the picture of those epochs that he included in the modern era, but that were antecedent to his own and therefore in many ways even quite different. However, these differences, rather of social and historical nature, do not seriously affect Leopardi's argument in so far as it concerns the nature of imagination in general, as it was possessed by the ancients, and the kind of imagination that is characteristic of the moderns. And the same is true of melancholy, which belongs much more conspicuously to the modern era, whether it starts with Dante, Petrarch, Shakespeare, or Ariosto.

What gives a characteristically melancholy tone to all modern poetry is the difference of attitude to suffering and its treatment in literature between the moderns and the ancients. The latter, generally speaking, deal with actual suffering undergone in one's real experience; the former base their melancholy poetry on the habitual contemplation of what Tennyson called "the doubtful doom of humankind" more often than on actual suffering or calamity itself. Leopardi believed that the ancients were always

greater, stronger, and more magnanimous than us [the moderns] in the excess of the misfortunes and in the consideration of the necessity thereof and of the invincible force which rendered them unhappy and tied them down to their misery, without any remedy or escape; they conceived of fate in terms of hatred and horror and blasphemed the Gods, declaring themselves in a certain way to be the enemies of heaven, even though impotent and incapable of victory or vengeance, but not therefore tamed or subdued, rather all the more desirous of vindicating themselves in proportion as their misery and necessity were great. . . . We, who neither recognize (nor believe in) fortune or fate, or any personified force and necessity which compels and rules over us, have no one against whom to vent the feeling of hatred and horror (if we are magnanimous and constant and incapable of yielding) except against ourselves.[36]

Hence the ancients were more in possession of the genuine feelings of terror and hatred than the moderns, and consequently not only had they more of firmness, constancy, magnanimity, and strength of character than the moderns, but also their way of looking at suffering and treating it in literature was conspicuously different. Today, the tragic sense has been replaced by the sense of a certain kind of comedy, which, in thoughtful persons, tends to be identified with the feeling of melancholy. "Because there are no more any spectators, all are reciting, and they do not have the virtue and the good qualities that they feign, and *nobody believes that others have them.*"[37] The melancholy comes from a vague sense of loss—loss of the many illusions which the ancients naturally and spontaneously possessed and which not only inspired certain virtues, but were also at times the very basis of and even identical with those virtues themselves. It is because of those illusions, for instance, that the ancients' attitude to suffering and their experience of tragedy and human destiny were so robust, inspiring and creative of the highest art. According to Leopardi, without illusions there cannot be great virtues as there cannot be great poetry; and so far as tragedy is concerned, it is also not possible either without illusions or without great virtues. In more philosophical and more eloquent language Nietzsche expounds somewhat the same connection between illusion and tragedy that one finds in Leopardi's comments. Referring to the hoped-for rebirth of tragedy and the faith in Dionysian life, Nietzsche tells us: "only from the Greeks can we learn what such a sudden and miraculous awakening of tragedy must signify for the inner fabric of a people's life. It is the people of the tragic mysteries who fight the battles with the Persians: and, conversely, the people who waged such wars required tragedy as a necessary healing portion. . . . Tragedy sets a sublime symbol, the myth, between the universal authority of its music and the receptive Dionysian hearer, and produces in him the illusion that music is only the most effective means for the animating, the plastic world of myth."[38]

Illusions, the sense of tragedy, and a powerful and fertile imagination unrestricted by too close and too factually definite a knowledge of the nature of the universe around us enabled the ancients to produce the sort of art they did and to live the sort of life of which their works are a living witness. Now, with the weakening of both illusions and imagination and the growing awareness and knowledge of the conditions governing existence which science and reason provide, the sublime and awe-inspiring sense of tragedy has given way to the feeling of melancholy, which is at times encouraged and at times overcome by the feeling of boredom—the Leopardian "noia" or the Baudelairian "ennui."

Thus the contrast between the ancient and the modern was an incomparably vital and effective means to Leopardi for understanding and interpreting others' experience as well as his own—experience both of life and of art, of all that renders the creation of art, and of poetry especially, possible.

CHAPTER FOUR

The Role of Melancholy and the
Concept of Poetic Inspiration

∽

IN SO FAR AS modern poetry is concerned, Leopardi, like so many poets before and after him, considered melancholy as something more congenial to poetic sentiment than cheerfulness. And it is not only more congenial to poetic sentiment, but also more conducive to the discovery of truth, and hence more useful to philosophers, than cheerfulness. At one point, and that through the creative philosophical value of melancholy, the antagonism, or what Leopardi himself calls the "unsurmountable barrier, a mortal enmity,"[1] between philosophical or scientific truth and poetic illusion, is broken down and a common ground is found where both can meet in harmony. If melancholy generates a poetic mood or poetic feelings, it is at the same time "the friend of truth, the light that can discover truth and that is less liable to err [than cheerfulness]"; a true philosopher, Leopardi adds, "in the state of cheerfulness cannot but persuade himself, not that the truth is good or beautiful, but that the evil, that is to say the truth, must be forgotten, and one must console oneself for it, or that one should give some substance to the things which do not really have any."[2] It is in giving substance and meaning to things which in themselves do not have it that the office of a poet and a philosopher approach each other. In fact Leopardi even goes so far as to declare that the two faculties, namely, the poetic faculty, whose goal is the beautiful, and the philosophical faculty, whose goal is the truth, have the closest affinity between them, that "the true poet is considerably disposed to be a great philosopher and the true philosopher to be a great poet, or rather neither one nor the other can be in his own kind either great or perfect unless he participates in more than a mediocre way in the other genre."[3]

Not that Leopardi always believed in the poetic efficacy of melancholy. In the period around 1818, he was at pains to demolish the romantic thesis, as approved and expounded by Lodovico Di Breme, according to which the element of pathos, often confused with what is lugubrious and melancholy, is considered to be an essential ingredient in modern poetry. As against the romantic thesis Leopardi advanced his own view that neither melancholy nor the pathetic note is an essential element in poetry and that poetry can just as well have other elements, such as the element of "the sublime, the exultant, the jubilant, . . . the carelessly gracious," and yet be poetry. But two years later, his own experience as a poet (he had already composed such poems as "Il primo amore," "All 'Luna," and "L'Infinito" among other poems), the psycho-religious conversion he underwent during his illness, and his anguished broodings on the destiny of man, dispossessed of his ancient faith and illusions, taught him to look upon melancholy as the most universally dominant feeling in modern poetry. It also led him to appreciate better the melancholy or tragic note in ancient poetry itself. He could now understand better why, for instance, even in ancient poetry the unhappy and unsuccessful hero of the *Iliad* is more interesting and more lovable than the happy and successful hero of the *Aeneid*.

But when it came to the discussion of the character and origin of modern poetry, that is to say of poetry written after Dante, Leopardi found it chiefly characterized by the note of melancholy, and thus he came to associate melancholy itself with poetic inspiration. Melancholy is seen as a natural outcome of the transition from the ancient poetry of imagination to the modern poetry of the heart or of sentiment. In the following passage Leopardi most explicitly lays bare his thought concerning this transition and the main distinction between the spirit of ancient and of modern poetry.

What is nowadays called heart among the human beings was little used in Homer's times, whereas imagination was used very much. Today, on the contrary (and thus also in the times of Virgil), imagination is generally speaking alloyed, frozen, torpid, extinct. . . . If the spirit of cultivated persons is still capable of any impression, of any living, sublime, and poetic sentiment, this properly belongs to the heart. . . . The poets of imagination today always manifest the labor, the effort, and the research, and since it was not imagination that moved them to poetize but they themselves, in order to express their brain and their talent and thus create and fabricate an artificial imagination, they seldom or never succeed in resuscitating and rekindling the true imagination, which is already dead in the spirit of the readers, and so they do not produce any good result."[4]

The fact that melancholy is a hallmark of the poetry that comes principally out of the heart and whose principal appeal is chiefly to the heart is related as a corollary to what Leopardi says concerning happiness or cheerfulness. Discussing the "essential and the only principal subject of" Homer's *Iliad* and Virgil's *Aeneid*, which is "a happy hero and an undertaking happily terminated," that happiness is useful only in so far as it excites the feeling of wonder, which itself appertains to the sphere of imagination, and not to that of the heart.

Now, since modern poetry is essentially a product of sentiment or heart rather than of imagination, melancholy is not only a necessary concomitant of poetry, but sometimes it is the very source and origin of poetic inspiration. Alfieri and Foscolo, says Leopardi, had a spark of genius because they were both melancholy by nature. Parini, on the other hand, tried to be cheerful, or at any rate preferred cheerfulness to melancholy in his poetry, just because he did not have a strong enough passion or sentiment to be a true poet. "Wherever melancholy does not reign in modern literature, the only reason for that is weakness." If happiness, whether "habitual or actual or momentaneous" is a necessary condition for "the development and exercise of imagination," it is unhappiness and "the misfortunes" that strengthen and deepen the sentiments, and hence the poetry of sentiment is bound to be melancholy. The poetic character of melancholy consists in this that it immerses "the spirit in an abyss of indeterminate thoughts, of which one cannot see either the bottom or the outline,"[5] and for the author of the poem "L'Infinito" what is vague and indeterminate, vast and immeasurable, is, as we shall see in a later chapter, the very soul and stuff of poetry. Hence melancholy and sentimental poetry—and the two epithets are complementary, if not precisely identical, in Leopardi's poetics—is "a breath of the soul"; one can say of poetry what is often said of love that the more the object of love has "a certain profound, melancholy, and sentimental character," harboring within itself something that does not come out, the better it is.

Poetic melancholy, however, must be distinguished from a morbid and uncreative kind of melancholy, which, as Giordani had occasion to point out to Leopardi, is "a poison that more or less destroys the power of the mind." It often lands a person into one of those situations, from the representation of which, to quote Matthew Arnold, "though accurate, no poetical enjoyment can be derived . . . in which suffering finds no vent in action; in which a continuous state of mental distress is prolonged, unrelieved by incident, hope or resistance." Leopardi himself described this kind of melancholy as "the state of resigned desperation, which is the last step of the sensible man, and the final sepulchre of his sensibility," being as it is "fatal to the sensibility and to poetry (in all the senses and extension of this term.)"[6] Poetic melancholy does not, and need not, always spring from real unhappiness or calamity, nor does it necessarily lead to unhappiness. In fact, melancholy is often compatible with the pleasure one finds in the discovery or even the very pursuit of truth, even though one knows about the utter incompatibility between truth and illusions, on which, when all is said and done, a large part of the happiness of most people, according to Leopardi, depends. And in so far as the transmutation of experience, experience even of the most melancholy and tragic sort, into art is concerned, it always implies a certain pleasure commensurate with the pleasure of artistic activity in general. Notwithstanding his personal unhappiness and his pessimistic philosophy of life, whatever they may have had to do with each other, Leopardi himself is a remarkable example of how one, who felt himself to be reduced to "a trunk that feels and suffers" by sorrow and disease, could still describe the time he spent in composing poetry to be "the best and the happiest period of my life." In his own life and work Leopardi bears out the truth of the parallel drawn by Shelley in his *Defence of Poetry* between the greatness of a man's poetry and his private virtues. Shelley merely touches upon this point, but does not develop it, as does Leopardi, according to whom there is a close relationship between virtue and happiness, on the one hand, and imagination and illusions on the other.

Even the poet's or the artist's pleasure, in the very act of transforming his sad experience into art, is something more than merely an aesthetic pleasure. It is often not unmixed with a certain feeling of pride and content in having more or less successfully grappled with and mastered even the most painful and most melancholy material and wrenched poetry out of it. This partly moral and partly aesthetic pleasure can be derived from and can coexist with, as it often does, not so much the kind of romantic melancholy as espoused by a Byron or a Chateaubriand, in which one revels, with an almost wilful hedonism, in gloom and melancholy for their own sake, as the one that arises from the contemplation on one's relation with oneself and with the universe. In a word, the Leopardian concept of poetic melancholy is more philosophical than romantic—a melancholy, as he says regarding the one produced by music, that "rather than pour itself out loves, on the contrary, to curl itself up, to gather within itself, and thus to confine the spirit as much as possible within itself."[7]

However, it is one thing to write or poetize about the general suffering of mankind and quite another to translate one's own suffering into art. The moment one starts doing so, one finds oneself involved in both an aesthetic and a moral problem at one and the same time. In order to give an adequate poetic expression to one's experience of suffering, it is not enough to feel it with a deep sincerity—in this connection one may recall Oscar Wilde's remark that all bad poetry comes from genuine feeling; one must also be able to detach oneself from one's own experience, so that one may relate it to a larger perspective and see it as being something more universal than a merely personal matter. The "bleeding heart" with which Byron wandered through Europe is poetically interesting only partly in so far as it is the heart of a particular individual—be it Byron, or Shelley, or Leopardi—but largely because we feel beating behind this heart the pulse of a larger and more universal heart, the heart of humanity. It is this union—and the greater the art, the more perfect it is—between the intensity of a personal emotion and the philosophical breadth of an impersonal or supra personal emotion, as we find, for instance, in Lucretius, that confers an artistic dignity and meaning to the expression of one's own sorrow and pain. Now, while this applies more or less to all emotions and experiences, it applies with a particular relevance to personal grief or suffering. Nowhere is what T. S. Eliot says regarding "the extinction of personality" so necessary and at the same time so difficult to achieve as when the poet is making his own pain or suffering the subject-matter of his song, or trying, to quote Leopardi, "as one often tries to consecrate my pain with poetry."[8] "The more perfect the artist," says Eliot, "the more completely separate in him will be the man who suffers and the mind which creates."[9] Indeed, it is not the theme or the subject-matter of melancholy or pessimistic poetry itself that can permanently delight or move us, but its artistic transmutation into something that acquires a greater meaning and also a greater aesthetic beauty

[71]

through that transmutation than what is inherently present in the experience.

It is in mastering his own experience of suffering —mastering in the only possible way it can be fully mastered by accepting it and giving it an appropriately artistic form, which is at once both personal and impersonal, particular and universal—that the poet's main business as well as pleasure lies. "If poets do find delight in the writing of sad poetry," says Geoffrey Tillotson concerning Pope's "Pastorals," "it is because of a consent that exists between sadness and poetry. Pope had more than his share of the actual sort that was anything but delicious."[10] Now Leopardi's share, as we know, was even greater than that of Pope, and yet if Leopardi himself could say that he experienced the greatest happiness of life in writing poetry, whose essential theme and matter was no other than that "share of sadness of the actual sort," it is not simply because of this natural, and, as it were, a priori consent between sadness and poetry, but because he had actually to forge or bring about such a consent, so that his poetry achieved the sweetness of song in proportion as it embodied the saddest thoughts or experience. And in order to be able to do so, Leopardi did not so much have to suppress, or escape from his own personality as to blend the terms and accents of his most personal sorrow with his *Weltschmerz*. A large part of his success in this direction can be attributed to the consistent and unfailing mastery with which he used the language—a language that he brought as close as any poet has ever done to the very core of his thought or passion. As regards what is personal and what is impersonal or philosophical about the origin of pessimism in his poetry, there is hardly any inconsistency between what Leopardi said to Giordani at the age of 22 and what he wrote to Louis de Sinner just five years before his death. "My pain," he wrote to Giordani, "derives more from the sentiment of my own unhappiness than from the certainty of the universal and inevitable unhappiness."[11] And about twelve years later he wrote to Louis de Sinner, complaining that "people have liked to consider by philosophical opinions as the result of my particular sufferings, and have persistently attributed to my material circumstances what I owe to understanding. Before I die, I should like to protest against this invention on the part of the weak and the vulgar, and pray my readers to try to confute my observations and my reasoning rather than blame my diseases."[12] For, the fact is that if the earlier Leopardi, who even at the age of twelve wanted his father to "read clearly in my heart those sentiments which I tried to express in words" without "exaggeration or lies," regarded poetry, much the same way as Wordsworth did, as a direct and spontaneous expression of one's deepest thoughts and feelings, the later and maturer Leopardi could very well assert, without substantially contradicting himself, that his views on life, as expressed in his poetry, are something much more than a simple outcome or reflection of his personal experiences and sufferings. He simply enlarged his earlier and relatively immature definition of poetry as an utterance of personal feelings into a larger and maturer definition, according to which poetry seeks to build something impersonally larger and more meaningful on the very basis of what is fundamentally particular and personal to the poet. Even what apparently seems to be the most personal statement may sometimes embody, if we are careful enough to probe beyond the surface meaning of the poet's language, something larger and impersonal. All great poetry has more than one layer of significance, and the language of poetry is to use Baccaccio's favorite expression, "polyseme," each layer and each grade of significance representing different layers of consciousness both in the poet and in the reader. Hence even the most subjective lyrical poetry ceases to be personal in the narrow sense of the term. While the personal note may ring as clear as ever, other notes of a less personal character, demanding a subtler perception and a more alert attention on the part of the reader, may have come to mingle with the personal note, enriching it and in turn being enriched by it. Thus the poem in question may attain to the level of great poetry where the distinction between personal and impersonal, subjective and objective, particular and universal ceases to exist.

Leopardi's defining modern poetry as essentially the poetry of sentiment, as distinguished from ancient poetry which is predominantly the poetry of imagination and his considering the sentiment of melancholy as the most indispensable factor in the poetic sentiment bring us face to face with the question of poetic inspiration itself, as Leopardi understood it. Though he did not actually identify poetic inspiration with poetic invention, he found the element of chance, both unpredictable and uncontrollable as it is by its very nature, to be an essential feature of poetic invention no less than that of poetic inspiration itself. It is on chance, observes Leopardi, that many discoveries in practically every sphere of human life have always depended. "An invention due to the genius or talent and meditation of a profound man is not considered accidental. But how many extremely accidental circumstances were required before man could attain to that capacity! Circumstances relating to the cultivation of his talent, to his birth, his studies; the extrinsic means of innumerable kinds, which, through their combination, have made him what he is and without which he would have been an entirely different person."[13] Thus not only poetic inspiration, but even poetic invention, like any other kind of invention, is very often a matter of chance, which, of course, does not mean that in order to make a worthy and fruitful use of it, the poet or artist need not prepare himself by way of study or training. And study and training, even though they cannot be a substitute for poetic inspiration, are yet necessary not only for the poet but also for the reader of poetry, if he wants to appreciate fully the meaning and beauty of what he is reading. Almost as if in contrast with his own conviction—of which more later—that a poet must and does write for the people in general, and not for the scholar or the specialist, Leopardi asserts that

the fine, intimate, and exquisite pleasure of the arts—that is to say the pleasure of perfected arts (and among the arts I include poetry and literature)—cannot be understood except by the connoisseurs, because it is one of those pleasures for the perception of which nature has not provided us with any sensory organ; it is custom that provides that, and custom means study and exercise. Hence, in order that people, who would never be able to have such a study and exercise, may enjoy the pleasure of literature, it is necessary that there should be available a less perfect literature. Such pleasure will always be inferior to the pleasure derived by the connoisseurs from the more perfect works of literature.[14]

It is the indispensable need and utility of study and exercise both for the poet and for the reader of poetry that brings into focus the question of poetic inspiration, because study and training are simply means whereby the poet can fully avail himself of what inspiration, and inspiration alone, can give him, and without which no creative activity is really possible. And even the reader of poetry himself can hardly appreciate what has been created through inspiration, without experiencing to some extent that very inspiration. Though Leopardi does not use the word "inspiration" very often in his discussion of poetry, he knew perfectly well, both as a reader of others' poetry and from his own experience as a poet, what inspiration meant and how indispensable it is in any creative and imaginative activity. In 1824, in a letter to his cousin Giuseppe Melchiori, who had asked him for a poem to be published in a collection honoring one Orazio Carnevalini, Leopardi explained why he could not bring himself to produce an occasional poem of the sort:

You have not been wrong in promising [that poem] on my behalf, because you thought that I was like others who write verses. But please know that in this, as in every other thing, I am very disimilar from and very inferior to others. And as regards verses, to understand my nature would help you from now on on similar occasions. In my life I have not written anything except very few and very short poems. While writing them, I have not followed anything else except inspiration (or frenzy) so that when it came up I formed the design and the distribution of the whole composition in just two minutes. Having done this, I usually wait that it may turn up again, and when it does so (which ordinarily does not happen except in a few months), I sit down to compose, but to compose so slowly that it is not possible for me to finish even the shortest poem in less than two or three weeks. This is my method, and if inspiration is not born of itself, it is easier for the water to come out of the trunk of a tree than for a single verse to come out of my head. Others can poetize whenever they will, but I have not got this faculty at all so that however much you might request me [to write a poem], it would be no use, not because I should not like to please you, but because I could not. . . . My verses would rather produce the contrary effect . . . for it is certain that to ask one, with a nature so difficult and so barren as mine, for verses is the same as to ask me for a bishopric: the latter I am not in a position to give, and the former I do not know how to compose, if not by sheer chance.[15]

Under the polite garb of modesty, however sincere it might be, one cannot but detect Leopardi's legitimate pride as an artist lurking subtly behind each and every line in this letter, which happens, at the same time, to be a kind of poetic manifesto concerning his own method rather than a criticism, couched in consciously or unconsciously ironical terms, of other poets' methods. And his own method obviously influenced his conception of poetry in general, and of poetic inspiration in particular. His small poetic output itself is due,[16] not so much to his ideal of perfection as to the importance which his innermost nature both as a man and as a poet made him attach to poetic inspiration. His conviction regarding the supreme value and utility of inspiration sprang more from his personal nature and experience than from any intellectual fondness for or interest in theories as theories. And even as regards his theoretical interest in the idea of inspiration, Leopardi had other mighty names in poetry as precedents, who had a similar interest and conviction about the incomparable and indispensable efficacy of inspiration, yet whose own poetic output was far from being small. "If poetry comes not as naturally as the leaves to a tree," Shelley had said, "it had better not come at all." And, according to Plato, "he who without the Muses' madness in his soul comes knocking at the door of poesy and thinks that art will make him anything fit to be called a poet finds that the poetry which he indites in his sober senses is beaten hollow by the poetry of madness." What actually limited Leopardi's output, among other things, was his conviction, backed again as it was by his practical experience as a poet, regarding the poet's need for knowledge and art. Inspiration, though indispensable, is not enough. Hence if Leopardi believed, along with Plato and Shelley, in the absolute indispensability of poetic frenzy or inspiration, he also believed, at the same time, with Dante in the necessity of cultivating art and talent through study and exercise. Like Dante, in *De Vulgari Eloquentia,* he considered them fools who "without art and knowledge and trusting in genius alone rush forward to sing of the highest themes in the highest style."

Another reason for Leopardi's small output was his continuous ill health and misfortunes. "You ask me," he had written to his friend Giordani, as early as 1820, when he was hardly more than 22 years old, "what I think and write. But for a long time I have neither thought nor read nor written anything, owing to the persistent imbecility of the nerves of the eyes and head: perhaps I would not leave behind me anything more than mere sketches of works which I have been meditating and through which I have been exercising, in the best manner I can, the faculty of invention which is now extinguished in the Italians."[17] Indeed, if anything, Leopardi's interest in poetic theory must have afforded him a powerful incentive, in so far as it led him to realize that the kind of lyric which alone he really considered to be worth the name (for instance the three poems of Petrarch "O aspettata," "Spirit gentil" and "Italia mia") was, on the whole, lacking in modern Italian poetry and to feel that it was not only high time to recreate it, but that he was endowed by nature and study to do so.

Moreover, Leopardi combined, as we have already noted, in an almost unparalleled degree, so far as Italian literature is concerned, a highly critical conscience with the creative gift. If Dante's or Milton's poetic output is larger than Leopardi's, it is, in part at least, because his life-span was obviously shorter than theirs. Nevertheless, the fiber of which the poetic genius of all these poets was composed is practically the same, and the basic principles and beliefs that governed their poetic compositions are also no less identical. Inspiration and art—art studied and cultivated with a self-conscious and painstaking industry and inspiration which cannot be forced, which must be obeyed if and when it comes, and without which no great poetry is possible—both Dante and Milton as well as Leopardi considered to be the two indispensable and inseparable aspects of the same process and experience.

But indispensable as inspiration is to a poet, it is of its very nature—and here Leopardi clearly anticipates Poe, Croce, and others—bound to be short-lived, and not only in the poet, but also in the reader of poetry. One noteworthy feature of Leopardi's theory of inspiration is that he views it not only in relation to the poet, but also in relation to the reader, who needs it almost as much as the poet himself in order to be able to recreate the poem in himself, more or less the same way as the poet did when he wrote it —a process which is implicitly and inevitably involved in the proper act of reading poetry.[18] "Enthusiasm and inspiration, which are so essential to poetry, are not durable things. Nor can they last very long in the reader of poetry."[19] Hence, poetry "consists essentially of impetus"[20] and the most propitious period for writing poetry is, generally speaking, the period of youth which is naturally richer in impulsive and emotional life than any other period. Leopardi calls it "the epoch of the perfection of man as well as of other things," including, of course, the poetic faculty, and "the youthful ardor" itself as "the greatest force, the apex, the acme of human nature."[21] That is why Leopardi considers enthusiasm, if not actually identical with inspiration, then at least the most requisite state of heart and mind in which, and in which alone, inspiration can be obtained. It is when coupled with enthusiasm that poetic inspiration shows itself to be most creative and renders the poet, especially the lyric poet, most capable of seeing things in a unique way—something which the poet cannot do with the help of "the longest, the most patient, and the most exact researches, experiences, comparisons, studies, reasoning, meditations, exercises of the mind, the talent, and the faculty to think, to reflect, to observe, and to reason."[22] Inspiration and enthusiasm, though they affect the poet in a much greater degree, can and very often do change even a common man's way of looking at things and enable him to see those things, to have those rare moments of vision, which neither he, nor even the poet or the philosopher, is ordinarily capable of seeing or having.

The lyric poet when inspired, the philosopher in the sublimity of his speculation, the man of imagination and sentiment when full of enthusiasm, or any man whatsoever when dominated by a strong passion or even in the course of weeping—and I dare add even a man moderately warmed up by wine—sees things as if from a higher level than the level from which an ordinary human mind is accustomed to see them. Hence it is that, by discovering at one and the same time many more things than he is usually capable of doing and by apprehending at one single stroke of the eye a multitude of objects, which are ordinarily seen by him one by one, and never all at once . . . he is in a position to perceive, together with these objects, even their mutual relationship; and because of the novelty of that multitude of objects which simultaneously present themselves to his mind, he is led to consider these objects and to note their inter-relationship better than he had done before or than he is used to do.[23]

Now, because the nature of inspiration and enthusiasm is, like that of youth itself, relatively short-lived and since poetry is essentially and exclusively the product of such inspiration, fervor, mania, or frenzy, a long poem of epic dimensions is, according to Leopardi, something "against the nature of poetry."[24] An epic poem requires, says Leopardi,

a plan well conceived and ordered in all coldness. But then what has a work that requires years and years of execution got to do with poetry, since poetry is essentially a matter of impetus? A long poem is also against nature itself in an absolute sense. It is impossible that imagination, the poetic vein, the poetic spirit, should suffice and should not fail in the course of such a long work on the same argument. Virgil's fatigue and labor are no less famous than manifest in the last six books of the *Aeneid,* which he wrote by dint of his willpower and not as a result of inner impulse or will.[25]

[82]

Leopardi, however, does not give an adequately detailed or convincing explanation of why Homer's *Iliad,* for instance, is to be regarded as an exception to this rule. His only explanation is that the epic poem itself, having a lyrical origin—in so far as the lyric is the "first-born of all" poetic genres—is, therefore, in a way, nothing but "an amplification of the lyric; that is to say, the lyric genre has, from among its other means and subjects, principally assumed and chosen the narrative form, poetically modified."[26] Hence, if Homer's *Iliad* is the most perfect epic, it is because of the excellence of those lyrics as lyrics that are woven together into this form by means of the narrative rather than in virtue of any epic qualities in it as an epic. It is not that Leopardi completely ignores the architectonic aspect of the epic or the characters in it; in fact, he goes so far as to point out that the *Iliad,* "besides being the most perfect epic poem as regards its design . . . is thus also as regards the principal characters in it, which are more interesting than those of other epic poems."[27] But in so far as it is poetry, it is so because it is nothing but a long series of many lyrics.

Even drama is also considered to be (and again because of the inherent supremacy of the lyric as well as the concept of poetry as something invented and created and not as something imitated) an inferior and less poetic form of literature. "It is not an inspiration, but an invention; offspring of civilization, not of nature; poetry in virtue of the conventions governing it and the will of the author, more than in virtue of its own essence. . . . The poet is driven to poetize by his own intimate sentiments, not by those of others. To pretend to have a passion, a character other than one's own (something so necessary to a dramatist) is something quite alien to a poet's nature. . . . The dramatist's inspiration is something feigned, because he must feign."[28] This judgment of drama is not simply the result of Leopardi's own strong predilection, both as a reader and as a writer of poetry, for the lyrical, but a result of his conception of the essence of the nature of poetry as well as of the nature of inspiration, which inevitably led him to this conclusion. The lyric was consequently considered by him to be the highest and purest kind of poetry, "the most excellent form of composition," "the top, the culmination, the summit of poetry," "a genre, which because it is the first in temporal order, is thus also eternal and universal . . . the only genre that remains for the moderns." Thus even though Leopardi was opposed to the romantics in theory, he came to look upon the lyric, just as they did, as being not only the most favored, but also intrinsically the best form of poetry, the one most suited to the genius, aptitude, and cultural and psychological experience of a modern poet.

Leopardi, therefore, not only asserted the view that the lyric is the highest kind of poetry, but he also discussed and analyzed, with an unparalleled lucidity, acuteness, and relevance, the essentially subjective nature of all that deserves to be called lyric poetry. It is this emphasis on the subjective nature of poetry that prevented Leopardi from conceding that by means of imagination and what Coleridge called "empathy" a dramatic poet can, as indeed Shakespeare so superbly did, enter into the mind and feelings of others as different from himself as they are different from each other and, while describing their feelings and thought, create poetry no less authentic than what Leopardi understands by lyric poetry, that even a manifestly lyrical and subjective poetry like that of Byron can at times be, as Leopardi himself was to point out, as "artificial" and as much "squeezed by force" as dramatic or epic poetry itself, and that even in a nondramatic poetry where personal subjectivism does not parade itself so ostentatiously one could nonetheless feel the same degree of lyrical depth and intensity.

It is the question of how Leopardi conceived of the nature of poetic inspiration, allied with that of the importance he attached to it in the creative process, distinguishing inspiration from consciously cultivated art and from assiduously acquired knowledge, that has much to do with Leopardi's exaltation of the lyric as the highest kind of poetry. What is not of itself authentically lyrical in poetry was not much esteemed in Leopardi's view. In a way therefore, Leopardi may be considered to be the spiritual father *malgré lui* (since in his own poetry he is something quite different) of what is termed "pure" poetry. As a poet himself, Leopardi like all good theorists of poetry, who are also good poets, occasionally took leave of what he had solemnly theorized about. For instance, he who had written so much in praise of illusions as the very life-source of poetic inspiration does not have much use for illusions in his own verses, which are, from first to last, in closest alliance with "truth"—the bitter and disillusioning truth—that, in Leopardi's theory of poetry, is supposed to be so detrimental to the poetic frame of mind. But the way he considered everything else that was not directly and indirectly conducive to a poem's lyricism as something extraneous to the real essence and meaning of poetry qualifies Leopardi as the principal originator of pure poetry among all the major poets and poetic theorists of his age in Italy and abroad.

CHAPTER FIVE

The Creative Use of Memory, Imagination, and Imitation

ᖰᖳ

THE WORLD is born with everyone who is born in the world,"[1] said Pascoli, who shared with poets like Blake, Wordsworth, and Leopardi the vision of childhood as being the happiest period not only in man's life, but, in a certain important and incomparable way, also, in the poet's. Leopardi himself, as we have already seen, regarded a child's imagination to be the only authentically Homeric type of imagination—an imagination that abounds in that quality of "the aery and the beautiful" which, according to him, constitutes one of the most essential characteristics of the poetic sentiment. Now, though the "first fine careless rapture" with which the child takes in the manifold marvels of "the mighty world of eye and ear," and the still greater rapture with which, on the basis of these marvels, he creates other marvels in his own extremely fertile imagination, may not be recaptured and repeated in the life and imagination of an ordinary man, memory, together with imagination, enables the poet to recall and recreate something of the lost splendor and glory of the child's vision of this world and of his feelings for it. The importance of memory as a creative factor in Leopardi's poetic theory as well as in his poetry itself is hardly second to that of imagination, and this all the more so because in him, to quote Pascoli again, "childhood was the whole of his life. That is why he is the poet more dear to us and more poetic, since he is the more childlike [than anyone else]; or I would rather say that he is the only child that Italy has in the canon of her poetry."[2]

In making creative use of the experiences of childhood, memory helps imagination in reliving them. Like Wordsworth, Leopardi believed that not the presence of actual emotion, but a relatively tranquil state of the recollection of that emotion is the ideal condition for the creative process, in so far as it involves—as it quite often does—the invention of a subject or theme.

In fine arts it is necessary to distinguish enthusiasm, imagination, heat [of passion], etc., from invention, especially of the subjects. The sight of beautiful nature excites enthusiasm. If this excitement happens to come to one who already has in hand a subject, it will afford him the force of execution, and also help him in the invention and originality of the secondary order, that is to say of the parts, of style, the images, in a word of all that concerns the execution, but little or not at all in the invention of the subject. In order that enthusiasm may be of any help, it is necessary for it to revolve around and be caused by that subject itself, for instance, the enthusiasm caused by a certain passion. But the vague, abstract, indefinite enthusiasm that men of genius often feel on hearing a piece of music, or at the sight of nature, etc., is not favorable in any way to the invention of a subject, and hardly even of the parts, because in those moments the man is almost beside himself. In those moments he abandons himself as if it were to an external force that transports him, is not capable of collecting or fixing his mind upon his ideas; whatever he sees is infinite, indeterminate, fleeting, and at the same so various and so copious, that it does not admit of any rule or order, or of any possibility of numbering, disposing or choosing, or even simply of conceiving in a clear and complete way, and still less of apprehending a point (that is to say a subject) to which he might reduce all the sensations and images which he feels in himself, but which have no center.[3]

Excess of passion and enthusiasm may often well lead to a sort of poetic barrenness; from Wordsworth's definition of poetry as "emotion recollected in tranquillity" we pass on to an analogous, but more detailed and more specific definition of the poetic faculty recovering itself from the excessive exuberance and multitudinousness of a powerful passion or excitement, in order to be able to operate—which effectively means to compose, organize, select, and polish—at all. While the poet's eye is rolling "in fine frenzy," the actual act of composing poetry has not even so much begun, or at the most it is in a very preliminary stage. While illustrating his thesis that a poet "when brimful of enthusiasm and passion is not a poet, that is to say, is not in a position to poetize," Leopardi goes farther than Wordsworth in exploring the psychology of the poet while he is under the influence of a certain passion and excitement, as well as while he is actually busy translating his poetic vision or experience or its recollection into words. "At the sight of nature, while his whole spirit is full of the image of the infinite, while ideas crowd together in his mind, he is incapable of distinguishing, choosing or grasping any one of them. . . . The infinite cannot be expressed except when one is not feeling it: or after one has felt it: and when the great poets wrote of those things which arouse in us the admirable sensations of the infinite, their spirit was not full of the sensations of the infinite; and while depicting the sense of the infinite, they did not feel it."[4] It is only when the heat and fury of the passion is spent, and the relative calm of the mind and spirit is returned that one can poetize; enthusiasm and inspiration themselves, which make for creative activity, are something subsequent to and not coexistent with the actual emotion. This does not mean that composing a poem is like solving a problem of algebra, or writing a postmortem report; but it does mean that the difference between the poet's psychological state while he is actually under the influence of the emotion and the state of mind while he is recollecting it, however moved and excited he might be in the course of this recollection, is not simply one of degree, but also of kind.

What is required is a period of force [meaning thereby emotion or passion] but tranquil force; a period of actual genius [or capacity] rather than that of actual enthusiasm . . . an effect of the past or future or habitual enthusiasm, rather than its very presence, and one may say its twilight rather than its very midday. Often that moment is the aptest [for writing poetry] when after a certain enthusiasm, after a certain emotion that one has experienced, the spirit, even though calm, surges up again, as it were, after the storm, and recalls with pleasure the past sensation. That is quite frequently the aptest moment for the conception of an original subject, or of its original parts. And generally speaking one can say that in the fine arts and in poetry, the demonstrations of enthusiasm, imagination, and sensibility, are rather the immediate fruit of the memory of the enthusiasm on the author's part, than of the enthusiasm itself.[5]

Some of Leopardi's own poems—for instance, "A Silvia," "L'Infinito," "Le Ricordanze"—are the outcome of "emotion recollected in tranquillity" rather than of the emotion itself, while it was bodily present. When Leopardi says that he never wrote poetry unless he was inspired—and hence, in a way, compelled—to write it, he means that he could not conceive of what to write and why to do so, unless inspiration gave him both the material and the emotion appropriate to that material, but the actual task of composing the poem came after inspiration had done its job. The first immediate fruit of poetic inspiration or emotion in Leopardi's case was not a poem, but a prose draft or outline of what might later, on a calmer and more suitable occasion, be utilized for the poem to be. In this respect, Leopardi's was a method of composition much similar to A. E. Housman's as described in the latter's *The Name and Nature of Poetry.* Describing the production of poetry as an involuntary, rather than a voluntary, process—a process comparable to a secretion, "whether a natural secretion, like turpentine in the fir, or a morbid secretion, like the pearl in the oyster"—Housman goes on to illustrate his own method of composition:

Having drunk a pint of beer at luncheon—beer is a sedative to the brain, and my afternoons are the least intellectual portion of my life—I would go out for a walk of two or three hours. As I went along, thinking of nothing in particular, only looking at things around me and following the progress of the seasons, there would flow into my mind, with sudden and unaccountable emotion, sometimes a line or two of verse, sometimes a whole stanza at once, accompanied, not preceded, by a vague notion of the poem which they were destined to form part of. Then there would usually be a lull of an hour or so, then perhaps the spring would bubble up again. I say bubble up, because, so far as I could make out, the source of the suggestions thus proffered to the brain was an abyss which I have already had occasion to mention, the pit of the stomach. When I got home I wrote them down, leaving gaps and hoping that further inspiration might be forthcoming another day. Sometimes it was, if I took my walks in a receptive and expectant frame of mind; but sometimes the poem had to be taken in hand, and completed by the brain, which was apt to be a matter of trouble and anxiety, involving trial and disappointment, and sometimes ending in failure.[6]

From what we have seen Leopardi himself saying about the creative process in general, and from the rough sketches of some unfinished poems that did attain to the finality of form and shape, we can conclude that Leopardi's method too was quite similar to Housman's.

In this process, therefore, the role of memory is obviously very vital. It is vital because memory is not merely a custodian of the past—and for Leopardi as well as for the romantics in general the past is intrinsically more poetic than the present, and the sense and sentiment of what is old and ancient, of the "old unhappy far-off things," or of what Baudelaire called "a far-off world, absent and almost defunct" is, according to Leopardi, "a very capital ingredient of the sublime sensations"[7]—but it also transforms the past, making it more poetically attractive. It is through memory that past continues to live in the poet's mind, not merely as a record of something dead and gone, but an active agent coloring and molding, to a certain extent, much that poetically interests him in the present. "Everything becomes poetry in remembrance," said Novalis. And it becomes poetry precisely in virtue of the fact that poetic memory is something more than mere memory in the ordinary sense of the term. "Availability, not mere possession," however, says I. A. Richards, "is what is essential. . . . What is in question here is not memory, in the stricter sense in which past experience is dated and placed, but free reproduction."[8]

But if memory and recollection are of great help to the poet, they are no less useful even for the reader of poetry. The full effect of a poetic image on the reader's mind, for instance, depends, to a large extent, not so much on his grasping the exact meaning and function of that image in the context where it occurs, as on his remembered experience of the object or the phenomenon on which that image is based. Whether this experience of which he cherishes the memory has been a firsthand experience (that is to say, something seen or touched or heard or undergone in his own real life) or a secondhand experience, whose source may be, among other things, books and poems read by him, makes practically little difference, so far as the reader's capacity to react to the image is concerned. And the capacity to react invariably involves the capacity to recognize or recall something already known to the reader. The sharper his capacity to recognize what is old and familiar, the more prompt his response to what is really new in the image would be.

But memory is only one of the aspects of the rather complex poetic process, imagination and imitation being the other two. Though Leopardi starts with the Aristotelian premise that art is the imitation of nature, he uses the word imitation in such a comprehensive and, at the same time, such a specialized sense that it often comes not only to mean something quite different from what Aristotle himself meant by it, but also to be identified with imagination or invention. As a result of this Leopardi sometimes seems to contradict himself; we deliberately say "seem" because in fact he does not really do so; he simply enlarges the meaning or explores new aspects of the same meaning or new reasons for the importance he originally attached to his statements regarding art as the imitation of nature. To begin with, by imitation Leopardi meant representation of both what is beautiful and what is ugly in nature, because he believed, even before Baudelaire, that the imitation of what is ugly in nature can be just as much a source of artistic delight as the imitation of what is beautiful. In the very act of imitating, art, in a very profound way, modifies or even transforms the very nature of the thing imitated. "That which when seen in the reality of things discourages or kills the spirit," Leopardi says, "when seen in imitation . . . opens and revives the heart."[9] The pleasure of reading a tragedy or seeing it performed on the stage does not come from the tragic theme or material or story itself, but from the way the material has been selected, molded into a well-wrought pattern, and given a definite form, which itself confers a new depth or a new dimension on the material treated. In tragedy, as in other forms of artistic imitation, the principle of selection as applied to what the artist picks up from out of the mass of material which everyday experience puts into one's hands, must not be confused with discrimination in the choice of experiences themselves as such. All experience, Leopardi insists, is valid as material for artistic imitation.

A plea for the inclusion in artistic imitation of what is ugly or unpleasant in nature did not imply for Leopardi, as it did, to some extent, for the later romantic-cum-aesthetic poets from Baudelaire and Gautier onwards, that the ugly imitated in art so as to look aesthetically interesting, and even beautiful in a certain way, ceased to be morally ugly or deplorable. In other words, artistic beauty, according to Leopardi, does not and should not be taken to mean as any condonation, acquiescence, or justification on the part of the artist with regard to what is intrinsically and inherently immoral in the object imitated or the argument treated—not that Leopardi does not at times seem to have conceived of artistic beauty or the beauty of form *per se*, that is to say, something isolated from and independent of the moral implications and attributes of the content as well as from the content itself. But the moment artistic beauty and the content it clothes or expresses are wedded together, art ceases to be autonomous and gets inseparably entangled with the moral implications of the content or the material in question. For Leopardi, as well as for Arnold, poetry divorced from morality is poetry divorced from life, inasmuch as the whole of life itself, and not merely three-fourths of it, is conduct, necessitating the presence and operation of moral criteria for its full and proper evaluation. This does not, of course, mean that an artist should make it his aim to preach morality, or even deliberately choose subjects which explicitly lend themselves for a strictly moral treatment more than others. Granted that the imitation of nature as it is or as the artist, by means of his senses and imagination, finds it to be, is the aim of art, it does not really matter whether the thing imitated is more beautiful or less beautiful in itself, more moral than immoral, so long as the imitation is perfect, that is, so long as it is a true and faithful imitation of the thing as it is in nature.

Not the beautiful but the true or the imitation of Nature in any form is the object of fine arts. If it were the beautiful, then what is more beautiful and what thus partakes of the perfection of beauty in the metaphysical

sense would please us more; whereas such beauty, instead
of pleasing us, nauseates us so far as the arts are concerned. . . . And that what is beautiful in nature is not
the only object of the fine arts is seen in all the poets and
especially in Homer, because if it had been so, then every
great poet would have done his utmost to look for what
is most beautiful in nature, whereas Homer has represented
Achilles to be infinitely less beautiful than what he could
have done . . . , then Anacreontes would have been a
greater poet than Homer. . . . The perfection of a work
of art is not to be judged according to whether it represents the most beautiful, but whether it is the most perfect
imitation of nature.[10]

Thus neither what is morally nor what is aesthetically
beautiful is the sole exclusive object of artistic imitation, but at times even what is its very reverse, so long
as the imitation is truthful, perfect, and natural. For
all his wide reading in the contemporary literature
on the ideas concerning the abstract concept of beauty
as well as in that of the past, and for all his own
musings and deliberations on the subject, Leopardi
never regarded beauty to be the sole object of art,
and there is consequently no truth whatsoever in
what Vossler says about Leopardi that he was "a
follower and a victim of that religion of beauty which
had mastered the spirits at the turn of the eighteenth
century."[11] Though one can deduce a system of
aesthetics from Leopardi's numerous reflections on
beauty and art or find in them the germ of what
would, later on in the nineteenth century, be elaborated and systematized into a whole philosophy of
aesthetics, Leopardi was, of course, by no means an
aesthete in the usual sense of the term. His concern

with art, for all its abstract and theoretical aspects, was something too much rooted in a solid grasp of the eternal values of great poetry as he found them actually represented and operative in the master-pieces of antiquity and of Homer in particular, to let him indulge in an altogether new theory of arts and aesthetics, or in what Nietzsche calls "a transvaluation of all values." At times, his thought does adumbrate the later philosophies of art and poetics, and in this, as we shall notice in a subsequent chapter, he is by far the most modern and most liberal-minded of all the nineteenth century Italian writers, and also a much greater pioneer in poetic theory than Croce and his followers in general have given him credit for. For instance, he anticipates in more than one way the cardinal points of Poe-Baudelaire-Gautier aesthetics. Poe had granted, for instance, while discussing the aim and function of art, that "the precepts of Duty, or even the lessons of Truth" may be introduced in a poem, but only in order "to subserve incidentally, in various ways, the general purpose of the work"; how-ever, a true artist "will always tone them down in proper subjection to that Beauty which is the atmo-sphere and real essence of the poem."[12] Baudelaire and Gautier, the formerly directly under the influence of Poe, came out with a more drastic onslaught against the utilitarian aim or element in poetry. Baudelaire even professed "a very decisive hatred against every exclusive moral intention in a poem," and Gautier declared in the perface to *Mademoiselle de Maupin* that "all that is useful is dull." In Leopardi, too, we have the same desire to disentangle the aim and *raison d'être* of poetry from its didactic or utilitarian motives, without, however, the adoption of a narrow and exclusive aesthetic creed.

The useful is not the aim of poetry, though poetry may avail itself of it. The poet may even aim at what is useful and obtain it (as perhaps Homer may have done) without, however, the useful becoming the end of poetry, in the same way, for example, as a farmer may avail himself of the axe for reaping oats or something else, even though reaping is not the function of the axe. Poetry can be directly useful, just as the axe can reap, but to be useful is not the natural end of poetry, which it can really do without, as it cannot do without the delightful, since to delight is the natural function of poetry.[13]

Thus, Leopardi's aesthetic or rather pseudo-aesthetic approach to poetry is just another way of his laying stress and expatiating on the essential aim and character of poetry as it always has been since the days of Homer. All the social, cultural, and historical changes, all the discoveries and inventions of science, and all the revolutions in the realm of thought and morals that may have taken place have not changed and cannot change the essential nature and function of poetry which is to delight more than anything else. And this delight, Leopardi maintains, can be procured as much from the imitation of the ugly and unpleasant in nature as from the beautiful; and though to teach or inform is not the function of poetry, it may incidentally do so, and, in fact, it very often does so, since the material treated by art is itself never amoral, any more than the artist's personality can be altogether so.

Whatever predilection a poet may have either for the beautiful or for the ugly in nature, he may very well satisfy it in his choice and even treatment of the subject, without, however, distorting the nature of the material utilized. The worst distortion in the course of artistic imitation or representation arises from an exaggeration of what the artist seems to have a fancy for, so that the imitation is no longer faithful, objective, and natural; and Leopardi condemned the romantics in general because they indulged too much in the representation of what is excessively horrible and terrible, whereby imagination and sentiment, "instead of being moved, are oppressed and crushed and they have no other alternative than to escape, that is to say, to close their eyes and shun what is presented to them."[14] Even while trying to delight, poetry should do so quite spontaneously, and the poet's intention should not be too evident in the poem. "Otherwise," says Leopardi, "nature is not imitated naturally."[15]

To imitate nature naturally, then, is for Leopardi the main business of the artist. Leopardi cross-fertilized, as it were, this Aristotelian theory of art with the neo-Platonic theory, according to which art does not so much reproduce the objects in nature as they are in their material and actual existence, as in their ideal qualities—qualities which, in turn, serve to evoke in the artist's mind, and consequently in ours, an image of what these objects are at best but a pale reflection. Leopardi's acceptance of the neo-Platonic theory of art, however, went hand in hand with his

outright rejection of the Platonic theory concerning eternal ideas. He regarded Plato's entire system as "chimerical, bizarre, capricious, arbitrary, and fantastic,"[16] and subscribed unreservedly to the scholastic saying that "there is nothing in the intellect what was not first in the senses," and to Locke's view of the falsity of innate ideas. Possibly as an indirect result of this, while Leopardi repeatedly emphasized that art is something much more than a mere copy or imitation of nature, based largely on our sense-perceptions, he did not at the same time go to the extent of saying with the aesthetes that the artistic or aesthetic experiences are *sui generis,* and that the world of art is, to quote A. C. Bradley, "a world in itself, independent, complete, autonomous." Imitation includes not merely the copy of the object as perceived by our senses, but also what we think and feel in relation to that object, and what we come to create and invent on the basis of our sense-perceptions. "A good imitator must have gathered and absorbed in himself what he imitates, so that true imitation is not, properly speaking, imitation . . . but expression, since the communication of one's own affections, thoughts, sentiments, or imaginations, in whatever way it may be done, I do not call imitation, but expression."[17] Imitation of what is outside oneself, colored as it inevitably must be in an artist worth the name, by "the force, the energy," of his own personality that reveals itself through the sentiments and thoughts provoked in him by what he happens to be imitating, cannot, therefore, be something objective in the strict

sense of the term. Even when the artist is not deliberately employing his own passions and sentiments,
even when he is the least conscious of them, his
imitation of what is clearly outside himself, of something he feels himself to be completely detached from
and observing with the utmost scientific and impersonal curiosity, cannot but be, in a more or less subtle
and unanalyzable way, an expression of his own
personality. In fact—and here Leopardi would fully
agree with T. S. Eliot—the more intentionally the
artist tries to conceal his personality or to escape from
it, the more effectively—if he is a good artist and if
he has at all any personality to escape from—he would
express it—express it, that is to say, in the only way
personality or one's own feelings and sentiments ought
to be expressed. Leopardi's concept of poetic imitation has the Aristotelian definition of art as its starting
point, but it goes impressively beyond it and thus
comes to acquire an altogether different emphasis and
a richer complexity of significance. It goes even
farther than what Tasso meant by poetic imitation
when he asserted—and quite rightly—that "imitation
cannot be unaccompanied by verisimilitude," for the
element of verisimilitude is firstly something quite
different from the expression of one's personality,
even though it helps and corroborates that expression
to a great extent; and secondly, it concerns itself more
with the relation between the truth of the objects as
they are in themselves and their artistic representation than with the relation between the artist's inner
world and his material or the object of his imitation.

Similarly, Leopardi even anticipates even Croce's theory of expression in a certain way, without going too far, as Croce did, into the extreme rigidity and dogmatism of a theoretical system, which, at times, seems to explain away art rather than interpret or analyze it.

Even though he had taken an active interest, in his early youth, in the controversy between romanticism and classicism, Leopardi had later on rejected, long before Croce did so, the real distinction between the two. He came to consider them as two complementary aspects of the same process, inasmuch as true art cannot afford to ignore and exclude the characteristic qualities belonging both to the classic and the romantic art. "Romanticism requires of art," says Croce, "above all the spontaneous and powerful effusion of affections, love and hate, of anguish and joy, of disappointments and exultations"; "classicism," on the other hand, "loves a calm and pacified spirit, the conscious design, figures studied with their studied character and precision of contours, ponderation, equilibrium, clarity; and tends resolutely towards representation as the other (art, namely, the romantic) towards sentiment."[18] The great artists, Croce goes on, "or the great works of art, or their great parts, cannot be called either romantic or classical, because they are at once romantic and classical, representation and sentiment."[19] And this is precisely what Leopardi's theory of poetic imitation as both imitation and expression essentially implies. Art is never complete, and therefore never mature or perfect, unless it steadily and infallibly pursues this dual end, that of imitation and expression.

That is why, Leopardi acutely observes, it is even more difficult to imitate than to create or invent—more difficult, because it requires of an artist an accurate and impassioned knowledge not only of the object to be imitated, but also of himself and of the human heart in general. as well as an "exact correspondence with nature and truth." While assessing the merit of artistic imitation, we must, therefore, in the last resort, after having studied the object of imitation as it is in itself, take recourse to our own heart, which is "the promptest, the severest, and the acutest judge of the truth or falsehood, propriety or impropriety, naturalness or affectation, efficacy or languidness of inventions, situations, sentiments, periods, and expression"[20] involved in the process of imitation. If a particular work of art is defective, the fault, says Leopardi, does not lie so much with the choice of the subject as such, or with the material itself, as with the artist's manner of imitating it, with his inability to cope with or mold his material, to absorb it within himself and to achieve, in a coherent and decorous way, an amalgam between imitation and expression. It is the very lack of propriety, proportion, and verisimilitude—themselves due to the absence of that amalgam—that accounts for the failure or defect of the artist's work. "Baseness, ugliness, deformity, cruelty, sordidness and pain," if imitated well, and in conformity with the principle of verisimilitude, would not be considered as unworthy of being treated in art, and would not seem to be defects at all.

Leopardi, thus, credits imitation with considerable transfiguring power, just as he credits imagination with great creative power. In virtue of this power, even what is unquestionably ugly and deformative in nature becomes aesthetically acceptable as well as artistically interesting, if well imitated. That is why those minute parts of an object, which we do not take notice of in reality, are keenly observed and even appreciated by us when seen in artistic imitation. Leopardi goes even so far as to assert that what is ugly or deformative derives from art and not from nature. It is the result of clumsy, mechanical, and uninspired imitation. Quoting Tasso, who says concerning two rival armies ready to engage in battle that "seen in such a beautiful [that is, vivid and lively] way even horror becomes beautiful, and delight is born out of the very theme."[21] Leopardi points out that "every lively sensation is pleasant, because it is lively, even though it may be painful or frightful."[22] He clearly disagrees with his friend Giordani, who had advised young and would-be painters to avoid the imitation of what is inherently ugly, unless they were "obliged to do so for historical necessity (and even then they should do so with grace and judgment)." It is, Leopardi asserts, not the beautiful or the ugly in nature, but nature itself, in its infinite variety, that the artist should try to imitate with verisimilitude. According to Giordani's principle, Leopardi argues, "Homer, Virgil, and other great poets must have erred an infinite number of times, and

Dante above all, who has so often represented the ugly. . . . Of course arts must delight, but who can say that to cry, to let one's heart throb and be horrified while reading a poet is not delightful? Rather, who does not know that it is most delightful?"[23] And the source of this delight lies not in the object of imitation, but in the very manner of imitation, selection, and coordination of the various parts into a meaningful and coherent pattern. Art, therefore, based as it is on the imitation of nature—and the closer and more faithful the imitation, the easier it is to produce the effect of verisimilitude, or the illusion of reality— does not borrow its beauty or its power to delight from the object imitated. This power is implicit in the very act and manner of imitation as well as in the personality of the artist and in his capacity to stamp his personality on nature in imitation.

But it is not merely self-expression that is almost always more or less involved in the process of artistic imitation, but even the very faculties of invention and memory both influence and are, in turn, influenced by that process. Attributing a very comprehensive, and, at the same time, a very complex significance to the word "imitation," Leopardi points out: "Memory is nothing but an imitation of the past sensation, and subsequent remembrances nothing but imitations of the past remembrances. Memory is almost an imitator of itself. . . . Man imitates even while he is inventing, though in a larger way, that is to say, he imitates the inventions by means of other inventions, and he does not acquire the inventive faculty (which seems to be something altogether opposite of the imitative faculty) except in virtue of imitations, and he imitates at the same time that he is exercising his inventive faculty, which is itself truly imitative."[24]

In this highly important role that Leopardi allots to imitation, it might seem that there is left hardly any place for creative imagination. And yet, as in the case of Coleridge, though not on such an elaborate and analytically detailed scale, it is when Leopardi is expounding the nature and function of imagination in creative art, and especially in poetry, that we get some of his sharpest and most characteristic pronouncements on the art of poetry. In some very interesting respects Coleridge's and Leopardi's thoughts on the subject of imagination, its nature and function in poetic art, run strikingly parallel, even though they were absolutely ignorant of each other's work or even of each other's existence itself, the only indirect link between them being the writings of Giambattista Vico. "That synthetic and magical power," says Coleridge apropos of imagination, "to which we have exclusively appropriated the name of imagination . . . reveals itself in the balance or reconciliation of opposite qualities . . . the sense of novelty and freshness, with old and familiar objects; a more than usual state of emotion with more than usual order; judgment ever awake and steady self-possession with enthusiasm and feeling profound and vehement."[25] And the chief gift of imagination, according to Coleridge, is "the sense of musical delight . . . with the power of reducing multitude into unity of effect and modifying a series of thoughts by some one predominant thought or feeling."[26] With this let us compare what Leopardi has to say. Concerning the unifying power of imagination we are told that, when truly moved, that is to say, when it is "in the heat of any passion whatsoever," it is capable of discovering the most vivid affinities between the things," "connections between the most dissimilar things," of finding out "comparisons and the most abstruse and ingenious similitudes." Imagination affords to the poet an insight into "the relationships of which he had never thought before, and gives him, in a word, an admirable facility to correlate and compare objects of the most distinct species, as, for example, the ideal with the most material, to embody most vividly the most abstract thought, and to reduce everything into images." It is at once "more varied than reason" and "the source of reason as well as of sentiments, passions, and poetry; the very faculty itself which we regard to be a principle, a distinct and determinate quality of the human spirit." And like poetic inspiration itself, imagination too is, in a certain degree, a requisite both in the readers and the judges of poetry.

Just as persons with little or no imagination and sentiment are not capable of judging poetry or writings of this kind and, while reading them and knowing that they are famous, do not understand why, since they do not feel themselves transported by them and cannot by any means collaborate with the writer, and all this even in spite of the fact that they have good taste and judgment, so also there are many hours, days, months, seasons, and years, when the same persons, endowed as they well may be with enthusiasm and imagination, are not in a position to feel, and to be transported by and, therefore, to judge such writings.[27]

This kind of reading and judging, when one's imagination and sensibility as well as intellect and reason are fully engaged, is what C. S. Lewis calls "receiving" a work of art, as distinguished from "using" it.[28] Whether in the poet or in the reader of poetry, whatever reason or analysis cannot achieve by way of comprehending and appreciating meaning and beauty, uniquely belongs to the province of imagination. And what is true of a poet or a reader of poetry is no less true of a philosopher or a researcher. "Whosoever examines the nature of things with pure reason, without the help of imagination or sentiment . . . would well be able to . . . analyze, that is to say, to dissolve and undo nature, but he will never be able to recompose it; in other words, he would never be able to draw an important and a general conclusion from his observations and analysis."[29]

Thus it is through imagination that we not only can enter into a world which is quite inaccessible to reason or reflection, but we can also better understand those very truths and concepts that reason has placed within our reach. "In any kind of imaginative work whatsoever," said Foscolo, "everything depends on incorporating and identifying reality and fiction."[30] And for Leopardi too the essence of art lies in its characteristic dualism, in its simultaneous commerce with the world of reality and with that of imagination and thought, and in its ability to blend the two in a harmonious fashion. It is from this dualism that the main source of artistic pleasure derives, i.e., "from the union of things and qualities that seem to be incompatible."[31] It is precisely this pleasure that Leopardi frequently concerns himself with defining as being both the result of the juxtaposition between the contrary qualities and things in art, and as something which one can obtain only through the possession and the exercise of the faculty of imagination. True as what he says of pleasure in general is, it is all the more true of artistic pleasure that "the causes and the nature of the greatest human pleasures are the most subtle, the most minute, and the most evasive. And the majority of them, it is found, derive from that which is not ordinary, and precisely because it is not ordinary. Wonder, the principal source of pleasure in fine arts, poetry, etc., whence does it come and to what theory does it belong, if not to that of the extraordinary?"[32]

One striking merit of Leopardi's discussion of the role and nature of imagination is that he does not treat imagination as just a poetic myth or a magical formula; while contrasting (much more than comparing) it with reason, he regards both as being two natural and inseparable aspects of the human personality, and the functions and the respective merits and demerits that he assigns to them have a basis in practical psychology as well as in poetic experience. "One can affirm with certainty," observes Leopardi, "that nature, and, let us even say, the universality of the things, are composed, conformed, and ordained to a poetic effect, or so disposed and destined as to produce a general poetic effect. . . . [Now] pure mathematics and reason would never be able to discover anything poetic, since all that is poetic [in nature] can simply be felt rather than known or understood. . . . It is for the imagination and sensibility to discover and understand all this."[33] If imagination seems to create something new, or to remove "the film of familiarity" from the objects and color them in "a light that never was on sea or land" it is, Leopardi points out, because it goes direct to the original source of both what is new and what is old—nature, or rather to the poetic part of nature which imagination alone can approach and interpret. Hence the final criterion of originality in imaginative art is not what is new in it, but the fact that it is so close to nature, to the poetic essence and meaning of nature which imagination, and imagination alone, can perceive. For however original art may be, it can never excel nature. Even the most fantastic things that imagination can depict or invent have ultimately to be referred to nature before they can have any meaning at all, even as fantastic things. Imagination may even transform, as it very often does, the sense-impressions into symbols, ideas and concepts into images, and thus seem to be, as it were, an instrument of poetic clairvoyance; however, all that imagination does, it succeeds in doing chiefly in virtue of its having a close contact with the parent-source of everything, namely, nature which gives both inspiration and sanction to whatever is conceived or invented by imagination. A poet's sworn allegiance to the faculty of imagination may imply, at least to some extent, a sort of rebellion against reason, intellect, or the sense, but never against nature. Even while rebelling against reason or intellect or the sense—and by "rebel" is meant more or less the same thing that Rimbaud meant by unruliness when he said that the poet makes himself a seer, a "voyant" by "unruliness of all the senses"—the poet asserts all the more clearly his special relationship with a particular aspect of nature, which is considered, in the realm of art or in the sort of creative activity in which the poet happens to be engaged, to be something more necessary and infinitely more valuable than those aspects of nature which seem to be neglected in his hands.

The extent to which a poet or an artist is endowed with imagination determines whether or not he is, besides being a man of passions, intelligence, and sensibility, also a seer. For a poet worth the name, according to Leopardi, sees things in a double way—the way they appear to his senses and reason and the way they appear to his imagination. Both the nature and the degree of that difference accounts for the difference between a truly imaginative poet and a clever and witty poet or philosopher.

"To a sensitive and imaginative man, who lives, as I have lived for a long time," wrote Leopardi, "continuously feeling and imagining, the world and its objects are in a sense double. He would see with his eyes one tower, one country; hear with his ears one sound of a bell; and, and at the same time, see another country and another tower, and hear another sound through his imagination. In the second category of things lies all that is beautiful and pleasant about the things. That life is sad (and yet such is life, commonly speaking) which neither sees, nor hears, nor feels except those simple objects, perceived by the eyes, the ears, and other senses."[34]

CHAPTER SIX

Poetic Sensibility and Illusion

◡◠

Each object seen in its double form—that is to say, as the object is in itself and as it appears to our imagination—is almost invariably colored by our sensibility, which gives that object, or to our reaction to that object, an emotional touch. By poetic sensibility is generally meant one's capacity to respond emotionally to things presented by imagination just as readily as one responds to objects, as they are in themselves, through one's sense perceptions. The more poetic this sensibility, the more powerfully and more spontaneously it reacts to the imaginative version of things, and the less hampered it is by "the obstinate questionings" of sense or intellect. Thus, for instance, the power that the poetic illusions have on us is the result of the joint operation of imagination and sensibility, or of their interaction upon one another.

Now, in Leopardi the word sensibility is used, partly under the French influence,[1] to mean something practically identical with the sentiment of pain and suffering, a state of feeling that follows the evanescence of all poetic illusions from life, or from the life of the mind. "The origin of the profound sentiment of unhappiness," Leopardi says, "or the development of that which is called sensibility ordinarily proceeds from the failure or loss of the great or living illusions. . . . The sensibility which is to be found in young people, who are still unfamiliar with the world and its evils, even though it is tinged with melancholy, is different from this sentiment and promises and affords to one who experiences it not pain but pleasure and happiness."[2] The ancients, because they were so happily endowed with such illusions, were stronger and richer in imagination, just as the moderns, with all their illusions more or less gone, are richer in sentiment or sensibility. Leopardi considers his own case as a typical example of this transition from the imaginative stage to the sentimental one. Like Wordsworth in "Lines Written A Few Miles Above Tintern Abbey," Leopardi traces his psychopoetic development from the stage of pure fantasy to that of "the philosophic mind," from what Leopardi himself calls the stage "of knowing the sure and certain unhappiness of the world to that of feeling it."

In the poetic career my spirit has traversed the same path as the human spirit in general. At the beginning my *forte* was fantasy, and my verses were full of images, and from my poetical readings I always tried to derive benefit for the imagination. I was, of course, very sensitive to other affections, but I could not express them in poetry. I had not yet meditated on things, and I had nothing but a glimmer of philosophy . . . with that usual illusion that we cherish that in the world and in life there must always be an exception in our favor. I have always been unlucky,

but my early misfortunes were full of life, and they dis-
appointed me because it seemed to me (not indeed to my
reason but to a very powerful imagination) that they stood
between me and happiness, which I thought others to be
enjoying. . . . The total change in me, and the transition
from the old to the modern state followed, one might say,
within a year, that is round about 1819, when deprived
of the use of sight, and of the continuous distraction of
reading, I started to feel my unhappiness in a much more
dismal way, to abandon hope, and to reflect profoundly
upon things . . . to become a professional philosopher
(instead of a poet that I had been) and to feel, rather
than merely know, the sure and certain unhappiness of
the world. . . . Imagination then was completely weakened
in me, and however much the inventive faculty may have
grown at that time, or rather it was then that it almost
started functioning, it was inclined principally towards
the prose things or towards sentimental poems. And if I
started writing verses the images came to me with great
difficulty, or rather imagination was almost dried up.[3]

Thus, illusions and sensibility are seen to be in
contrast with each other in Leopardi's poetic theory
—a contrast that is caused by the fact that it is dis-
illusionment that makes man not only unhappy, but
also deeply conscious of his unhappiness and that
sensibility chiefly means the knowledge and feeling
of one's unhappiness. Leopardi virtually identifies
happiness with illusions and unhappiness with sensibility. Since even persons who are by nature endowed
with a highly developed sensibility are not always
sensitive, or are sometimes more and sometimes less
so, sensibility itself depends on the recurrence of, or
at least it is concomitant with, a great desire which
cannot be satisfied. The symptom of the return of

sensibility is always "a discontent, a living and energetic melancholy, a desire for something which one himself does not know, a kind of despair that one likes, a propensity to a more vital life, to more deeply felt sensations"; sensibility, therefore, is nothing but "the energy of the faculty of the spirit" and as such it is "the companion of discontent and desire, and hence of unhappiness, especially when nothing corresponds to internal activity."[4] It is not that Leopardi does not consider sensibility to be in itself just as capable of feeling the sensations and sentiment of pleasure and happiness as much as those of pain and unhappiness. But—and this is the cardinal point of Leopardi's theory of pleasure, with which his theory of poetic sensibility is closely allied—"the sensations whether physical or, what is even more true, moral which a man can experience are by no means solely pleasant, but are either indifferent or painful."[5] Hence, though sensibility, when absolutely considered, is "indifferently inclined to feel every kind of sensation, it comes to signify in substance nothing more than a superior capacity for feeling pain."[6] Like Keats' identification of beauty with truth, Leopardi brings about, in his poetics, the identification of sensibility with unhappiness, as well as that of truth with unhappiness. In the absence of illusions, the mind turns back on itself and meditates upon things as they are in their naked (and very often) bitter reality. Matthew Arnold calls it "the dialogue of the mind with itself," and Leopardi describes it as something caused by "the superabundance of the inner life," each of which leads more often than not to unhappiness.

If other proofs were needed to show that truth is something altogether unhappy [that is to say that, unlike illusions, its knowledge invariably leads to unhappiness], would it not have been enough to see that the persons of profound sensibility, character, and imagination who are incapable of taking things superficially and accustomed to ruminate on every incident in their lives are always irresistibly dragged towards unhappiness? Hence, to a young man of sensibility, however prosperous his circumstances might appear, one can predict without any doubt that sooner or later he would be unhappy.[7]

In his moral dialogue "Torquato Tasso and His Familiar Genius," Leopardi explicitly brings out the contrast between truth and illusion, between sensibility and happiness. Explaining the difference between truth and dream, the Genius tells Tasso: "Know that between truth and dream, there is no other difference than this that the latter is sometimes much more beautiful and sweet than the former can ever be." The Genius goes on to explain what is the very quintessence of Leopardi's theory of pleasure:

Pleasure is a speculative subject, and not something real; a desire and not a fact; a sentiment of which man conceives with his thought, but does not experience; or rather, a concept, and not a sentiment. Do you not realize that during the very moment of your delight, even if infinitely desired, and obtained by indescribable labor and trouble while not being able to content yourself with the enjoyment of each one of those moments, you are expecting a greater and a truer enjoyment, in which that pleasure really consists, and you are almost continuously trans-

ferring yourself to the future moments of the same delight? But tell me if at any moment of your life you
remember to have said with full sincerity and conviction:
I am enjoying myself. Each and every day, however, you
may well say and you do say sincerely: I would enjoy
myself, and many times, though with less sincerity: I
have enjoyed myself. For pleasure is always either past
or future, but never present.[8]

This conception of poetic sensibility as something
more prone to, and more frequently nourished by, the
sentiment of pain and unhappiness than that of
pleasure and happiness, inasmuch as happiness and
pleasure are themselves no more than mere illusions,
is a key to the understanding of an important aspect
of Leopardi's attitude to poetry. Theoretically in an
irresolvable contrast, these two elements of the poetic
feeling, namely, sensibility and illusions, are in practice not only capable of coexisting, but also of acting
upon each other as cause and effect. Illusions themselves—or as Leopardi calls them by various poetic
names, "the delightful images," "pleasant deceptions,"
or "dear and delightful appearances"—in order to have
any poetic value at all must be taken for something
which represents both what is real and what is unreal
at one and the same time. And it is the function of
sensibility, arising as it does from the loss of illusions
and from the realization of the bitter truth of the
things as they are themselves, to make us feel the
illusory nature of the illusions and to desire at the
same time that the illusions were true. This is what
Leopardi's poetry does, for it is the poetry at once of
illusions and of the bitter truth which has replaced

those illusions in the poet's spiritual and psychological universe.

Illusions, in Leopardi's theory of poetry, are something more than what imagination may present to our mind, and what we may be persuaded to believe in, for the nonce, as something real, through the operation of what Coleridge called "the willing suspension of disbelief." They are, to begin with, an act of willing belief rather than of willing suspension of disbelief, in so far as they represent a more or less stable state of mind, which willingly submits to their sway both before, during, and after the Coleridgean suspension of disbelief. Secondly, in so far as they exist at all, and being the kind of illusions that they are, they both emerge from and, to a certain extent, influence our attitude to life itself, and our very conception of the universe around us. They are something more than a passing mood or a momentarily appealing fancy, which lasts long enough to inspire a poem or a poetic idea. "The illusions," Leopardi points out, "are in nature, inherent in the very system of the world; the moment they are altogether or almost altogether removed, man becomes unnatural; and every unnatural people is barbarous."[9] Leopardi's own pessimism, in so far as it is based on the philosophical conviction of reality being equivalent to nothing or Maya, to use a term of Vedantic philosophy, is closely connected with his theory of illusions as being at times a cause and at times a consequence of that theory. "It seems absurd," says Leopardi, giving us a cold prosaic paraphrase of what he summed up with such a superbly laconic and pure art in his great lyric "A se stesso," "and yet it is exactly true, that everything that is real being nothing, there is no other reality or substance in the world than illusions."[10] To what extent these illusions, so natural to a child or to the childhood of the world (that is to say, to the ancients who represent that childhood), and so necessary to the poet, can be seriously affected by the advance of scientific knowledge and by what Thomas Hardy called "the plethoric growth of knowledge" in all directions, is most aptly illustrated in the poem "Ad Angelo Mai," where, referring to Columbus' discovery of the New World, Leopardi tells us that what had seemed to the eye of imagination, before that discovery, to be an "unknown and immense earth" had now shrunk into something definitely known, measured, and defined in terms of geographical boundary. And in proportion as the world of geographical reality extends, the world of imaginative curiosity irreparably shrinks. The charm of the indefinite, the unknown, and the mysterious, on which imagination so gloriously feeds, as, for instance, did the imagination of the ancients, is replaced by the pathos, and the consequent melancholy, of the poet's concern with the inner life, with "the dialogue of the mind with itself."

Now however paradoxical it may seem, the fact is that Leopardi's emphasis on the element of illusion as an essential factor in poetry prevented him from indulging in the most favorite illusion of his times— the pantheistic illusion, according to which a romantic poet saw an image of what he felt and conceived within himself on the face of nature. Discarding, or going beyond what the testimony of the senses or of scientific reason would warrant—something which Leopardi with all his theoretical opposition to reason could not succeed in doing, and hence the fundamentally illuministic and, one may say, rationalistic nature of his prose and poetry—the romantic poets created a world of their own, based on their feelings and idealism, and identified it with the outer world. They not only received from the outer world "but what we give," but they also did not want to receive anything else. Leopardi seldom or never does so, and he is therefore remarkably free from the pathetic fallacy of the romantics. If he turns to the moon, or to a broom or to a sparrow, it is, of course, with a view to giving vent to his feelings and to using them as spiritual interlocutors, but he never identifies himself with them. In fact one almost always notices the sharp contrast that Leopardi draws between himself and his lot and these objects; his comments regarding what is outside himself, even though he feels drawn to it for its aesthetic charm and for the wealth of sentimental associations that such an object, say the moon or a sparrow, evokes in him, are always made in the form of conjectures, tinged with deep agnosticism or with sceptical curiosity as to the way they fit in the general scheme of things. Hence one cannot well say with Vossler that "in the history of Leopardi the poetic motive is a kind of sentimental Titanism or imperialism, that is to say the tendency to subdue the whole world and the history of humanity to his own sentiment of life and to sentimentalize destiny";[11] for, while it is true that Leopardi's own feeling and experience of life did influence his poetic philosophy and, as such, his very poetry—which poet's sentiments and experience do not?—Leopardi never tried to achieve and never could have achieved that identification between himself and the outer world or nature, which is essential to that sentimental Titanism or to the tendency to subjugate the whole universe.[12] A Wordsworth or a Keats, and even a Coleridge or a Shelley could do so much more easily than Leopardi. What indeed actually strikes one is not the sense of identity between Leopardi's inner world of sentiments and the outer world but precisely the very sharp and the apparently unbridgeable contrast between the two.

This illusion which Leopardi himself did not possess and which he found to be possessed by the romantics in a very spurious way, inasmuch as it was not in consonance with nor implicit in their real and honest attitude to the outer universe (about whose scientifically true nature they knew as much as a disillusioned Leopardi) but merely a projection of their inner sentiments and sensibility on to the canvas of nature, was a prerogative and almost a monoply of the ancients. For the ancients knew much less about the physical universe than the moderns. But even a modern poet may have his illusions, though they may not be of quite the same type as the illusions of the ancients. And so far as Leopardi is concerned he thinks that "a poet or a poem without illusions,

without passion, are terms that exist only in logic"
and that "if a poet cannot illude he is no longer a
poet, and a rational poem is the same thing as a
rational beast."

It is from the necessity of illusion as an indispensable source of the poetic sentiment that Leopardi
derives another principal theme—a theme that frequently recurs in *Zibaldone* and that plays such an
important part in Leopardi's theory of poetry—namely,
that poetry aims at producing the effect of the vague,
the indefinite and the indefinable, that what is vague
and indefinite is in itself poetically more appealing
than its opposite, and that what is clear, precise, and
definite cannot afford us the same pleasure, or at least
in so far as its artistic representation is concerned,
as what is not. It is in the very nature of illusion,
and especially poetic illusion, that it should produce
in us the sense of the vague, the indefinite, the
indefinable, and the fundamentally mysterious. Leopardi is among the very first poets to emphasize the
importance of the irrational element in poetry as well
as in the poetic language. "Certain daring modes of
expression, epithets, phrases and metaphors, which
are so much recommended in poetry, and also in the
rest of literature, and which have been so much used
by Horace are often nothing but the result of the
beautiful use of that something so vague, and as
regards construction in a certain way, so irrational,
which is so necessary to the poet." Leopardi goes on
to illustrate and exemplify what he means by the
vague and the irrational, especially as applied to

poetic expression, by analyzing certain phrases in Horace's poetry—an analysis that reveals to us by the way Leopardi's power and quality as a reader of poetry, and that puts him in the first rank of the modern critics whose principal concern, while studying and criticizing a poem, is verbal and structural analysis.

As in Horace where the hand of necessity is called the hand of bronze—a clear idea but expressed in a vague way, by dragging in, as it were by chance, the epithet into what he happens to be talking about without caring if it suits him well or not, that is to say if the two ideas that present themselves to him (the one regarding the object and the other regarding its quality) can be immediately put together, as for instance calling the wind "hard" because it is difficult to break through its flood when one is going against the current.[13]

This kind of analytical reading is possible only if there is something vague and hidden, something apparently irrational and inexplicable, something that Empson would call "ambiguous," in a poem, including its style and diction, to analyze. Leopardi distinguished between analyzing and analyzing. There is, for instance, a kind of analysis that looks for the logically and mathematically exact in a work of art, and endeavors to measure a work's beauties and excellences in terms of logic and reason, making thereby all the beauties disappear, instead of revealing them. "Mathematics, which measures when our pleasure would not like to be measured, defines and circumscribes when our pleasure does not want limits . . . analyzes when our pleasure does not want either analysis or the intimate and exact knowledge of the thing that pleases (even when such knowledge does not reveal any defect in the thing in question, and rather makes us regard it to be more perfect than we thought, as it happens in the examination of the works of art, that while discovering all the beauties one makes them disappear), mathematics, I repeat, must necessarily be opposed to pleasure."[14] Poetic illusion and poetic vagueness can thus be made the subject of critical analysis, provided we look for the right thing in a poem—the source and the nature of the pleasure we get out of it (and, according to Leopardi, the greatest pleasure is the pleasure of what is unlimited, indefinable, and therefore vague)—and provided we do it the right way, that is, by analyzing the richness, the complexity, and the vastness of the concepts fused into what has rendered the poem or its particular aspect, say, the phrases, the metaphors, or the images, so fascinatingly and so provocatively vague.[15] It is only a creative kind of reading, analysis, or criticism that can achieve this result, and Leopardi's idea of what that kind is is practically the same as, for instance, that of a modern critic like F. R. Leavis. "Analysis," Leavis remarks, "is the process by which we seek to attain a complete reading of the poem—a reading that approaches as nearly as possible to the perfect reading. There is about it nothing in the nature of 'murdering to dissect'. . . . We can have the poem only by an inner kind of possession; it is 'there' for analysis only in so far as we are responding appropriately to the words on the page. . . . Analysis is not a dissection of something that is already and passively there. What we call analysis is, of course, a constructive or creative process."[16] Similarly Leopardi tells us that "in order to know perfectly well the excellences of a perfect or almost perfect work of art . . . it is not enough to be used to writing oneself, but one must be able to do so almost as perfectly as the writer himself whom one is going to judge . . . because that excellence cannot be totally known or enjoyed unless through one's own practice and exercise, and unless as it were, that excellence has been transferred in oneself."[17]

Hence, the less analyzable a certain quality in a given poem is—and every poem has or ought to have something that cannot be fully analyzed or even understood—the more job there is for the right type of reader and the more use for the right type of analysis. Connected with the notion of poetic illusion and poetic vagueness in Leopardi's theory of poetry is the thought that for the human spirit to be completely satisfied it is necessary that it should be presented with the sense or illusion of the infinite. More than anything else it is art that goes a long way in satisfying the soul's craving for the infinite, precisely because art, unlike mathematics, does not deal with what is precise, clear, definite, and therefore finite, but with what is vague, indefinite, and infinite. This notion of art was not peculiar to the romantic age, nor even to Leopardi himself, for it found favor with exponents of art and poetry in the age of the Enlightenment as well. For Dr. Johnson implies the same sort of thing when he refers to "the grandeur of generality" in poetry. "Great thoughts," he tells us, "are always general and consist in positions not limited by exceptions and in descriptions not descending to minuteness." The poet who pursues his thoughts, Dr. Johnson goes on, "to the last ramification . . . loses the grandeur of generality . . . ; what is little can be but pretty, and by claiming dignity becomes ridiculous. Thus all the power of description is destroyed by a scrupulous enumeration, and the force of metaphors is lost, when the mind, by the mention of particulars, is turned more upon . . . that from which the illustration is drawn than that to which it is applied."[18] Similarly Wordsworth too tells us that imagination "recoils from everything but the plastic, the pliant and the indefinite."[19] Leopardi's chief merit, in so far as this line of thought is concerned, consists in his having elaborated this idea of poetic vagueness by affording us a wealth of illustrations and arguments, with their subtle psychopoetic implications, and by fitting them all into his theory of poetic illusion and of poetry itself. And in so far as poetry is supposed, first and last, to delight, the theory of pleasure itself, and not merely poetic pleasure, is also brought in. At times like a true romantic *malgré lui,* Leopardi tells us that "all pleasures from far-off are great and from near small, arid, empty, and null."[20] It is because the poet is attracted to what is vague and indefinite, more than to what is clear, concrete, and precise, that his language, even when it does not contain a full-fledged image or simile or metaphor, does to a certain extent partake of the character of an image or a symbol, both saying and suggesting something much more than what it commonly would outside poetry. Leopardi even goes so far as to declare, like Vico, that the maximum part of any human language is composed of metaphors, and he quotes Beccaria *(Trattato dello stile)* to the effect that "words not only present the idea of the object signified, but also more or less accessory images."[21] The poet, therefore, instead of being tied down to what is mathematically and geometrically exact and calculable, and logically sound and comprehensible, lets his mind "wander in the realm of the vague and indeterminate, in the realm of those childlike ideas which are born out of the ignorance of the whole,"[22] and which constitute the true and legitimate province of poetry and all imaginative arts. And that is why poetry deals more frequently and more readily with sentiments than with thoughts, in so far as "ideas are . . . definable" whereas "the sentiments are almost never so."[23]

The identification, in Leopardi's theory of poetry, of the vague with the poetic, as of the exact and the definite with the scientific and the prosaic, hails, to a certain extent, from his conception of the poet's way of knowledge and the kind of knowledge that is most suitable for him. With the subtle scepticism of a Hume, Leopardi questioned not only the capacity of reason or intellect to discover the whole truth about the nature of things, but also the very validity, and indeed even the utility for the poet of the sort of truth discovered through reason and intellect.[24] Lamenting not merely "the impotence of human knowledge" but also its "blindness, misery, futility, and harmfulness," Leopardi goes on to tell us that "the ultimate grade of knowledge consists in knowing that all that we were looking for lay right before us at our feet; we could have known it and indeed we did know it without study; in fact it is study and the desire to know that has prevented us from knowing it; our looking for it has prevented us from finding it."[25] This may sound strange, coming as it does from one who strongly recommended the study of classics and the pursuit of knowledge as one of the happiest and the most fruitful occupations of human life—"commerce with the wise," Leopardi tells us of himself "is not only useful, but necessary to me"—but then Leopardi distinguishes between the kind of knowledge that is useful and even necessary to a scholar or a scientist or a philosopher and the one that is useful and, indeed, necessary to a poet. What fundamentally interests a poet is not the truth or the truths in their isolation and independence from one another and from the rest of the poet's experience of things in general and of himself, but the interrelationships between those truths and the sense, vividly felt, of the underlying unity among them in spite of their infinite variety and diversity. "All the truths and all the existing things are bound together, one with the other, more strictly and more intimately and more essentially than the whole community of philosophers think or can ever think or imagine."[26]

Now, it is only by refusing to get himself involved in the pursuit of the knowledge of the particular truths as well as the general truths, as they exist in isolation or as they are perceived by a philosopher or a scientist, in other words by lapsing deliberately into the state of what Keats happily called "negative capability" that a poet can perceive the subtle and almost mysterious interunion, interrelationship, interdependence, and interpenetration of what seem to be, and, indeed, of what are both for the philosophers and the scientists and for the common man the most diverse and unconnected things. Describing "negative capability" as the capability of "being in uncertainties, mysteries, doubts, without any irritable reaching after fact and reason," Keats found it, for example, wanting in Coleridge, in spite of the latter's plea for "the willing suspension of disbelief" in the reader as well as in the poet as a kind of *sine qua non* of poetic appreciation and indeed of poetic creation itself, and criticized him because he would "let go by a fine isolated verisimilitude caught from the Penetralium of mystery, from being incapable of remaining content with half-knowledge."[27] Leopardi's idea of the poetically vague is in essence similar to the Keatsian concept of the "negative capability," and as a principle of poetic art it is even wider in its application, for it concerns not merely the poet's state of mind, whether occasional or habitual, as in the case of the "negative capability" doctrine, but also the nature of the influence of this state of mind on the poet's style and on his treatment of the subject. The very fact that the poet deliberately cultivates this state of mind, during which his imagination and creative activity are the busiest, and that what attracts and interests him during this state is not truths as they can be scientifically demonstrated or mathematically proved, but those hidden and abstruse and yet, to the poet's eye and mind, so profoundly visible and meaningful relationships between apparently diverse and dissimilar things, means, of necessity, that such visions and experiences cannot but be expressed, or rather adumbrated in a vague way. Hence it is that all great poetry has a fundamental vagueness or ambiguity, with which may be correlated Coleridge's profound observation that "poetry gives most pleasure when only generally and not perfectly understood," for the perfect understanding of the meaning of a poem is not only likely to limit the pleasure that we may derive from our reading of it, but at times even to kill it. The more vaguely this meaning is presented, the more it arouses our curiosity and sense of wonder, and the more irresistibly it calls forth the most wide-awake and most earnest response from within us. What the poet is chiefly concerned with, and what alone really matters in his poetry is not what he asserts, supposing he asserts anything at all—for, as I. A. Richards has truly pointed out "if we look closely we find that the greatest poets, as poets, though frequently not as critics, refrain from assertion"[28]—but the complex state of his own mind and heart which cannot be fully or properly evaluated or even explained in terms of a moral or a rational significance. It is this general complex state—and not the particular state of one's mind and emotions, which depends on the particular event or situation that produces it—which is antecedent to as well as coexistent with the particular poetic emotion or inspiration, which Keats describes as the "negative capability," and whose essential characteristic Leopardi identifies with vagueness.

Poetic pleasure is thus closely connected with poetic vagueness, which in turn derives from the perception and knowledge of the truth about things and oneself acquired not so much with the help of reason or inquiry, as with that of imagination and sensibility. And our pleasure in what is perceived or created by imagination can never be exhausted, since what is so perceived and so created is itself inexhaustible, being by its very nature vague and indeterminate. Even a small thing known in a poetically vague way is greater, more meaningful, and more capable of affording pleasure than a big thing, whose size and range is clearly and definitely known.

The human spirit is so made that it receives a greater satisfaction from a small pleasure, from a small idea or sensation, whose limits we do not know, than from a big one, whose limits we see and feel. . . . Science destroys the principal pleasures of our spirit because it determines the things and shows us their limits, even though in many things it has materially enlarged our ideas. I say materially and not spiritually, since, for example, the distance between the sun and the earth was much greater in the human mind, when it was thought to be only a few miles, though one did not know how many, than it is now when one knows precisely how many thousand miles it is. Thus science is the enemy of the greatness of ideas, although it has immeasurably enlarged our opinions concerning nature. It has enlarged them as clear ideas, but a very small yet confused idea is always greater than a vast but clear idea. The uncertainty as to whether a thing is or is not there is the source of a certain greatness that cannot but be destroyed by the certainty that a thing is really there.[29]

The connection between truth and knowledge on the one hand, and the poetic pleasure and illusion on the other, is one of the cardinal points in Leopardi's theory of poetry. In distinguishing between the kind of knowledge that is useful to a scientist, and the one of which the poet can profitably avail himself, Leopardi classifies them as "material cognition" as opposed to "philosophical cognition," "physical cognition" as opposed to "mathematical cognition," and "the cognition of the effects" as opposed to "the cognition of the causes." "The former is necessary to the fecundity and variety of the imagination, to the propriety, truthfulness, clarity, and efficacy of the imitation; the latter cannot but prejudice the poet. . . . Erudition can help the poet greatly only when the ignorance of the causes enables him to attribute, not simply in the respect of others, but also in respect of himself, the effects which he knows or sees to the causes which his fancy figures out for itself."[30] In other words, the poet cannot illude others unless he can illude himself; the causes, scientifically irrelevant, unverifiable, and even untenable as they may be in proportion to their being poetically efficacious and appealing, of what he knows and sees all around him, must be emotionally and also, as far as possible, otherwise accepted by him, before he can render them into the proper material of poetry. And what is beyond the reach of scientific inquiry or analysis, what cannot always conform to and be interpreted by the logic of facts as we see them in our daily prosaic life must, of necessity, be at bottom vague and indefinable. It is chiefly in virtue of their ability to invent or imagine the causes of things which had not hitherto been scientifically studied or verified that "Homer and Dante, for their age, knew so many things, and, indeed, more than what most of the cultured people do today, and that not only in relation to their times, but also in an absolute manner."[31] Even their very ignorance, too, of what we have now learnt from science and other departments of knowledge afforded their imagination a wider scope and a stronger incentive.

The notion of the poetic vagueness, or of what Edgar Allan Poe called in "The Poetic Principle" the "suggestive indefiniteness of vague, and therefore of spiritual effect," is linked with the contrast between the finite and the infinite, the relative and the absolute, which itself is regarded as a factor conducive to poetic feeling. Proceeding from his favorite argument that reason tends to restrict one's ideas and views about things and imagination to enlarge them and to give them "an almost unlimited extension," Leopardi observes that in poetry we prefer "the aerily beautiful, the infinite ideas" to everything else. The ancients' superiority over the moderns consists also in this that there was in them a far greater sense of the infinite, and consequently of something indefinite and indefinable, concerning their attitude to life and the universe than is the case with modern man. This enabled them to be far more spontaneously sensitive and appreciative of "the aery beautiful" in life and nature than the moderns can afford to be. Instead of having, like modern man, particularized and definite information about this or that aspect of the physical universe as well as of their own life and mind, the ancients' imagination tried—and how often it succeeded!—to embrace within its orbit the whole of life and the universe. However, the change from the ancient to the modern does not mean any change in the natural desires and aspirations of man who is always as enthusiastic and desirous of the infinite, and as resentful and unsatisfied with what is narrow and circumscribed, as before. What renders this sense of the infinite so poetic is the contrast between man's consciousness of the finite from which he not only cannot escape, but which is the only reality that he can perceive in his daily normal experience, and the insatiable longing of his inmost soul for something that is infinite, something that knows no limitations. This contrast is, in a way, fundamental to all poetry, inasmuch as it symbolizes the blending between the particular and the universal, between personal and impersonal. For "the idea of something terminated of which there is nothing more, of something that has ended forever and that will never come back again,"[32] is always a melancholy idea, and yet it excites a poetic sentiment because it is so vast and indefinite. The poetic quality of the sense of the infinite depends precisely on this that we can never have a clear idea of infinity; the more this sense teases us "out of thought," the more poetically rich and pleasant our experience of it becomes. Poetic imagination does justice both to our soul's inmost craving for what is infinite and to our deep-rooted consciousness, verified by our everyday observation and experience, that we can never have a notion of infinity. "Not only the cognitive faculty, or the faculty to love, but even the imaginative one is incapable of the infinite, or of conceiving infinity; it is only capable of the indefinite, and of conceiving indefinitely. . . . The spirit, seeing no limits, gets the impression of a kind of infinity and confounds what is indefinite with what is infinite."[33]

But even the very impression of the indefinite implies the element of what is definite or well-defined, which serves as a starting point for the imagination; it is the very sense of limitation that goads the imagination to transgress the limits and sends it "voyaging through the sea" of the indefinite and the unknown. Leopardi's own poem "L'Infinito" is an ideal example of how by means of what is characteristically limited and particularized Leopardi succeeds in evoking the sense of the infinite, or how he can bring his personality, to borrow G. Wilson Knight's words, in "direct contact with the eternity dimension." Like poetic illusions themselves, the sense of the infinite depends on imagination, and disappears with the application of analytical reason. But the expression of the sense of the infinite in poetry—that is to say, the sense of something that may be suggested by the

words or the poetic image, but the full significance of
which is not limited to the sense of the words, and
aspires to something which may be called a sense
beyond sense—like that of any other poetic emotion, is
not possible while the emotion or the sense is actually
present: "When the greatest poets wrote about the
things, which evoke in us the remarkable sensations
of the infinite, their spirit was not possessed of any
sensation of the infinite; while depicting the infinite,
they did not feel it."[34]

In Leopardi's emphasis on the element of the
vague and the indefinite one may detect the germ of
the impressionistic theory of poetry—a theory that is
generally supposed to have derived its origins from
Poe through Baudelaire. According to this theory, the
poet describes a given object or a situation or a state
of mind or feeling not so much by giving definite facts
and details about it as by reproducing in the reader,
by means of suggestions, images, direct or indirect
associations and evocations, a similar state of thought
or feeling, a reproduction that is bound to have a
certain amount of vagueness and indefiniteness about
it. Nevertheless, the emphasis on the vague, the
indefinite, and the irrational in Leopardi's theory of
poetry does not in the least warrant for carelessness
or wilful ambiguity of style, or what Leopardi himself
called "the savage obscurity and confusion." "Clarity,"
said Leopardi, "is the first duty of the artist." Antici-
pate as Leopardi very clearly did by at least a century
or so some of the fundamental positions of what may
be called the modern theory of poetry, he nowhere

differs from the modern poets and the modern theorists of poetry so much as in his unswerving allegiance, both in theory and in his own practice as a poet, to the principle of clarity. A passionate and devoted admirer of the Homeric style, he was far from mistaking poetic vagueness with the wilful or clumsy obscurity or intricacy of style or diction. And by the clarity of expression, he principally meant the poet's ability to render not simply a particular idea or feeling, but also all the subtle and complex emotional responses and the intellectual echoes and associations that that particular thought or emotion causes to arise in an attentive reader's mind, or that are implicit in the very nature of the poetic inspiration itself or of the subject in question. The more vague and more complicated is the pattern of poetic thought and feeling in the poet's mind, the more incumbent it is for the poet to render it in as clear a way as possible, by achieving, that is to say, what F. R. Leavis calls "a paradoxical precision-in-vagueness," and by persuading "the elusive intuition to define itself, without any forcing, among the equivocations of 'the dream-crossed twilight.' "[35]

CHAPTER SEVEN

The Poetic Image

∽

IT IS THROUGH a poetic image that the poet best can convey the sense of the vague and indefinite, of something that is at once finite and infinite, particular and universal. A poetic image enables him to transcend and transform the more or less definite significance one normally attaches to words as words. An image, however simple and unitary it might be, evokes not one, but several ideas in the reader's mind, precisely because it expresses, better than could have been done in any other way, the poet's perception and meaning of something, which is itself complex, multiple, and vague. Thus, a poet tries to escape the tyranny of facts and ideas in their limited isolation and concreteness—facts and ideas that are represented by the material sense of the words as opposed to their figurative and metaphorical sense. So long as a poet uses words and phrases in their definite, material, and, in consequence, relatively narrow sense, his art does not necessarily differ from a sort of versified description of things, however eloquent and dignified may be the language of that description. The element of vagueness in poetry is nothing but a proof as well as a consequence of the superimposition of a wider, richer, and, hence, both more particular and more original significance on words than they will normally bear in any other context or use.

Talking of Chiabrera's images, Leopardi draws a distinction between essential or primary images on the one hand, and accidental and secondary images on the other, that is to say, between images which the poet has in his own mind and which he, more or less consciously, aims at evoking in the reader's, and images which, without there being any intention on the poet's part to evoke them, happen to be evoked by what Leopardi calls "the fortuitous collocation of words."[1] But in so far as the poet's intention goes, he should, Leopardi says, avoid as far as possible the secondary or illusory images inasmuch as they cannot but interfere with the effect of the essential or primary images. While analyzing a certain stanza in Chiabrera's poem "In morte di Orazio Zanchini," Leopardi comes to the image where personified Florence is seen beating its head and weeping on the tombstone of Zanchini and makes the following criticism:

The sense is clear, and that "beats" has nothing to do with "on thy tombstone," and is something as distinct from it as it could possibly well be. But the casual collocation of the words is such that, I wager, all those who read Chiabrera's poem with their minds so open to receive images, at first sight, imagine personified Florence . . . beating its head and breaking its crown on Zanchini's tombstone, however immediately though one may come to realize one's error, and understand the poet's manifest intention. Now, aside from the question whether the image is a suitable one or not, it is sure that the poet did not want it to be there and hence he must avoid this illusion, however momentary it might be . . . unless he happens to like it; but then it should be so only if the illusory image does not harm the true image, and there is no need for an error to enable one to perceive the latter, since one cannot see two images at one and the same time, though one certainly can see them one after the other.[2]

Hence, it may well seem that Leopardi is against the poet's evoking anything but the deliberately planned image or response in the reader's mind—something that indeed contradicts his fundamental proposition that poetry evokes the sense of the vague, the indefinite, and the infinite rather than of the definite, the concrete, and the limited in range, in meaning, and in suggestive power. But Leopardi himself adds to what he has said concerning the utility, if not the absolute necessity, of letting the primary image have its free play and its full effect on the reader's mind. Without harming the primary image, and the context, the poet may try, if he wishes, to evoke the illusory or secondary images, since it is good that "the reader be always in the midst of images."[3] In fact these secondary images, and the illusion they create, are often the source "of great art and of a very great effect that procures that sense of the vague and the uncertain, which is so appropriately and in such a high degree poetic."[4] The *raison d'être* of these images is almost hidden, and they seem to be accidental, and by no means procured by the poet, "but almost inspired by invisible and incomprehensible things and by such an ineffable state of vacillation in the poet that when he is really inspired by nature, by the country, or by anything else he does not really know how to express what he feels, except in a vague and uncertain way; and hence it is but natural that the images aroused by his words seem to be accidental."[5]

A judicious juxtaposition of the primary and the secondary images, of the ones that the poet deliberately seeks to present to the reader's mind and the ones which result from "a fortuitous collocation of the words" is, therefore, a very essential part of the poet's craft. Besides expressing what the poet wants to express, poetic images also adumbrate the sense of something unexpressed and inexpressible that is so indisputably a part of the poet's meaning and experience. It is these images—and the more objective they are, the more truly they partake of the nature of what G. Wilson Knight calls "inward thought and feeling"—that distinguish as well as liberate the poet's language from the material sense of the words. Leopardi's differentiation between the material sense of the words and the sense of "that vague and uncertain" which poetic images, and poetic images alone, can communicate is in line with what the modern American poet Karl Shapiro has said: "Poetry is not language, but a language *sui generis* which can be understood, paraphrased, or translated only as poetry. . . . The same word used in a line of prose and a line of poetry is really two different words, not even similar, except in appearance. I would designate the poetry word as 'not-word' . . . a poem is a literary construct composed of not-words which, in their retreat from meanings, arrive at a sense-beyond-sense. The aim of a poem is not known."[6]

A poetic image is, therefore, not merely a poetic substitute for description, an epitome or a symbol of what the poet's inner world of thought and emotion is like under the spell of creative impulse and inspiration, or even what T. S. Eliot calls an "objective correlative"; it is also a spur, and a very potent spur indeed, to the reader's own imagination, which the image sets operating, sometimes even beyond the scope intended or even foreseen by the poet himself. It is, at least partly, in this sense that one has to interpret what Leopardi said apropos of Byron's own notes on *The Corsair,* providing historical examples of the effects which the sort of passions and characters treated in his work are likely to arouse. Even though Leopardi's criticism of Byron's poetry, or of that part of it which Leopardi had really read—for there is no mention, for instance, in *Zibaldone* or *Epistolario* or anywhere else to show that he had read *Don Juan* or even *Childe Harold's Pilgrimage*—is not on the whole acceptable, there is no doubt that some of the observations that he makes have a particularly apt relevance, not so much to Byron's poetry as such, as to the theory and art of poetry in general.

Lord Byron in his annotations to *Corsair* (and perhaps to other works as well) cites historical examples of those effects of the passions and of those characters which he describes. It is bad. The reader must feel and not learn about the conformity which his (the poet's) description has with the truth or nature, and that such passions and such characters under such circumstances produce such effect; otherwise the poetic pleasure disappears, and the imitation, applying itself to unknown things, even though it may be the most exact, does not produce the sense of wonder. . . . And poetry is transformed into a tract, and its action passes from the imagination and the heart to the intellect. In effect the poetry of Lord Byron, even though the warmest, is, nevertheless, and that for the same reason as prevents that warmth from being communicable, for the most part a very obscure tract of psychology, and even as such not very useful, since the characters and the passions that he describes are so strange that they do not, in any way, appeal to the reader's heart; they happen to fall upon us, in the most unsuitable manner, from nooks and corners, as it were, and thus the impression that they make on us is much more external than internal. . . . The one thing that the poet must show is that he does not understand the effect which his images, descriptions, and sentiments are likely to produce in the reader.[7]

In other words, the poet's intention in using a particular image, passion, or theme must be implicit in and justified by that image, passion, or theme itself or by their treatment and representation in the poem concerned, and not imposed on the reader from the outside or communicated to him indirectly. In this connection Leopardi's thought runs closely parallel to Keats', who, though in a more colored and more metaphorical language, said practically the same thing: "The rise, the setting of imagery should, like the sun, come natural to him (the reader), shine over him, and set soberly, although in magnificence, leaving him in the luxury of twilight."[8] "The luxury of twilight" may, in a sense, stand for Leopardi's concept of the poetic vague; in any case, each one of these is likely to be achieved only if the poet has no "palpable design" on the reader.

Moreover, however useful and indispensable a poetic image may be, it does not, and need not, express the whole of the poet's meaning or purpose; while expressing or suggesting one part or aspect of it, it does not always even adumbrate the other, which may all the time be there and of which the poet himself may not always have been conscious. This enables the reader—and even the poet himself, when he comes to read what he has written—"to expatiate with the help of imagination concerning what one does not see."[9] Hence it follows that the economy of words—and brevity as the soul of wit concerns itself largely, if not exclusively, with the expressional rather than any other aspect of wit—is just as important in the construction of a poetic image as in style or diction itself. "All true poetry is economical of words," says Robert Graves, and so is all true imagery. A poet, and especially a lyric poet, should, if need be, pack the whole image in one single phrase, or perhaps even in a single word or two. "The richer and the vaster a language is," says Leopardi, "the fewer the words it needs in order to express some particular thing."[10] And the same thing may be said of the art and the stylistic and linguistic resources of a poet. The more developed his art, the richer his vocabulary, and the surer his command over the language and the technique he is going to use, the fewer words would he need in order to construct a poetic image, which may be sometimes even superior in the effects of intensity and vividness to a full-fledged and elaborately detailed Homeric or Miltonic type of image. Hence the characteristic difference between Ovid's and Dante's images. "A most faithful painter of the objects, and a most persistent and most acute hunter of the images," Ovid has, nevertheless, a weaker style than Dante, and this chiefly because his images, unlike Dante's, are based, for the most part, on "an abundance of words and verses, which cannot evoke any images without a long circumlocution, and thus there is little or nothing of the simultaneous, or rather the spirit is conducted to see the objects bit by bit through their parts."[11] Dante's style, on the other hand, is strong because "each word in him is an image."[12]

Ovid, whose way of depicting amounts to enumerating . . . leaves almost nothing for the reader to do, whereas Dante, who with just two words arouses an image, leaves much for the reader's imagination, without overexerting it, since the [reader's] imagination spontaneously conceives of that image and adds to it what is missing in the poet's outline, which is nevertheless clear enough to remind one inevitably of the whole.[13]

Ovid describes, Virgil paints, Dante . . . not only paints like a master with a couple of strokes and draws a figure with just with one stroke of his paint brush; and not only paints without describing (as Virgil and Homer also do), but he carves and engraves before the reader's eyes his own ideas, concepts, images, and sentiments.[14]

Being himself, after Dante, the most successful master of brevity in art in Italian literature—a brevity that is especially manifest in the diction and imagery of his poetry—Leopardi conceived of the poetic image as something more than an ornament, something often indistinguishable from the very meaning or thought of the poem. It is in the poetic image more than in any other aspect or ingredient of poetry that one finds clearly illustrated the principle of the inseparableness of form and content, meaning and medium, the thing said and the way of saying it. If poetry need not mean but be, so also needs a poetic image. To what extent a poetic image is merely an accessory, and to what extent it is what, according to Leopardi, it should be, namely, an aid to the reader's imagination to receive from the poem something more than the poet has put therein, to give a more definite form and more substantial meaning to what has been merely adumbrated by the poet, depends on the degree of fusion between emotion and thought, between what is capable of being interpreted and analyzed as logical thought or statement and what is not. Of course, not all images, even in a great poet, belong or even need belong to the second category; many of them are just no more than ornaments or accessories. But in the case of a truly great poet, and especially if he is great in virtue chiefly of his distinguished style, many of his poetic images would belong to the second category; these images:

(sometimes compressed even in a very short phrase, or even in a single word) must only be hinted at; and

similarly their connections and relations with the subject
and with other images, ideas, sentences to which they
belong, and to which they refer should also be merely
suggested or hinted at. And this is always pleasing to
the [reader's] spirit, because it obliges him to act continuously, to supply what the poet himself does not say,
to terminate what he has just only started, to color what
he has merely outlined, to discover those remote relationships which he has scarcely indicated. . . . That is why
sometimes the very omission of words, phrases, and concepts turns out to be a source of beauty, because it agree-
ably obliges the spirit to act and does not leave it in
leisure.[15]

Thus Leopardi's thought clearly opposes itself to the
"natural tendency," as I. A. Richards calls it, "to suppose that the more clear and vivid an image the
greater will be its efficacy."[16] In so far as an image
itself is the product of the poet's imagination, it can
be best appreciated if the reader's own imagination,
too, is called into play; and this is possible only if the
image is not described or developed in all its details
and dimensions. For the fact is that a sensitive and
imaginative reader too no more "watches and receives
in wise passivity" than does the poet; both more or
less create while watching and receiving. "Man hates
inactivity, and should like to be liberated from it by
the fine arts," says Leopardi.[17] And it is precisely by
letting the reader's imagination operate, by leaving
something for it to fill up in the outline of the poetic
image or any other form of poetic representation,
that the poet can best help the reader to liberate
himself from the lethargy of inactivity. Referring to
that part of Blake's and Shakespeare's poetry, which

he describes as poetry "neat, or adulterated with so little meaning that nothing except poetical emotion is perceived and matters," A. E. Housman tells us that "that mysterious grandeur would be less grand if it were less mysterious; if the embryo ideas which are all that it [a poem by Blake, beginning "Hear the voice of the Bard"] contains should endue form and outline, and suggestion condense itself into thought."[18] It is these "embryo ideas" and that "mysterious grandeur" which constitute the quality of vagueness that is such an indispensable element in all great poetry.

This element of poetic vagueness, whether it concerns poetic diction or poetic imagery, must not be secured, however, at the cost of clarity and naturalness; nor should the device of signifying the whole by means of the parts, and of leaving something for the reader's imagination to supply, be exaggerated or abused so that it may result, as it did in the case of the English metaphysical poets and the Italian *seicentisti*, notably Giambattista Marino, in the construction of too far-fetched, too abstruse, and too incomplete images, which always betray the lack of a sufficiently strong imagination to enliven those images or of a style powerful and efficacious enough to clothe them in an appropriate form. Such qualities of style, Leopardi points out, can easily exceed the due limit, as it happened in the seventeenth century, and cease to delight. It is only "a never to be interrupted action, vivacity, and freshness of imagination" that can render these images poetically alive and efficacious; without that, "however imaginative may be the style, however poetic the invention and the quality of the things treated and expressed therein," the poetic images and their effect as well as the effect of the whole poem are bound to be the very reverse of the poetic, and this "by way of contrast and inappropriateness which would be great in proportion as they [style and images] and the invention are imaginative and poetic."[19] Leopardi's criticism of the excessive or exaggerated use of that very method of conceiving the poetic images, which he considers to be, if and when used with judicious discrimination and moderation, the only proper method of creative composition,[20] sums up, in a way, both the negative and the positive aspects of the criticism of the metaphysical poets from Samuel Johnson down to T. S. Eliot. Johnson's definition of the metaphysical wit as "a combination of dissimilar images, or discovery of occult resemblances in things apparently unlike" reminds us of Leopardi's own definition of poetic imagination as "the ability to know the connections, the affinities, the resemblances, etc., whether true or apparent or poetic, among the various objects or to discover or invent them,"[21] just as his remark that "imagination, to a large extent, does not differ from reason, except for the style or manner, while saying the same things," even though these things reason would never be able to know or express in such a way as the poet and as he alone can do, refers, at bottom, to the same relationship between thought and imagination, between reason or intellect and poetry that is implied by Eliot's definition of the essence of Marvell's Horatian Ode as something consisting of "a tough reasonableness beneath a slight lyric grace." And when Leopardi comes to warn against the dangers of the excessive use of this device of hinting by means of parts, and by means of the vague outline of an image, and of discovering connections between the obviously dissimilar and unconnected, a kind of *discordia concors,* his warning anticipates, in many essential points, Housman's criticism of the Metaphysical School of poets. "Simile and metaphor, things inessential to poetry," says Housman, apropos of the metaphysical poets, "were their great engrossing pre-occupation, and were prized the more in proportion as they were further fetched. They did not mean these accessories to be helpful, to make their sense clearer or their conceptions more vivid; they hardly even meant them for ornament, or cared whether an image had an independent power to please: their object was to startle by novelty and amuse by ingenuity a public whose one wish was to be so startled and amused."[22]

The concept of poetic vagueness, then, as applied to poetic images no less than to style and diction does not in the least make for obscurity or intellectual over-subtlety in poetry. One of the best safeguards against obsecurity or abstruseness is the poet's insight into the true nature and meaning of a word or a phrase as something in itself representing an image. Leopardi, together with Wordsworth and Coleridge, believed that certain words are intrinsically more poetic than others, i.e., more capable of stimulating our imagination and vivifying our thought and sensibility. Such words as "night," "nocturnal," "far-off," "ancient," "eternal," "solitude," "irrevocable," "silence," etc. were considered by Leopardi as being particularly beautiful, much more so than other words of common use, independently of the context where they occurred. And this because they evoke in the mind a picture of something vast, indefinable, and vague. Thus one can see the germs of certain typically modern theories such as the symbolist and the imagist theory of poetry in Leopardi's conception of a poetic image and of poetic vagueness.

CHAPTER EIGHT

The Concept of Poetic Style

∽

To pass on to posterity one's own language, more highly developed, more refined, and more precise than it was before one wrote it, that is the highest possible achievement of the poet as poet," says T. S. Eliot in connection with Dante.[1] After Dante the one Italian poet who may be said to have done so—and done so, at least so far as the poetic use of that language is concerned, even far more than Manzoni —is Leopardi. As the recreator of the Italian lyric, which had considerably lost its force and originality in the hands of the imitators of Petrarch and as the originator of the philosophical lyric in Italy (De Sanctis rightly calls Leopardi "the first in Italy who has let poetry spring from philosophy, and who, in conformity with our times, has given the predominance to the truth"),[2] Leopardi's views on poetic style and diction are of unique importance and interest. "In order to become mediocre," says Leopardi, concerning style, "one must aim at the best." And there is no doubt that Leopardi himself did so, as is evident not only from his own poetry, which is the fruit of a very high stylistic conscience[3] as well as of poetic genius, but also from the profound and indefatigable concern shown in his *Epistolario* and *Zibaldone* with the nature and problem of style. His interest was not simply that of a poet anxious to carve out an individual style for himself and for the expression of his own genius, but was also something dictated by a genuine desire to reform and reconstruct the language and literature of his own country.

Aspiring to create in Italy "a philosophy and a modern and philosophical literature, which it has never so far had,"[4] Leopardi set out to study the relation between language and poetry not only from the poet's point of view, but—which even not many critics and theorists of poetry ever do—also from that of a philologist. Not that Leopardi was oblivious or ignorant of the merit or achievement of an Alfieri, a Metastasio, a Parini, or a Foscolo, but he felt that their achievement was not, on the whole, so considerable as to enable Italian literature to be fitly compared with the French or English literature, especially in so far as the lyric and prose are concerned. From the study of "our best lyric poets," he tells Giordani in a letter, that he has derived nothing but boredom and that lyric poetry itself, "the chief genre of [poetic] composition," if we leave aside that of Petrarch, is yet to be born in Italy.[5]

It was from his study of philology, which was his first passion and which, even after his so-called literary conversion later on,[6] did not altogether lose its hold on him, that Leopardi came to regard words with a kind of mystical reverence, and to be deeply familiar with their subtlest and finest shades of meaning, and above all with their poetic and musical value. A meticulous verse-stylist—the only English poet with whom he may be compared in this respect being Milton—Leopardi firmly believed that the ultimate secret of style and of poetic originality itself lies in the way a poet manages to revitalize the language, injecting a new quality in the words he uses, rather than in anything else. "The language and the style," Mario Fubini aptly remarks, "seem to him to have a perfection of their own, independent of the ultimate value, so to speak, of the work of art."[7] But then the ultimate value of art itself is something indistinguishable from the perfection of style and language as such —perfection in the sense in which Leopardi conceived of it.

And yet, for all his interest in philology, Leopardi's conception of language, or rather his ideal of what it ought to be, is more that of a poet than that of a prosewriter or scientist or a philologist. This ideal has a direct bearing on, as it is organically linked with, his conception of poetry itself. Leopardi was drawn to philology, as Vossler points out, by "an innermost necessity," so that his researches and labors in that field became, as it were, "the custodians of his lyrical purity." Vossler wishes that some such equally severe discipline could restrain the "lust of our contemporary poets."[8] The drafts of his poems, in which he continued making several significant emendations of verbal and stylistic order before the poems finally

achieved their definitive form show what an indefatigable craftsman Leopardi was and how just by
substituting a single word or phrase he could infinitely improve the expression and enhance its poetic
merit. Indeed, the immense stylistic and linguistic
pains Leopardi took while composing poetry seem to
ill accord with his definition of a lyric as something
natural and spontaneous, something that is or ought
to be "a free and frank expression of a lively and
well-felt sentiment of man,"[9] and, in a way, also with
his own confession that he seldom or never composed
poetry except when truly inspired. But then, as we
have already seen, poetic inspiration in Leopardi's
case as well as in that of Housman dictated the
essential mood and spirit of the poem, and in a vague
way even the form that the poem was destined to
take; but the perfecting, polishing, and embellishing
of the form of expression, the choice of appropriate
diction was to be done later on. Hence there is no
contradiction between originality and artistic labor or
the so-called poetic pains, between the Leopardian
conception of a lyric poet "inflamed by the maddest
fire, whose spirit is in total disorder, and who is in a
state of extraordinary feverish vigor (principally, or
rather almost indispensably corporal) and almost of
intoxication"[10] and his idea of a meticulous and painstaking artist.

The principle of spontaneity, however, does play
an important part in Leopardi's conception of poetic
style and diction. If the ancient poets were superior
to the modern poets even in point of style as well as in

other things, it is, Leopardi points out, because their style, and, to a large extent, the style of the Italian *trecentisti* and *cinquecentisti* also was as a rule more spontaneous and bore fewer signs of elaborate conscious artistry than that of the moderns. The ancient poets did not have to guard themselves against the corruptions of time, language, and customs, for instance, as the moderns have to do.[11] Like children, the former were ignorant of certain vices, which the latter know all too well and try desperately to avoid. What the ancients succeeded in achieving in a natural and almost instinctive way, the moderns have to use all their craft, cleverness, and industry in order to manage to achieve, and even then they cannot do it so well. We, the moderns, have more knowledge and experience of art than the ancients; consequently, we cannot commit the same mistakes as they happily committed. Our art cannot be guilty of the "vices of Homer, the conceits of Petrarch, the coarsenesses of Dante." And yet, in spite of all that, or rather just because of it, our works are devoid of that originality, that naturalness and ingenuousness in which their works manifestly abound. We know too much, are too much guided by experience of the past literatures and models to be able to achieve these qualities, especially in so far as poetic style is concerned. We are too much tradition-ridden to be free. But from this position, Leopardi does not proceed to argue, as one should have expected him to do, against deliberate efforts and industry aimed at the cultivation of style, or against the acquisition of the knowledge of past models and tradition. On the contrary, he lays it down as an absolute requirement that an artist, in order to be able to accomplish any style at all, and to write really effectively must buckle himself down to a patient and painstaking study of the ancients, their language and literature. "He who has not read and studied, and, in a word, who is, as they say, immune from the prejudices of art, or innocent, does not write with simplicity at all, but just in the opposite way."[12]

Leopardi's emphasis on the poet's or the artist's need for study, and especially the study of the classical literatures, sums up some of the fundamental arguments advanced by T. S. Eliot concerning the importance of the Classics in the training and education of a man of letters, with the difference, however, that while for Leopardi such a study merely or at least principally helps one in the acquisition or cultivation of a certain taste and style, in Eliot's thought it has a much broader function, in so far as it is supposed to affect one's very sentiments and sensibility.[13] Leopardi, on the other hand, following evidently the lines of Rousseau's thought in this matter, lets nature have an upper hand, rather than study or books, in the training or molding of one's sentiments and sensibility.[14] He even goes so far as to assert that in this respect the study of sentimental books like Goethe's *Sorrows of Werther,* far from helping us, may even harm us to some extent, by letting us acquire "a false sensibility," as he calls it, which we did not naturally have, and by corrupting the one we had. "A mortal enemy of affectation, especially in so far as the

affections of the heart and spirit are concerned . . .
I have always tried to leave nature alone as a completely free and spontaneous agent. . . . In any case,
I have realized that the study of books has not
produced in me either the affections or the sentiments
that I did not already have."[15]

But it is when we come to the question of the
cultivation of style by means of the study of the
ancient poets and writers, who were themselves so
natural and spontaneous and without any models, and
therefore all the more original in their style, that we
find Leopardi's distinction between naturalness and
originality on the one hand and affectation on the
other to be very illuminating. What was neither possible nor necessary for the ancients—namely, a deliberate study of models of poetic style and of literary
tradition in general—is almost an indispensable need,
even if at times Leopardi himself may regard it as a
necessary evil, for a modern poet; and this all the
more so today, inasmuch as even Cicero, in the realm
of eloquence—and for Leopardi the art of poetry and
that of eloquence have much in common—had to
study the art of writing, including grammar and
diction, in order to be able to achieve what he did,
and even Virgil, without a conscious cultivation of
art, could not have been Virgil. The question of the
distinction between what is natural and what is
affected, in so far as poetic art and style are concerned, is related, in Leopardi's theory of poetry, to
the larger question of the difference between art and
nature. Affectation, like its opposite, as Leopardi

himself admits, is a relative term. An innovation in style or diction, a new idiom or a neologism may seem affected today, but when time, training, and habit have made it acquire a certain consuetude, it may cease to look affected at all. Affectation, in other words, may, at times, be just another name for a healthy, constructive, and desirable sort of innovation or peculiarity in poetic diction, idiom, or technique, and the poet cannot but wait and see the reader develop that change of taste in himself whereby he can properly judge and appreciate the nature and importance of the innovation. "The charge of affectation," as Francis Thompson noted, "has been hurled in turn at the outset of their poetic careers against Coleridge, Wordsworth, Shelley, Keats, Tennyson and Browning."[16]

But it is not this kind of affectation that Leopardi has in mind when he condemns it not only in its manifestation in the realm of feeling and sentiment, but also in that of language and poetic style. He distinguishes between affectation which is "the extraneous quality of things" and naturalness which is "the manner of treating things in a natural way." He regards affectation as "the mother of uniformity," "the cursed corrupter of all that is beautiful in this world," and "the general vice of all the fine arts," which even "embraces almost all the other vices." He draws an even further and subtler distinction between naturalness and affectation. In the ancients, simplicity and naturalness were positive and spontaneous qualities; in the moderns they are the result, when this result is really obtained, of a deliberate avoidance of what is feared to be affectation, or a deliberate pursuit of what is thought to be simplicity and naturalness. And this deliberate act of pursuit or avoidance may itself, at times, result in affectation, of which the poet himself may not always be conscious. "Even negligence, careless ease, and inaffectation itself may be affected, may show up."[17] Hence, the more diligently the art of style is cultivated—and some element of affectation cannot but be implicit in any attempt at the cultivation of art or style on the part of a modern poet, as distinguished from an ancient poet, who was simple, natural and unaffected without any efforts—the more imperative it becomes for the poet to hide the signs and effects of that cultivation. Sometimes affectation may be just due to the ill-concealed efforts on the part of the artist at the attainment of the qualities of simplicity and naturalness in his style, qualities which constitute "the summit of art," even though these qualities may have been achieved by him in a highly conscious and deliberate way. Thus for Leopardi, as Fubini has pointed out, there is no distinction between stylistic perfection and the so-called ultimate value of art. But, then, after all, in what does this ultimate value of art consist, or at any rate in what way can it be perceived and analyzed, judged, and discussed except in terms of what the poet has done with the very words he uses? Whatever content, thought, idea, or feeling a poem may express, it cannot in the last analysis be distinguished or divorced from the way it has been expressed, and its very meaning and relevance in the poem, both as seen by the poet and by the reader himself, vitally depend on that expression, on the form and pattern that the words, conveying it, have assumed in the poem. "It is in the highest degree unphilosophic," said Wordsworth, "to call language the *dress* of thoughts"; he preferred to call it "the incarnation of thoughts." And similarly for Leopardi, too, the ultimate essence and value of art, in a good poem, is almost always indistinguishable from the form and expression through which it has been rendered. "Ideas are enclosed and almost bound together in words, as gems in rings; rather they incarnate themselves as the soul in the body, making together with them, as it were, one person, so that the ideas are inseparable from words, and once they are separated from them they are no longer what they used to be; they would escape our power of comprehension and conception, as it may happen to the spirit as soon as is disjoined from the body."[18] Though Leopardi does not go so far, as some modern critics do, as to assert that words are the "matter" of poetry, in the above passage and elsewhere he practically does mean what such a statement, if understood and interpreted in a more than merely literal way, would in essence mean. For the one most important union that art can and does effect is not so much the union between the subjective and the objective, the particular and the universal, the poet and poetry, the writer and the reader, as the one between the matter and the form, the meaning and the words.[19] The chief value of art, which is also its chief function and attribute, lies in the fact that it brings perfectly close together the poet's capacity of thinking, feeling, suffering, and experiencing with his power and ability to communicate—so close together, indeed, that they become almost indistinguishable and inseparable, not merely because, as F. R. Leavis observes, "we should not know of the one without the other, but [also] because his [the poet's] power of making words express what he feels is indistinguishable from his awareness of what he feels."[20]

Some of the qualities which Leopardi considered essential to poetic style *per se,* as distinguished from an individual or personal style in a given case, are best illustrated and explained in his criticism of Petrarch—the one Italian poet whom he studied with particular care and thoroughness, inasmuch as he edited his poems with a critical comment. Leopardi judged Petrarch an incomparable master, both among the ancients and the moderns, of the tender and pathetic vein in lyric poetry, which "while dazzling the less, moves and persuades the more." "All that glitters is not gold" in poetic style is a principle to which Leopardi constantly draws his own and others' attention, while evaluating poetry. Talking of Petrarch's poetry in general, and of three lyrics in particular ("O aspettata in ciel beata e bella," "Spirito gentil che quelle membra reggi," and "Italia mia"), Leopardi tells us that it has "a simplicity and a candor all its own, which, however, submits and adjusts itself admirably to the nobility and magnificence of the speech . . . and it submits itself best to the images, in which the three poems abound—images, which are grafted into the style and form, as it were, its very blood."[21] These qualities, together with the fact that "Petrarch gives us his very heart, while other poets, even the most excellent among them, anatomize it" and that "while other poets merely talk about the heart, Petrarch makes it talk," account for "the softness and almost the unctuousness, as of the smoothest oil, of his songs."[22]

However, this simplicity and this natural fluency of style and diction hide a good deal of art, an art so great, indeed, that it can hardly be perceived or noticed. One feels it, without being able to analyze it or pin it down as being due to this or that element in poetry. One reason, however, why the quality of simplicity in Petrarch, so different as it is from the simplicity in the ancient Greeks, cannot be explained is perhaps the fact that there is a greater degree of familiarity in Petrarch's poetic diction, and a greater affinity between it and the language of prose than was the case with the Greek poets. Leopardi's implied praise, therefore, of the language of everyday speech as the language of poetry reminds us of Wordsworth's advocacy of the same principle, except for the fact that Leopardi did not go, like Wordsworth, to the length of declaring that there is hardly any difference between the language of prose and the language of verse. While upholding with Paciaudi that prose is "the nurse of poetry"—and in this how near does Leopardi's thought come to twentieth century thought and practice concerning poetic diction—he maintained, at the same time, that there is a clear, easily perceptible, and quite palpable difference between the two.

The poetic language and style in a literature that is already formed . . . is to be distinguished from the language and style of prose, and from the vulgar speech, not only because of the expressions and phrases, which, even if they can be understood, are not used in familiar discourse or even in prose—expressions and phrases which belong to a diction that has become obsolete except in poetry—but also, and above all, because of the different material inflection of the same phrases and expressions which are still used in prose and in the vulgar speech. . . . Hence one should not think that the inflection of a particular term or word is more elegant both in prose and verse, because it is more in conformity with its etymological meaning, but just because it is less wornout by familiar use, and because it is both well-understood, and at the same time does not seem to be far-fetched. (Rather quite often an etymologically regular inflection is most trivial, whereas the same expression maimed in a particular way is most elegant and most poetic.[23]

The secret of poetic style and diction, therefore, emerges in a clearer and more consistent form in Leopardi than in many a poetic theorist of that age, including Wordsworth. And the secret lies in this: the use of a language that is not wornout by familiar use, and at the same time that is easily well-understood, and that does not give the impression of being far-fetched. Now, whatever we might think of this principle of Leopardi's in the light of our knowledge of modern poetry, in which the trivial in expression and diction is deliberately cultivated and the apparently poetic and elegant assiduously shunned, there cannot be any doubt that some of Leopardi's postulates concerning the difference between the language of prose and the language of poetry, and the relationship between the two are broadly and essentially incontrovertible. The difference between prose and poetry, so far as their diction is concerned, lies not merely in the choice of words, but also in the degree and quality of imagination that the poet or the prose-writer may display while using those words. For instance, so far as Parini's or Monti's poetic diction *qua* diction is concerned, Leopardi has not any real fault to find with it, inasmuch as it is, together with that of Alfieri and Foscolo, to use his own words, "much more properly and perfectly distinct from the language of prose than that of any of our poets including particularly the most classical and the most ancient among them."[24] And yet, at least so far as Monti and Parini are concerned, he calls them "men of letters of the finest judgment rather than poets,"[25] and elsewhere he calls Monti "a very excellent translator . . . a very shrewd and very fine modernizer of the old style and the old language"[26] and Parini regards as devoid of "enough force of passion and sentiment to be a true poet."[27] Leopardi's estimate of these two poets, it may be noted in passing, is, on the whole, much more sound as well as much more in tune with their modern critical estimate than, for instance, that of Foscolo who not only whole-heartedly shared the exuberant admiration of his contemporaries for Monti, but who even went so far as to declare Parini as the new Italian Virgil. One cannot, therefore, but concur with Wellek's view that "in critical ideas and temperament Leopardi seems to me much more original and striking [than Foscolo]."[28]

It is, thus, neither a special kind of vocabulary which, because of its association with the classical tradition, may be considered to be in itself poetic, nor a prose vocabulary and the use of the idiom of everyday speech which by itself may lead to the achievement of an intrinsic and effective poetic style, but a discreetly peculiar choice and combination of words belonging to either category, determined by a sense of their appropriateness both in themselves and in their relation to the context where they occur, that constitutes, according to Leopardi, the legitimate language of poetry. If a certain poet happens to use a special kind of vocabulary, it is not so much its novelty as such, but the degree of its intrinsic as well as contextual appropriateness that will determine its success. It is this very principle of appropriateness that may either justify or condemn the use of those words which, while they were once current in prose and verse, have now gone out of fashion. If these words are used not simply because they evoke literary echoes and impress us in virtue of their novelty and uncommonness, or in virtue of their archaism—and Leopardi strongly disapproves of archaisms in poetry unless there is an absolute need for their use—but also because they signify something particular in the given context, as distinguished from what they originally signified, or from what the new words that have taken their place in current vocabulary signify, they can contribute as much as newly-coined words, or prose words that a particular poet is going to introduce for the first time in poetry, to what is characteristically and unmistakably poetic about the diction.

But it is not merely the choice of words and the kind of words one uses that distinguish the language of poetry from that of prose, but, and most significantly, also the very different aims that the poet and the prose-writer generally have in using any language at all. The poet generally tends to make his language look as simple and natural as possible, the prose-writer to make the very inherent simplicity and naturalness of a language look as artistically cultivated and polished as he can in conformity with the theme and the context. That is what Leopardi implied when he observed that there is more scope for the display of art in prose than in poetry,[29] and that he would find it much easier to imitate Dante than a letter of Annibale Caro.[30] Together with A. E. Housman—declining the office of Public Orator at Cambridge, Housman observed: "You, none of you, have any notion what a slow and barren mind I have, nor what a trouble composition is to me (in prose, I mean: poetry is either easy or impossible)"[31]—Leopardi regarded the art of prose writing as something much more arduous and complex in its nature, and requiring a greater training and study, than that of versification. In a letter to Giordani, written when he was hardly nineteen, he says:

I don't think that one can cite an example of a true poet who has not started writing verses when he was very young; nor can one show many poets who achieved excellence in prose, and even those very few who have done so seem to have been poets first and prose-writers afterwards. And in fact it seemed to me that, in so far as words and the language itself are concerned, it is much more difficult to preserve propriety, without affectation and with full ease and frankness, in prose than in verse, since in prose affectation and effort are seen . . . like a buffalo in the snow. But they are not so easily seen in poetry—firstly because many things seem affectations and distortions in prose, but not in poetry, whereas there are very few things which are not affectations and distortions in prose but are so in poetry; and secondly, because even those things which are really affectations in poetry, are easily hidden by the harmony and diction of poetry, so that they are scarcely noticed.[32]

Himself an equally great master of prose and verse—something that may be said of very few of his contemporaries, whether English or Italian—Leopardi considered prose style, with its typical strength, clarity, and poise to be a far more difficult accomplishment than verse style. But then so far as even verse style is concerned, that, too, depended, though not in quite the same way nor in the same degree as prose style, on what Leopardi calls "infinite study and hard work." Inspiration and originality, indispensable as they are in the writing of poetry, cannot by themselves make of poetry what it ought to be in its accomplished form. Once they have done their work and furnished the poet with the central theme and vision as well as with the mood and atmosphere which must control his creative activity and which indeed set it into operation, it is for the assiduous craftsmanship of the poet to engage itself in what may well seem to be the never-ending search for the most appropriate expression, the most suitable style. "One does not finish a work," says Rimbaud, "one merely abandons it." And so it is with the search for the most appropriate expression and style. But before the search is abandoned, it must have been sincerely and earnestly made, and for Leopardi "infinite study and labor" are the necessary parts of that search.

And yet for all his emphasis on style, Leopardi is by no means an exponent of style for its own sake. Not only does he distinguish between style for its own sake, that is to say, style as an end in itself, and style as just a means, but he also distinguishes between genuine and spurious style, that is to say, between a style that is intrinsically poetic and a style that is merely extrinsically so and that having apparently all the qualities of a poetic style, yet almost invariably fails to produce a genuinely poetic effect. Chiabrera, for instance, was "robust in images, sufficiently fertile in invention and novelties, easily warmed up, inflamed and sublimated, like Pindar even by the most tenuous things, and able to bestow upon them, at the first stroke, a grand and excellent air. . . ."[33] And yet in spite of what is undoubtedly a poetic style, but poetic in the merely extrinsic sense of the term, he seldom or never could attain to the felicity of expression and the beauty of composition as manifest in the poems of Horace. A truly and intrinsically poetic style, on the other hand, informed as it is, both from within and from without, by a veritable poetic sensibility and imagination, not only can by itself be a source of poetic delight, quite irrespective of the material or the subject in the treatment of which it is employed,[34] but can, at times, even entitle one to be regarded as a poet, even though he may not have any other qualifications. Such is for example the case, according to Leopardi, with Horace who passes as a lyrical poet chiefly in virtue of his style—a style so remarkably agile and vigorous that it keeps our imaginations continuously absorbed and active, carrying us, at times even abruptly, from one thought, one idea, or one image to another. A poetic style, like that of Horace, indeed, possesses and overwhelms us in virtue of the multitude and variety of images it presents to our minds—images, not necessarily always powerful, vivid, or beautiful in themselves, but presented so strikingly that one experiences "the same sensation of vigor as one feels while walking fast, while being driven by swift horses, or while being in the midst of an energetic action or at the point of a climax in something."[35] It is, for instance, such style, and the sort of use it makes of language, that distinguish, according to Leopardi, Cicero from Demosthenes—the former being a poet, and the latter not, even though, so far as Demosthenes' emotions and concepts are concerned, they are more poetic than Cicero's. And it is style again that accounts for the indisputable superiority of Virgil over Lucan, even though Lucan was perhaps a greater genius than Virgil. It is not for nothing, therefore, that Virgil himself believed—Robert Graves calls it one of the evil bequests of Virgil's to posterity[36]—that style is more important than subject. And Leopardi himself concludes that, "in the last analysis, the force of art in human things is much greater than that of nature."[37]

Nevertheless, this concept of poetic style as the very *sine qua non,* or even the very soul of poetry or poetic greatness, a style that may even compensate for the lack of other qualities in a poem or in the poet himself does not go unchallenged by Leopardi—a challenge that may seem to lead him into self-contradiction, but that really attests to his earnest and untiring efforts at thoroughly examining the various aspects of the proverbially thorny problem of poetic style. In fact Leopardi himself admits how difficult, and well-nigh impossible, it is to separate style from other factors in a work of poetry, and to assert whether a particular poem is poetical only in virtue of its style, or also on account of other factors as well. Of course, there is no doubt that very few parts of even the most poetical work would still seem to be poetical, if their stylistic qualities were taken away. Like Coleridge, and later on Poe and Croce, Leopardi, too, believed that no poem of any considerable length can be all poetry, that "the epic poem is against the nature of poetry,"[38] that "the weakening and the exhaustion of imagination, of warmth, and enthusiasm in a long poem are so natural and almost inevitable even in the case of the truest and the greatest poets," and that *"The Divine Comedy* is nothing but a long lyric."[39] Now this belief was in large part dictated by Leopardi's conception of the poetic style and its place and importance in the totality of the pattern that comes to be presented to us as a poem. Being in its essential nature concise and swift —and this because "the rapidity and the concision of the style appeal to us, since they present to our mind a crowd of simultaneous ideas, or ideas so rapidly succeeding each other that they seem to be simultaneous" so that our mind "has no time to be idle"[40] —a poetic style worth the name cannot but manifest itself, at its best, in relatively short compositions, and when it does manifest itself, it is one with everything else that constitutes poetry. Such style, however, cannot by itself constitute poetry, even though it may go a long way to make up for the deficiencies of other things in a poem. In the following passage we have Leopardi's sharply analytical but clear account of the working of the poetic style:

To what I have said elsewhere regarding the reasons why the rapidity of the style, especially the poetic style, is so appealing, may be added this: that from this sort of writing there needs must be born, all of a sudden, something quite unexpected, which itself derives from a number of things—from the collocation and order of words; from the metaphorical senses which oblige you, as you read, to give to the words you already know a meaning, quite often, altogether different from the one you had thought; from the very novelty of the metaphors; from the remoteness of the ideas (in their mutual relation) which the author has brought together. All these things, besides affording us the pleasure of surprise, delight us in other ways as well, inasmuch as the very act of discovering unexpected things keeps the spirit in continuous activity and exercise, supplying it with the novelty, with the material and with the partial marvel deriving from this or that word or phrase or from a daring expression.[41]

Novelty and originality of images being one of the basic ingredients, and perhaps the most important ingredient, of poetic style, it necessarily follows that the same force and quality of imagination, sensibility, and sentiment that enlivens poetic images must also enliven poetic style; hence it is practically impossible to separate, in the last analysis, style from other factors which constitute poetry. Criticizing those who consider the whole value of a poem to be in its style alone, Leopardi tells us that these people

not only despise, but cannot even conceive of, the novelty of thoughts, images, and sentiments; and having neither thoughts, nor images, nor sentiments, they believe themselves to be perfect and classical as poets, in sheer virtue of their style. These people would be quite surprised if they were told not only that one who is not good in images, thoughts, and sentiments is not a poet . . . but also that he who does not know how to create images, think, feel, and invent cannot possess a good poetic style himself . . . or judge it, that the art, the faculty, and the use of imagination and invention are as indispensable to poetic style as they are, though in an even greater degree, to the discovery, the choice, and the disposition of the material, the sentences, and all the other parts of a poem. Hence, one cannot be a poet just for the sake of style, if one is not at the same time also a poet for all the rest as well.[42]

This integral and organic view of poetic style as something more than a bundle of rhetorical devices and tricks, as something more than a merely external form or guise of the poet's thoughts or sentiments is typical of Leopardi's philosophy of creative expression as the combined result of the working of imagination and sentiment on the one hand, and of sheer craftsmanship, training, and study on the other. A mere playing of the sedulous ape to one or more than one master of poetic style, necessary as it is as far as it goes, is however not enough, unless one's own imagination and sensibility come to one's help, not simply in the acquisition of a personal style, but also in the just and adequate appreciation of that of others, including, above all, those, whom one endeavors to imitate. A "continuous and uninterrupted action, and the vivacity and freshness of imagination" are just as necessary to poetic style as to poetic invention, and it is this quality of imagination which renders Virgil's style "the most poetic of all . . . and perhaps the *non plus ultra* of poeticalness. . . . And whenever this quality languishes, the style also languishes, however poetic and imaginative the invention and the quality of the things treated and expressed therein may be. The things would be poetical, but not the style; and the effect would, then, be all the worse, than if those things had not been poetical."[43]

But if the absence of a truly poetic style renders the treatment or expression of things and material which are in themselves poetic (that is to say, poetically conceived) awkward and inartistic, a possession of the poetic style, too, cannot, by itself achieve much unless the poet is both master of himself and of the material he is dealing with. Being a master of one's material and of oneself is tantamount to having the courage and the sincerity to say what one feels, and to say it "without the mincing of words," even though it may at times adversely affect the quality of one's style. Being like Hardy a staunch advocate of candor in literature, Leopardi thought that it is better to violate, if one is forced to make this choice, the principles of good style than to distort the truth as one sees it and as one feels like expressing it. In other words, between one's integrity as a writer and one's ideal of poetic style, in case they should ever come into conflict—something that may sometimes happen, showing thereby that the style is not always the man—a writer should always sacrifice the latter. While discussing the contemporary state of literature in Italy, Leopardi makes this thought abundantly clear.

It is not enough that the writer should be master of his own style. It is also necessary that his style should be master of the things [it deals with]; it is in this that the perfection of art and the excellence of the craftsman consist. There are but few among the writers of modern Italy worth the name who show themselves to be masters of style. There are but few whose style is steady and uniform, not topsy-turvy, nor always on the edge of precipices, nor uncertain . . . but free, easy, and flexible; there are but few whose style can expand and unfold itself and flow, whose style is assured that it will not say what the writer does not intend to say nor say it in a way he does not wish, that it would not get mixed up with another style or assume a quality that the writer wants to avoid. . . . Such writers are masters of their style. But their style is not master of the things; that is to say, these writers are not free to express through their style all that they want. . . . Many things, which may be useful or necessary to the theme in question and which they [the writers] should like to express and to conceive of in a perfect and even original way, they, however, run away from, hardly touch or mention except indirectly or obliquely. . . . This has never happened to truly great writers, and it is fatal to literature.[44]

Thus, Leopardi's concept of poetic style is broader, based as it is on the discussion of a wider range of problems than, for instance, Buffon's celebrated definition, which Leopardi himself quotes with approval: "Works that are well-written are the only ones that will pass on to posterity; the quantity of learning, the singularity of facts, the very novelty of the discoveries are no sure guarantee of immortality . . . the style is the man himself. . . . If the style is elevated, noble, sublime, the author would always be admired in all epochs."[45] While agreeing with Buffon that it is above all style that endows writings with a perennial charm and interest, even when the ideas and the subject-matter come to lose at least part of their interest and relevance with the passage of time, Leopardi ably contends that style itself is not something to be cultivated in isolation from the rest of what is in a work of art and what that work of art, in its organic wholeness and unity, stands for. Like the poem itself and the images it contains, the style too is chiefly the product of the poet's imaginative capacity, which includes, being both clearly dependent on and a reflection of, his very personality, character, taste, and sensibility. Indispensable though study and training are as aids, in so far as style owes at least part of its power and originality to them and part to natural inborn talent, they are not of much use unless the writer is also endowed with what Leopardi calls "the spark of genius," a spark which Bembo, for example, with all his massive learning and study, lacked and as a result of which his style is characterized by "aridity, sterility, nudity." One can therefore say that that part of the style which can be cultivated through study, training, and imitation is incomplete and unfruitful unless it is fertilized by what is innate in every writer, what is so inextricably linked with the weft and woof of his very being, and what his imagination helps him discover in himself and communicate to others. Says Remy de Gourmont, who was familiar with Leopardi's writings: "Si rien, en littérature, ne vit que par le style, c'est que les oeuvres bien pensées sont toujours des oeuvres bien écrites. Mais l'inverse n'est pas vrai; le style seul n'est rien. Il arrive même, car en esthétique comme en amour tout est possible, que le style, que fait vivre un temps certaines oeuvres, en fait périr d'autres prématurément. . . . Le signe de l'homme dans l'oeuvre intellectuelle, c'est la pensée. La pensée est l'homme même. Le style est la pensée même."[46] Leopardi would wholeheartedly agree with such a statement, adding, however, something of his own—a plea for the combination of those formal principles in style which Buffon insists upon and those principles which Remy de Gourmont expounds, in order to arrive at a synthetic and comprehensive view of style, like the one that he discusses with such a thoroughness and detail in *Zibaldone*.

CHAPTER NINE

The Language of Poetry

ભ

THE QUESTION of style is inseparably bound up with the question of language—a question which in Leopardi's theory looms much larger than any other. And this is not merely because of his philological interest, but also because of his conviction that in the last analysis it is what the poet does with words, how he transforms them in order to make them express what no other words or what the same words in no other context or as used by no one else would have expressed, that determines and that indeed makes one aware of ultimate value of art. The very qualities and elements in a poetic style are sometimes absolutely indistinguishable from the qualities and potentialities of a given language in its present stage of development, and as it comes to be treated by the poet concerned. Though in a great and original poet this difficulty may not arise at all, it is often not very easy to analyze to what extent the beauties of a certain poetic style are the creation and achievement of the poet, and to what extent they are the result of the historic growth of the language and of the inherent qualities in the language as such. The mark of a great poet is that he injects into words a quality that was not there, leaves on the language he uses the unmistakable stamp of his personality and genius, so that his style cannot easily be confounded with that of any other. The study of a poet's style, therefore, must necessarily entail a consideration of the qualities inherent in the language itself as well as of the qualities which the poet has bestowed on it—qualities which he alone could have bestowed.

In all the languages a large part of the style belongs to the language itself, and in no writer can the one be considered without the other. The magnificence, the force, the nobility, the elegance, the simplicity, the naturalness, the grace, the variety, all or almost all the qualities of the style are so connected with the corresponding qualities of the language that while considering them in any writing whatsoever it is quite difficult to know and distinguish how many or what part of them (as well as of the contrary qualities) belongs to the style properly so-called, and how many to the language itself.[1]

And yet the poet's own contribution to the making of the poetic style is, and should be, generally evident from the way he has chosen to arrange the words in a given context and according to a certain pattern of harmony and meaning, the awareness of which on the poet's part almost always precedes, even though in a vague and unanalyzable form, the actual composition of the poem. It is this arrangement of words, how it is brought about and what type of words the poet comes to prefer, in that pattern, that distinguish one poet's style from another's. ". . . Such is the force and authority of the words in the style that the moment they or their form or order is changed, each and every quality is changed or lost, and the style of any writer or writing, whatsoever changes its character in such a way that it is no longer, nor is it recognized to be, what it originally was."[2]

A poet's style ought to reflect, as in most cases it almost invariably does, not merely the artist and the poet but the man as well. Leopardi, for instance, attributed the characteristic qualities of Galileo's prose-style as well as of his way of thinking—"that frankness and liberty of thought" and at the same time "the decorous disdain of his style"—to his noble character as a man, to "a certain magnanimity, a praise-worthy self-esteem and self-confidence, and a generosity of spirit"—qualities that are rather inborn than acquired.[3] It is, in fact, the triple combination —the intrinsic qualities of the language as such at the particular stage of its development where the poet finds it, the application of conscious craftsmanship to language with a view to engrafting a personal quality on words, and, lastly, the very qualities that determine a writer's character as man—that is at the basis of poetic style, or even of prose-style for that matter. What is simple and natural or at any rate what seems to be simple and natural in a poet's style and diction belongs less to the inherent qualities of a language than to the poet's own personality as such, and, above all, to his conscious and diligent art. That is why simplicity and naturalness of style and language, Leopardi points out, cannot be really appreciated by "simple and natural men"—men who paradoxically prefer what "is cultivated, studied, and affected to what is simple and natural," but rather by cultured and learned people who alone are in a position to distinguish between the simple and the natural.[4] Nature may be, and according to Leopardi, it is, the first and ultimate source of poetic inspiration and poetic art; but that part of style or art which goes by the name of simplicity and naturalness—"those fundamental values of any writing whatsoever, those indispensable and primary qualities, without which all other qualities matter little or nothing"—Leopardi attributes to art—"they are nothing but the fruit and effect of art,"[5] and of the conscious and elaborate effort behind it. So far as these two fundamental qualities of writing are concerned, art has a double role to perform: to produce these qualities, and at the same time to conceal itself and to create the illusion of artlessness. Hence the so-called natural beauty, in so far as it depends on the simplicity and naturalness of style and language, is more artistic than natural, even though the art behind it has been adequately concealed—and the more successful the concealment, the greater the artist.

In order to discuss Leopardi's conception of the language of poetry, we should briefly glance at his theory of language in general, of which the poetic language is a part or a development. And much of what Leopardi has to say about language concerns the nature, growth, and development of Italian and the similarities and the dissimilarities between Italian and other languages, especially French. Following Vico, he regards the history of language as something corresponding with and, in a certain way, even revelatory of the history of the human mind, and the great variety of languages and dialects that are spoken within a relatively limited space as a sign of the lack of civilization among the people who speak them. As to the influence and diffusion of a particular language, it has not much to do with the greatness and influence of the nation speaking it, though it may also be due, to some extent, to the intrinsic character of the language itself. What tends to make a language universal is those qualities which can be easily appreciated and mastered by those who are not born in it, as distinguished from those qualities which only those born in it can fully appreciate.

The universality of a language derives principally from the geometric regularity and ease of its structure, from the material exactness and clarity, from the precision and certainty of its meaning—things that can be appreciated by all, in so far as they are based on dry reason and on pure common sense, but have nothing to do with the beauty, the richness (on the contrary, richness confounds and creates difficulties and prejudices), the dignity, the variety, the harmony, the grace, the force, and the clarity which cannot confer the quality of universality on a language, since they cannot be intimately felt and appreciated except by those born in that language.[6]

Similarly, the golden age of a language is not the age when it is in the state of formation, but the one when it is used, when the material and potentiality that it has gradually acquired come to be fully exploited, as was the case with Italian in the sixteenth century. What keeps a language fresh and alive, in view of the ever-present need to keep itself competently abreast of the new thoughts and new experiences that it is called upon to express is the introduction or coinage of new words. That language which does not grow, while the material and the themes keep constantly changing or multiplying, soon falls into barbarism. In order to enrich a language one need not borrow words from a foreign language, if the nation speaking that language has a life of its own, full of variety, action, and movement. However, these things alone are not enough, nor is it enough that the language simply be spoken and used in everyday life; it must also be put to a literary use, without which it cannot be said to have been really formed and established. To write a language is not the same thing as to put it to a literary use, that is to say, to employ it in the creation of the best kind of literature, not merely in this or that genre, but in all possible genres. The health and growth of a language, therefore, depend on the growth and development of the literature written in it.

One of the fundamental aspects of Leopardi's linguistic theory is the contrast between the literary and the scientific use of a language.

Words, as Beccaria *(Treatise on Style)* points out, do not present just one single idea of the object signified, but also, more or less, accessory images. It is the supreme excellence of a language to have these words. The scientific words present the naked and circumscribed idea of that object, and hence they are called terms, because they define and determine the thing in all its parts. The more a language abounds in words, the more appropriate it is for being used in literature and fine arts.[7]

Elsewhere, Leopardi follows this distinction between words and scientific terms through more analytical details:

It is the duty of the poets and the literary writers to cover as much as possible the nudity of things; as it is the duty of the scientists and the philosophers to reveal it. Hence, precise words suit the latter, as they do not suit the former. . . . For the scientist the most convenient words are those which are very precise and which express one bare idea. To the poet and to the man of letters, on the contrary, it is vague words, words which express either an uncertain idea or more than one idea at one and the same time.[8]

And yet it is prose and not poetry that may be taken as a measure of the perfection of a particular language, prose being its most customary and most natural part. The perfection of a language itself Leopardi identifies with the liberty of that language— "liberty is the most beautiful and the most useful quality of a language"[9]—by which he means the ability of the language to imitate "the genius and the spirit of any other language whatsoever, and of any author in it."[10] Such a language, Leopardi points out, "contains in itself, so to say, virtually all the languages. . . . It has that which is an equivalent of what the other languages have, though it is not precisely the same. It can, therefore, represent and imitate, by means of its own forms, the mode of others, while remaining the same and preserving its own character which is quite distinct from others."[11] It is this ability to imitate and reproduce the elements of other languages, while keeping its own individuality intact, that makes for the richness, the liberty, and the vitality of a particular language. Leopardi distinguishes three kinds of liberty in a language. Some languages are naturally and factually rich, like English; some by nature, but not in fact, as Italian used by the pedants in Leopardi's time; and some, like French, are neither actually nor naturally free, "bound more than any other language, whether ancient or modern, cultured or uncultured."[12]

It is the sign of the richness and maturity of a language that fewer words are needed to express oneself in it than in a less rich and less mature language. And the reason simply is that in a rich and well-developed language it is the metaphorical rather than the scientific and the literal meaning of the words that counts; and a metaphor obviously requires less words than a prosaic description or statement. Another sign of a mature and perfect language is that it can be both "definitely poetical" and "definitely mathematical" and contain in itself all the possible grades between these two extremes.[13] The ability to form and to preserve in use compound words, too, is a sign of the richness of a language. Modern languages have more or less lost this faculty, with the multiplication of the roots, which do away with the need of forming compound words. Sanskrit, for instance, "prodigiously rich as it is, derives its richness from just a few roots, by means of the great use it makes of the composition and derivation of the words."[14] Ancient Greek similarly allowed the writer to form the compounds he needed. In Latin, on the other hand, it was more difficult to write well and to form compounds, because, with more roots, it was necessary to master all of them before one could write well at all.

With these considerations about language in his mind, Leopardi draws a contrast between Italian and French—a contrast that indirectly throws some light on what the language of poetry ought to be like. Italian is the language, which, of all the modern languages, comes nearest to the ancient languages in character and spirit because in no other language does imagination, instead of reason, reign so powerfully as in Italian. It lends itself to all kinds of style, being as capable of the precise style as of the elegant; among the modern cultured languages it is the one most free, free by nature, though, thanks to the pedants, not in actual fact. Its immense richness and variety, however, are not known except to the few, even among the most learned Italians themselves. Consequently many words which are perfectly Italian and of a perfectly good quality are not to be found, even in the dictionaries or the texts cited. Italian is particularly well adapted for translations, since it can well preserve the spirit and character of the author translated. It has never had to suffer from any reform coming from a single source and authority. French, on the other hand, in spite of its boasted ductility, is always uniform and monotonous; its universality is an evidence of its poverty and uniformity, a proof of its being not very beautiful. It has just one style so that whosoever chooses to write in French cannot help writing in a more or less good style. The style of its writers does not differ from the familiar style. Its flexibility and facility do not derive from its being a pliable instrument, but from its being a small instrument and therefore easily manageable. Being extremely capable of precision, it is incapable of elegance, of a poetic style, or of a lyrical grace. Though derived from Latin, it has alienated itself from Latin much more than any other language. Easy to be translated into other languages, it is incapable of translating those languages, and this because it has no distinct prose or poetic styles.

French poetry and French prose are often taken for each other, since France has no true distinction between prose and poetry, not simply because its poetic style is not distinct from its prose style, but also because it has really no poetic language as such . . . and its poets (especially the moderns) are writers, thinkers, and philosophers more than poets; Voltaire, for example, in *La Henriade* writes with the same *enjouement,* with the same *esprit,* in the same conversational tone, with the same *tour* and play of words, phrases, and sentiments, as in his prose . . . because French prose is a kind of poetry.[15]

In other words, the distinction between prose elegance and poetic sublimity in French cannot, in general, be defined or perceived so easily. French prose cannot be elegantly written without the writer's using a style which is, to all intents, emphatically poetic and tends to be lyrically eloquent. But when it comes to writing poetry, the French rarely succeed in achieving the truly lyrical tone. Commenting on a certain passage in Horace, Leopardi says: "The liveliness and the excellence of all this . . . consists in nothing but the frequency and the length of the leaps from one place or one idea to another, which are due to the ardor of the material eloquence. The French language being incapable of this ardor, it is also incapable of the poetic style, and it is thousands of miles away from what is lyrical."[16] And this is true because the spirit and genius of the French language is predominantly inclined towards precision and definiteness, rather than, as a potentially poetic language should be, towards vagueness and indefiniteness. The contrast between the mathematically and scientifically precise and definite and the vague and the indefinite that lies, as we have seen, at the very core of Leopardi's concept of the poetic sentiment and its expression in language also influences Leopardi's attitude to the question of language.

Not only the elegance, but also the nobility, the grandeur, and all the other qualities of the poetic language, or rather the poetic language itself, consists, if one carefully observes, in the manner of one's talking in an indefinite, or not very definite, or always in a less definite manner than in the prosaic or vulgar way of talking. . . . All that is precisely defined may sometimes find a place in the poetic language, since one must not consider the nature of the language except in its totality, but strictly speaking, it is not poetic in itself. The same effect and the same nature one may note in prose, which, without being poetic, is, however, sublime, elevated, magnificent, and grandiloquent. Even the true nobility of prose style uniformly consists in something indefinite. . . . Hence there is not much difference between the indefinite of the poetic language and that of the prose or oratorical language.[17]

Thus, the difference between the language of prose and the language of poetry, while it is constantly emphasized by Leopardi to be something relative, and not absolute, something that may be accounted for in terms of degree rather than in those of kind (and this all the more so because what among other things renders a language so poetic—the elements of indefiniteness and vagueness—is quite often to be found in prose itself), is most clearly to be seen in the contrast Leopardi draws between French and Italian. Much of what Leopardi says in praise of Italian is incontrovertibly true, and one cannot explain it away by charging Leopardi of showing a partiality for his own mother tongue or by alleging that he did not know and hence could not well appreciate a foreign language so well as he could his own. For, apart from the fact that Leopardi, like any cultured Italian of his times, and in a degree far greater than him, knew French thoroughly, his analytical distinction between French and Italian contains and is indeed based on those observations regarding the two languages and their essential characteristics, which even one tolerably well-versed in these languages, and having no philological learning and linguistic intuition like Leopardi, could not help noticing. As to the superior degree of the distinction separating the language of Italian poetry from that of Italian prose as compared with a similar distinction in other languages, we have the testimony of a critic like Coleridge, who, while comparing English and Italian, says: "I cannot but deem it likewise an advantage in the Italian tongue, in many other respects inferior to our own, that the language of poetry is more distinct from that of prose than with us."[18] The reason why, according to Leopardi, Italian is more poetic and has a poetic language more distinctly marked out from the language of prose, than is the case with French, is that, more than any other modern language, it has preserved its ancient richness, that is to say, those ancient words and phrases which are now more or less obsolete but which are very beautiful and can be very useful. It is partly on this availability of archaic and more or less obsolete words, which can, however, be used with the utmost poetic efficacy, and partly on the number and variety of the authors that the essential richness of a language consists. Such words, Leopardi says, even though they have gone and are day by day going into disuse, are nevertheless "fresh and flourishing . . . since they can be used without any scruple" so that everyone would understand their significance and recognize them as Italian. These words exist in Italian, but not in French, because "the Italian language has never had to undergo a reform like the French—a reform, coming as it did from one single source and authority, namely the Academy, and recognized by the entire nation that required the national use of only those words which were current at the time of the reform or which would become so henceforward, depriving it thereby of the liberty to use what was good, unaffected and intelligible in the store of the language, things no longer in customary use, though used by ancient writers."[19] As to the influence of the Accademia della Crusca in Italy and on the Italian language, Leopardi justly considers it to be negligible, and at best ineffectual. In any case what the Accademia della Crusca proposed to do was something just the opposite of what the French Academy did, that is to say, to restrict the language to its ancient founts and cut it off from the modern ones—something, says Leopardi, which "goes against the nature of the living language."[20]

It is, then, not the language of prose as such, which too can be elegant and lyrical, if the writer chooses to make it so and if he is indeed capable of doing so, that Leopardi opposes to the language of poetry, but the language of exact sciences, such as logic and mathematics; and he almost invariably characterizes French as being preeminently the language of science, and Italian as that of poetry. Being the only modern language that has been able to inherit and preserve the beauty, force, variety, and copiousness of ancient Greek, Italian, too, Leopardi noted, had started to degenerate and lose its characteristic virtue in modern times by falling "into the arid, the monotonous, and the mathematical."[21] The language of science and reason is "the meagerest and the driest," because it makes its sole appeal to the intellect; the language of poetry, on the other hand, makes its principal, though not its exclusive appeal to the heart and to imagination, being, as it infallibly is, full of "blood and color." Leopardi was, therefore, anxious to see that Italian did not become unitary, monotonous, and arid like French, that it did not reduce itself, as Fénelon said of French, to "a procession of collegiates." Leopardi's criticism of French is also corroborated by that of Victor Hugo himself, who described French as "dry hard, neutral, colorless, insipid."[22] It is not that the French have no poetry at all, but that their poetry, Leopardi points out, is hardly to be distinguished from prose and their prose from poetry. "The French do not have poetry which is not prosaic, nor do they even have prose which is not poetical. This, while confounding the two languages, which by their very nature ought to be so distinct from one another, harms the power of expression of our thoughts and is opposed to the nature of the human spirit, which never talks poetically when arguing in a calm and quiet mood, as the French are obliged to do when they want to write what they consider to be elegant, witty, and orderly prose."[23] The poetic element in prose may have some justification, only in so far as it serves to bring into focus those very qualities of prose which sharply and unmistakably distinguish it from poetry properly so-called. These qualities some of the classics of French prose themselves—such as Madame de Sévigné, Madame Lambert, Racine, Boileau, and Pascal—so admirably display—qualities like gravity, simplicity, familiarity, and severity, which Leopardi considers to be the hallmark of a good prose style. While Leopardi recognizes that good prose should have something poetical about it, just as good poetry is undoubtedly to gain something by absorbing some of the qualities peculiar to prose, and while he was perhaps the very first poet to advance the idea of writing poems in prose, he was far from asserting with Wordsworth that "between the language of prose and that of metrical composition, there neither is, nor can be, any *essential* difference." Not merely does he expound with clarity and consistency the qualities and characteristics that distinguish poetry as poetry, from the characteristic qualities of prose, but he also analyzes the respective and typical aims of both prose and poetry—the one aiming at the mathematically precise and scientifically lucid and objective representation of what is definite or definable, and the other at the presentation of what is intrinsically vague, indefinite, and unanalyzable, including also what is irrational, which Leopardi considers to be not only tolerable but also desirable in poetry.

Leopardi's own *Operette morali* affords an ideal example of what he meant by prose poems, for they are, to quote Francesco Flora, "fundamentally poems in a prose which is quite firm, and also, if you will, unlyrical. But they are poems."[24] One reason why Leopardi was drawn to this kind of writing, this species of prose-poems, was his growing dislike for rhyme which, he said with characteristic frankness and lucidity, makes the poet say things only in part as he would like to say them, and in part as the rhyme requires him to say. "In rhymed verses, however spontaneous the rhyme may appear and however

far it may seem to be from being wrenched out, it
may be said, in the light of the experience of one
who composes, that the concept belongs half to the
poet and half to the rhyme, sometimes only one third
to the poet and the rest to the rhyme, and at other
times it belongs entirely to the rhyme. There are
very few of those concepts which belong entirely to
the poet alone, even when they do not seem to be
labored, or they rather seem to be born out of the
thing itself."[25] The chief artistic merit of the *Operette
morali,* therefore, lies in their being able to weld in a
remarkably harmonious and impressive way the freedom that is of the very essence of a poet's inspiration
—and especially if he is a lyrical poet—and the discipline that a good prose-writer willingly imposes upon
himself. The first person to recognize this merit was
Manzoni himself, who did not hesitate to inform
Sainte-Beuve that the *Operette morali* constituted
"the best writing in prose that has been composed in
Italy for a long time."[26]

The contrast between French and Italian in Leopardi's theory of poetry is closely connected with, as
it is frankly indicative of, Leopardi's views on the
nature of the poetic language itself—a language characterized by elegance, sensuousness, sublimity, and a
certain element of vagueness, just as the language of
prose, especially the language of scientific and philosophical prose, is generally characterized by precision,
monotony, and dryness. The language of science, and
even of much of the prose that is not strictly speaking
scientific, abounds in terms that have a definite and

precise, but also very limited significance; the language of poetry, on the other hand, uses words which mean something larger, even though less precise, something deeper and richer, even though less definite and clear, each word standing not for one particular idea only, but for a group of ideas, which lead our minds to "wander in a multitude of concepts, and in their vague, confused, indeterminate, and uncircumscribed [nature]."[27] And not only do these words mean something different in poetry from what they mean in prose, but they also acquire a different shade of meaning in the case of each one of the different poets who happen to use them. "Each time a word is used by a good poet," Professor Tillotson remarks, "it is a partly new thing; the good poet is a voice, and only the bad poet that mindless thing, an echo—to adopt Goethe's useful distinction between genius and talent."[28] As to why a word, when used in prose does not produce the same particular effect on us as it does when used in poetry, Leopardi refers to the force of habit and opinion as being the main cause of this. "The force of opinion, of habit, etc., and how everything is relative, can be seen in the words, the modes of expression, the concepts and the images of prose and of poetry, when compared with each other. This comparison can be easily instituted by showing, for example, how a word, a common ordinary sentence, which does not produce any effect in prose, because we are used to it, does so in verse."[29]

In a poet's hands, therefore, each word is, as it were, a potential metaphor—a metaphor that conveys something much more than the basic material significance of the word. Moreover, words arouse in our minds—and certain words do so more than others—in addition to the ideas proper to them, what Leopardi calls "the concomitant ideas." The more numerous these ideas are and the wider is their range, the more poetic the words are. These concomitant ideas are, in a way, independent of the proper meaning of the word concerned, and yet they are tied up with it, in virtue of the circumstances in which this word has usually been heard and of the associations one has formed with it, just as closely as the proper meaning itself. They are, Leopardi points out,

very often tied up with the word (which in the human mind is inseparable from the thing itself, is its image, its very body, even if it is a material thing, or rather which is one with the thing itself; and it may be said that a language, in so far as the mind of its user is concerned, contains not only the signs of the things, but almost the things themselves) more than with the thing itself, or tied up with both in such a way that once the thing is separated from the word (since the word cannot be separated from the thing), the thing does not evoke the same ideas any more.[30]

A full and proper appreciation of a word, especially when it is used in poetry, inevitably involves, therefore, penetrating into all the minute details, parts, and ideas contained even in the words which have the simplest meaning.

It is words with such concomitant ideas, when they are studied and understood in the manner suggested above, that constitute what Leopardi calls the "propriety" of a language, as distinguished from its precision. And the expressive quality of a language itself derives—Leopardi points out, while clearly anticipating Croce, in so far as the main aspects of his theory of expressionism are concerned—from this "propriety." For a word is more or less expressive in proportion as it is more or less capable of arousing in our minds "a crowd of concomitant ideas, derived from the vivid impressions which accompanied those words in that age [childhood], and from the fecundity of the child's imagination."[31] That is why each word has a personality of its own, consisting as it does of the variety of associations or concomitant ideas which shape and enrich the very meaning of the word itself, closely related to the personality of the person using it. "There is perhaps no man," says Leopardi, "to whom the same word . . . means precisely the same thing as to another . . . perhaps no individual (as no nation in respect of others) has precisely the same ideas as another concerning the most identical object. . . . Thus men conceive very different ideas regarding the same thing, while expressing that thing through the same word, which (that is to say, the word itself) they understand in a different way . . . they think that they are in agreement, but they are not."[32]

But not only do words differ as to their significance and effect in relation to the difference of character between the two people using them, but they sometimes also have an intrinsic difference between them. Some words are more poetical than others, quite irrespective of the fact whether they are used in prose or poetry, or whether by this person or that. It is not merely that words acquire a particular poetic value from the context in which they are used, or from the way they are combined with other words—"poetry depends on combination more than on single words— that is why words that singly are words of prose become words of poetry when combined," observes Professor Tillotson[33]—but that simply in virtue of what they are in themselves and what accessory images or what concomitant ideas they convey, they happen to be more poetic than others. Now for this notion of his, that certain words are in themselves more poetic than others, Leopardi has sometimes been criticized, especially inasmuch as the practice of modern poets in Italian—notably Montale—as well as in other languages has shown that it is not always so. Criticism is based on a gross misinterpretation of what Leopardi actually means or implies. He neither means nor implies that the same effect cannot be produced by other words that are in themselves not so poetic; nor does he mean that this special quality of poeticalness applies as a rule to all words more or less, that words in a language can be classified as being more or less poetical. It is only a few words, to begin with, that he regards as being extraordinarily poetical; and then what really matters about Leopardi's notion is not these words in themselves, but the reasons he gives for finding them more poetical than others—reasons which are closely connected with the poetic virtue of all words and with the criterion for recognizing and for distinguishing it from other virtues. One has to examine this notion in the proper context of Leopardi's theory of the poetic sentiment which identifies it with whatever is vague and indefinite, vast and infinite, as opposed to what is mathematically numbered, geometrically bound and circumscribed, scientifically precise and logically or rationally analyzable and explicable. Words like " 'descendants,' 'posterity,' . . . 'future,' 'past,' 'eternal,' 'long' (in point of time), 'death,' 'mortal,' 'immortal,' and hundreds of words like them have a sense and a significance as poetic and noble as indefinite, and hence they are the cause of the nobility and beauty in all the styles."[34] Again, words like " 'far off,' 'ancient,' and others are extremely poetic and pleasant, because they arouse in us ideas that are vast and indefinite, confused, and indefinable." As an illustration, Leopardi quotes a certain stanza from Ariosto, where, in the verse "The pine tree which he used to see from far," "the effect of the words 'from far' is united with that of the words 'used to'—words whose significance is equally vast because of the abundance of the memories they contain. Take away these two words and ideas and the effect of the verse is lost; or separate the one from the other and the effect is diminished."[35] Similarly, words like " 'night,' or 'nocturnal' " are very poetic, because " 'night' confounds the objects, and the mind cannot conceive but a vague, indistinct, and incomplete image thereof . . . and so also words like 'obscurity,' 'profound,' etc., etc."[36] Hence, words which indicate multitude, abundance, greatness, length, width, height, vastness, etc., whether as to force or to extension, are intrinsically poetic, and so also the corresponding images which express them. Leopardi gives another example by quoting a verse each from Petrarch and Ippolito Pindemonte, where the word "tanto" (so much)—"Te solo aspetto, e quel che *tanto* amasti," (I wait for you only, and for that which I loved so much) by Petrarch, and "Fermossi alfine il cor che balzò *tanto*" (The heart it stops at last which bounded so much) by Ippolito Pindemonte—is used because "being indefinite, it produces a greater effect than the words 'molto' (much), 'moltissimo' (very much), 'eccessivamente' (excessively) or 'sommamente' (in the highest degree) would have done. Similarly words, like 'ultimo' (last), 'mai più' (never more), 'l'ultima volta' (the last time), etc., are of great poetic effect, because of the notion of infinity they convey."[37]

However, these words, intrinsically more poetic as they are than most other words, cannot always help the poet, who must choose the kind of words most appropriate to the theme and the context concerned; that is why, for instance, the vocabulary that is so appropriate to Byron's *Don Juan* would be highly inappropriate to Wordsworth's *Prelude* or to Byron's own *Childe Harold;* that is why, in Leopardi's own work, one finds a palpable difference between the diction of the *Canti* and that of *Paralipomeni della Batracomiomachia.* "Different styles require a different sort of words, and as what is noble and best for prose is quite often ignoble for poetry, so what is noble and best for one kind of prose is very often unfit for another."[38] Leopardi's regarding certain words as being poetically more suitable than others should not lead one to suppose that he was in favor of creating a pure and stereotyped diction for poetry, from which what is unpoetic should be cautiously avoided. In what Leopardi means by poetic diction, it is not so much the choice and discrimination of certain words and the avoidance of certain others that chiefly matters as it is the utilizing of all the possible resources of a language, including the idiom of contemporary spoken speech as well as words of ancient literary origin, which are no longer in use but which have somehow preserved a certain kind of efficacy and freshness. His preference for words that express something vague and indefinite was, as we have seen, part of his notion of the nature and effect of poetry itself, poetry which he sharply distinguished from and contrasted with science or mathematics. Thus it is practically the same thought that Sir Walter Raleigh, who was familiar with Leopardi's writings, also expressed when he said: "All words, the weak and the strong, the definite and the vague, have their offices to perform in language, but the loftiest purposes of poetry are seldom served by those explicit hard words which, like tiresome explanatory persons, say all that they mean. Only in the focus and centre of man's knowledge is there place for the hammer-blows of affirmation, the rest is a flickering world of hints and half lights, echoes and suggestions, to be come at in the dusk or not at all."[39]

In theory as well as in practice, Leopardi believed, together with Dante and Wordsworth, that the basis and source of a poet's language, in the main, is no other than "the real language of men,"—"the popular language" or "the popular idiom," as Leopardi calls it—that no language did or would ever have the qualities of force, beauty, variety, and novelty unless it obtained them from the common language of speech, using it, of course, not as the people in general use it but in such a way as to reduce it to the universal forms and laws of literature. The source of the poet's language being, first and last, the spoken language of the common people, the poet indeed may, as in practice he almost invariably does, select from this source and thus write in what Wordsworth called "a selection of the real language of men." Of course, this selection is not to be made according to any fixed laws except those of the poet's own taste and of the particular contextual or thematic or atmospheric contingency which renders one kind of words selected more appropriate than another. The final test of poetic merit lies, no doubt, in what the word becomes in a poet's hands, and not from what source it comes. "The highest poetry can be written," says Saintsbury, and Leopardi would have wholeheartedly agreed with him, "in what is, literally speaking, the vocabulary of the most ordinary prose; but when it is—for instance, 'The rest is silence,' or 'To-morrow and to-morrow and to-morrow,' or 'Put out the light'—there is always some *additional* meaning which, in ordinary prose use, the words would not bear."[40]

Thus, so far as the diction of poetry is concerned, and indeed so far as the whole question of language itself is concerned, Leopardi is by no means a purist. Not only did he advocate the intermixture, in the maximum degree possible, between the prose idioms and the diction of poetry, but he also supported the idea of borrowing words from a foreign source. To conserve the purity of the language he says, "is an imaginary thing, a dream, an abstract hypothesis, an idea, never to be realized in act, unless a nation has never received anything from a foreign country either with regard to literature or doctrine, or with regard to life itself."[41] Leopardi, therefore, attacks the narrow-minded purism of Antonio Cesari—"a Bembo of the nineteenth century"—who rather than approve of borrowing words from a foreign language, when one needs them and does not find them in one's own language, recommends the use of circumlocutions. New ideas, new institutions, new sciences and philosophies entail the use of a new vocabulary and demand the use of what the purists called "hateful neologisms and barbarisms"—neologisms that are more or less common to practically all the languages of Europe. Not to give due recognition to these neologisms, and not to absorb them into Italian is, Leopardi points out, tantamount to keeping Italy out of contact with this world and with this century.

Leopardi's attitude to poetic diction is, in essence, the same as that of Milton—"that great exemplar of diction" as Sir Walter Raleigh justly called him—to poetry (meaning thereby for the most part, the

language of poetry) that it ought to be simple, sensuous, and impassioned. The one word that Leopardi
so frequently uses in order to denote all these qualities at one and the same time is "elegance." Leopardi's
use of this word is subtler and at the same time
richer and more comprehensive than that of Hazlitt,
for instance, when he complains about the lack of the
"feeling for the classical or elegant" in Coleridge.
For Leopardi "elegance" is not merely something that
has got to do with the external aspect of a language,
distinguishing it from prose or from the spoken
language, but a kind of poetic grace that may be
found not simply in one particular style, but in all
kinds of poetic styles, whether ornate or simple,
classical or baroque, epic or lyrical. Poetic elegance
is the name of that "additional" quality which a poet
injects into the words or the language he uses. And
in so far as the language itself can contribute something to the achievement of this quality, it is on two
principal sources that it mainly relies—the popular
idiom with its perennial freshness and energy, or as
Leopardi calls it "the infinite tenacity of the vulgar
speech," and the ancient literary language which is
no longer current today. As regards the first source,
what Leopardi means is quite clear, namely, that
nature being the source of all beauty, it is how the
common people speak, without the help of art or
literary training or scholarship, that, when judiciously
used, can make for the quality of elegance. And it
can do so if the words of common speech are used
in a way that the common people would never be

able to use; and the common people themselves, knowing those words full well, cannot but feel the pleasant shock of surprise when they see them charged with a new and additional meaning, force, and beauty. That is why, as Tillotson so truly observes, "words in poetry show themselves as words, and rouse us to look at them as if for the first time";[42] it is this new and peculiar way of using the same words in poetry that one reads or uses in prose without being struck by them, which accounts for that essential difference between the language of prose and of metrical composition, the existence of which Wordsworth so categorically denies and Coleridge so convincingly asserts. "I appeal to the practice of the best poets," says Coleridge, rebutting Wordsworth's thesis, "of all countries and in all ages, as *authorizing* the opinion . . . that in every import of the word essential, which would not here involve a mere truism, there may be, is, and ought to be an *essential* difference between the language of prose and of metrical composition."[43] Thus while drawing from the language of everyday speech, the poet uses what he draws in such a way that it is capable of producing an effect, conveying a shade of meaning and a kind of emotional depth that the language of prose or conversation, whether in the case of highly educated and learned people or in that of uneducated or illiterate people, cannot do.

Another source of poetic elegance in language is those words which were used by ancient writers and which still preserve a literary flavor, but which are not in current use. Such words are not to be confounded with archaisms, and Leopardi is himself at pains to draw a distinction between them—a distinction, however, which does not seem very clear:

> I hate archaisms; these ancient words, even if they are very clear, expressive, beautiful, and useful, always seem to be affected, deliberately sought after, far-fetched and labored, especially in prose. But our ancient writers abound in words and modes of expression which have fallen into disuse today, but which besides having a very clear significance, accord with the language of ordinary discourse so naturally, so softly, and so easily, are so far from any semblance of affectation, effort, or study about their use, and, in a word, so fresh and at the same time so beautiful that the reader who does not know whence they come cannot realize that they are ancient and cannot but consider them very modern, as if coming straight from the mint: words and modes of expression whose antiquity one may know, but cannot feel. Whereas the archaisms may be compared with things which have become stale, rancid, and moldy with the passage of time, these (i.e., the literary words that have gone out of current use) resemble fruits conserved in a wax-plaster to be eaten out of season; and when they are taken out of the plaster they seem to be fresh, vivid, colorful, and beautiful as if they had been just plucked from the trees. Even though they had been long discarded from the written or the spoken language, they do not seem to have been altogether forgotten, but rather to have been set apart and preserved in order to be taken up later on."[44]

The use of such words borrowed from antiquity serves to distinguish the language of poetry from that of prose—words which seem intolerably affected and far-fetched in prose, but which, to quote Ben Jonson, "doe lend a kind of Majesty to style. . . . For they have the Authority of yeares, and out of their intermission doe win to themselves a kind of gracelike newness."[45] It is at least partly in this sense that Gray's famous statement—"The language of the age is never the language of poetry, except among the French, whose verse, where the thought or the image does not support it, differs in nothing from prose"[46]—has got to be interpreted. For, while these words from old writers, whether in prose or verse, cannot be used today in prose or everyday speech, they can very well be used in poetry, and they, in fact, constitute "a very abundant source of elegance" in the poetic language. The choice and use of these words has to be determined according to the particular need and the context where they occur, and whether these words, used even in poetry, contribute to heighten the degree of poetic elegance or not depends on the poet's own individual capacity to exploit the linguistic material and resources at his command. In the case of an indifferent or bad poet, these very words may serve to produce just the contrary effect, and may seem uncouthly archaic and affected.

Leopardi's qualified condemnation of archaisms, therefore, amounts to his condemnation of the wrong, inadequate, or injudicious use of archaisms, whether in poetry or prose—a use that cannot but produce the impression of something being grotesquely affected and artificial. This, though, would not happen in the case of a good poet, even if he used the same words, however archaic and obsolete they might be. Moreover, since what contributes to elegance in poetic diction does not necessarily do so in prose, archaisms in prose stand self-condemned. But not always so in poetry, where going back to Nature, to the origin of language—and this is what the use of archaisms really involves—may be, and in the hands of a good poet often is, quite profitable. "True archaism does imply," observes Owen Barfield, "not a standing still, but a *return* to something older, and if we examine it more closely, we shall find that it generally means a movement towards language at an earlier stage of its own development. Nothing further, it is hoped, need be said as to the general reasons why language at an earlier stage of its own development should be more suitable for poetic expression, or why a return in that direction should correspond in some degree with a return to 'Nature.' That the two do in fact often go together is palpable from the history of European literature."[47] And Leopardi, too, delineates the growth of a language from the primitive and poetically more propitious age to the more geometric stage, as he calls it, in its complex modernity. Identifying nature with poetry, and reason with science and philosophy, Leopardi points out:

Those qualities [in the languages] which, on the one hand, are of help to reason and, on the other, depend upon it, grow and develop with the passage of time; those which depend on nature decline, decay, and are lost. Hence, languages gain in precision, clarity, order, and regularity, in proportion as they remove themselves from the primitive stage. But in so far as variety, efficacy, and beauty are concerned, the further they get away from their primitive stage, the more they stand to lose. The combination of nature with reason takes place when they are

[211]

applied to literature. Then art corrects the roughness of nature, and nature corrects the dryness of art. Then one can say that the languages are in a state of relative perfection. But they do not stop here. Reason advances, and with the advance of reason, nature recedes. Art is no longer counterbalanced. Precision predominates, beauty succumbs.[48]

Poetry, by using the words of ancient literary origin, helps preserve the primitive character and purity of the language.[49] Of all the modern languages, Leopardi considers Italian to be the most capable of preserving this original purity as well as of achieving that kind of poetic elegance which is possible through the use of the ancient literary words on the part of the modern writers endowed with "true judgment." And this is because Italian has remained closer to its parent source (that is to say, not simply Latin, but also, and above all, the language of the *trecentisti* and the *cinquecentisti*) than any other modern language, and, therefore, it is in a better position than other languages to utilize words "as remote from daily use as need be so that they may have about them such a degree of extraordinariness and rarity as may not affect the clarity, the ease, and the harmony between these words and the modern words and phrases."

How true all this is may be seen from the example of modern Italian poets like Montale and Quasimodo, in whose poetic diction both ancient and extremely modern words sometimes rub shoulders and thereby produce an admirable poetic effect. The old Italian writers and poets themselves, while trying to achieve in their diction "that rare quality of forms, phrases,

and expressions" which makes for elegance, took fre-
quent recourse to Latin and enriched their poetic
diction with many Latin words and expressions. It
is thus not simply languages that, as Tillotson observes, shed their defects in the hands of poets, but
even individual words in the same languages; and
they not only shed their defects—for instance, the
defect of archaism or obsoleteness—but they even come
to acquire a peculiar force and charm which they
never had before, even in the writer who originally
used them, and which no modern coined words or
expressions could convey. In other words, the quality
of elegance and rarity is something like a dormant
element which the poet has to awaken and vivify;
that is what Emerson meant when he said that "Language is fossil poetry"; it has to be revitalized each
time a great poet comes to handle it. What is rare
and elegant about a certain word today may not be
so tomorrow, and it may not have been so yesterday.
These qualities have to be constantly rediscovered,
recreated, and rebreathed into the words and into the
style.

In his ceaseless quest for the qualities of elegance
and rarity in the words he uses, a poet is not at all
helped, or rather he is positively hindered, by the
abundance of synonyms in a language. Far from
being a sign of the richness of a language, synonyms
are a proof of its poverty, of its lack of subtlety and
sensibility with regard to those "small and fleeting
differences," as Leopardi calls them, "between the
meanings of the words invented not for the sake of

luxury, but for the sake of need and utility."[50] For, according to Leopardi, the true richness of a language does not consist in its ability to signify the same thing by means of different words, but in its ability to express or at least suggest the subtlest shades of difference and the various grades of appropriateness and the wealth of associations underlying the use and meaning of two different words *apparently* signifying the same thing. For Leopardi, therefore, as well as for Sir Walter Raleigh, there are no synonyms; language, to quote the latter, "halts far behind the truth of things, and only a drowsy perception can fail to devise a use for some new implement of description."[51] Sometimes, in fact, the very limitedness of the range of vocabulary in a given language may constitute its richness and strength. That is why, as Leopardi points out, the more developed a language is, the fewer words one needs to express oneself in it. And so far as the task of a poet is concerned, it principally lies in his creatively expressing himself within the range of the vocabulary at his disposal, that is to say the vocabulary of the present spoken language as well as the literary and poetic vocabulary of the old classics, on which he may from time to time draw. Even from within the range of this vocabulary he has obviously to select. The secret of what renders his language so poetically effective lies in the nature of this selection as well as in his ability to extract a new significance from the ordinary commonplace words and clothe them in an altogether new light. Synonyms, where they exist, are a perpetual temptation to the poet, not indeed so much to make use of them as to spare himself the trouble of digging into some hitherto undiscovered or unexploited layer of a word. But in spite of what he says against archaisms, or rather against the abuse of archaisms, Leopardi would have basically agreed with Nietzsche's statement in *The Wanderer and His Shade* regarding the poetic potentiality of a deliberately or naturally limited vocabulary.

To use neologisms or archaisms in the language, to prefer the precious and the strange, to aim at the richness rather than the limitation of the lexicon is always the sign of a taste that is either not yet mature or that is already corrupt. A noble poverty but within the limits of a perfect real control and a masterly liberty is what distinguishes the ancient Greek artists of speech: they should like to possess less than what people possess—for it is always the people who are the richest in things old and new—but that little they would like to possess it better.

Besides taking recourse to ancient literary and poetic words—now no longer in use—in order to achieve the quality of elegance, the poet can also use the words of everyday speech in a peculiar and unusual way, by means of what Leopardi calls "the different material inflection." Since the very quality of poetic elegance itself depends on what is "new, extraordinary, irregular, . . . rare, and unusual" in the language, the best way of achieving this is by departing from the monotony, unimpressiveness, and even triviality of etymological exactitude and propriety, or by even distorting the original etymological meaning of the word. "Every beauty," Leopardi

[215]

points out, "whether of a language in general (except for the harmony and the richness of the words and their inflections), or of the way of saying, in particular, is a spite against the universal grammar, and an express, though more or less serious, infraction of its laws."[52] It is not merely a question of delving deep into the etymological meaning of a word, but of actually departing from the meaning it would normally have in its logical or syntactical relationships with other words.[53] This departure, instead of causing any obscurity, adds to the expressive power of the language. There is no writer in Greek or Latin or in any other ancient tongue who is easier to read than Xenophon, and yet, "he is full of locutions, modes, and figurative forms which are extremely irregular . . . contrary no less to the Greek syntax than to the universal logical order of the discourse."[54] Poetic rashness of the right quality, George Meredith has said, enriches the language. And for Leopardi too grammatical, etymological, and logical rashness is the very basis and origin of poetic rashness. Of course, this rashness ought not to be exaggerated; for, then instead of serving as a fount of poetic beauty and elegance, it will be a cause of ugliness.[55] In a passage that closely reminds one of a similar passage in Coleridge's *Biographia Literaria,* Leopardi clearly explains the difference between the poetic language and the language of prose in so far as the relative propriety of certain expressions in prose and poetry is concerned. While discussing Wordsworth's theory of poetic diction, Coleridge says:

The true question must be, whether there are not modes of expression, a *construction*, and an *order* of sentences, which are in their fit and natural place in a serious prose composition, but would be disproportionate and heterogeneous in metrical poetry; and, *vice versa*, whether in the language of a serious poem there may not be an arrangement both of words and sentences, and a use and selection of (what are called) *figures of speech*, both as to their kind, their frequency, and their occasions, which on a subject of equal weight would be vicious and alien in correct and manly prose.[56]

And Leopardi, with even more analytical details, makes the same point:

The poetic language and style in an already formed literature—a literature that has at all any poetic language and style of its own—distinguishes itself from prose and from vulgar speech not simply in virtue of the use of the phrases and expressions which, even though they can be and are understood, are no longer used in prose or in the familiar discourse—phrases and expressions belonging to ancient dictions and locutions which have fallen into disuse except in poetry—but also in virtue of the different material inflection of the same expressions and phrases from the one used in prose and in common discourse. Hence very often a certain phrase or expression, if written or pronounced in a certain way, is poetic, but if pronounced and written in another way, it is definitely prosaic, and sometimes even altogether unpoetic, or rather quite ignoble and vulgar. . . . This method of distinguishing and separating the language of poetry from that of prose and of the vulgar speech, by inflecting or conditioning in a way quite different from the normal a certain prose or familiar expression, is most frequently adopted in every language that has a distinct poetic language of its own, as the Greeks always had and as the Italians have; nay, while talking purely of the language and not of the style, it may be said that this method

[217]

is frequently adopted in order to achieve the desired end, and perhaps more frequently than that of employing unusual phrases and expressions.[57]

But while the use of ancient literary words that have now fallen into desuetude, as well as the use of current vocabulary in an unusual, unfamiliar, and etymologically irregular way, makes for the quality of what is poetically elegant in a diction, the use of dialect words does not. On the contrary, the use of dialect words tends to deprive the poet's language—and consequently his very poetry and its appeal—of its universality. Moreover, poetry written in a language with a strong admixture of dialect words seems rather trite even to those who speak that dialect. It is Dante's use of dialect words, says Leopardi, that, among other things, has prevented him from being a popular poet in the same way as Homer was popular among the Greeks. Not that Homer, too, did not make use of words belonging to a certain dialect, but then those words were understood in all the Greek provinces, or at any rate in those provinces which Homer considered to be his audience. This was not so with Dante's use of dialect words. Leopardi even remarks that the poetic language of Italy neither is, nor ever was, that of Dante. And this is partly, or principally, because between the poetic and the prose language of Dante's times there was hardly any difference. Italian then did not have enough antiquity behind it to serve as a source of those words which often render language poetically elegant and distinct from the language of prose. "And without the quality of antiquity," says Leopardi, "there cannot be a poetic language."[58]

Together with elegance, there is another quality in words and language as they are used in poetry which Leopardi contrasts with the quality of precision and regularity, whether logical or mathematical, in the language of prose or vulgar speech—the quality of propriety. This quality he deems to be so important that he affirms that a language cannot be beautiful without it. What exactly Leopardi means by "propriety," he himself sums up in the following passage.

Now, what does one mean when one says that a language has propriety? Nothing but that it is a bold language, that it is capable of deviating in its forms and modes from the order and dialectic reason of discourse, inasmuch as within the limits of this order and this reason there is nothing that is proper to any language at all, but everything is common to all the languages (meaning thereby, of course, the forms and the faculties, and not the naked words or their inflections, considered in isolation). Hence if the form of a language that has no propriety, neither is nor can be beautiful, the language itself also neither is nor can be beautiful, if in its form it is all or almost all mathematical, and in conformity with the universal grammar. And thus once again one cannot but conclude that the beauty of the forms of a language (that is to say of the forms in general as well as each one of them individually) must needs be in opposition to the general grammar, and it cannot but constitute a major or a minor violation of its laws.[59]

Propriety, therefore, amounts to the very individuality of a language, which in the hands of a poet becomes something even more individual and more particular. The reason why the ancient poets' language had more of this quality than that of the modern poets is that it was "nearer to the earliest stage when the meaning and formation of the words was determined, and to the formation of the words and their meanings themselves, not for the sake of luxury, which was unknown to the ancients, but for the sake of need and utility." It is in virtue of its possessing this propriety that one can say of a language that the richer and the vaster it is, the fewer words it needs to express something, and that, *vice versa,* the more words it needs to express the same thing, the more restricted it is. Propriety is, therefore, a token of its richness and vastness. And it is the richness and vastness of a language rather than its paucity and restricted character that lead one to desire and achieve brevity of expression.

Leopardi's theory of poetic language, therefore, is largely influenced, as we said, by his conception of Italian as, of all the modern languages, the one where the distinction between the language of prose and that of poetry is most manifest. It is "among the illustrious modern languages the one most distinct from, and the least dominated by, usage . . . because in Italy there are fewer social classes than in any other cultured nation, because literature with us is something much more exclusively a property of the *letterati* than elsewhere, and because Italy does not have an illustrious modern language."[60] In any nation whatsoever, Leopardi says, a poetic language as such is and, of necessity and by its very nature, must be materially different from the vulgar tongue. It is more or less poetic in proportion as it is more or less

different and distinct from the vulgar tongue. Thus
Leopardi takes a diametrically opposite stand against
Wordsworth and fundamentally agrees with Coleridge.
Knowing that Italy did not possess a modern language, that is to say, a language suiting the scientific
and philosophical needs of the changed and changing
times, Leopardi undertook the attempt to create one—
an attempt in which, as is proved by his *Operette
morali,* he succeeded to a remarkable degree. One
of the profoundest observations to be found in Leopardi's *Zibaldone* concerning the relationship between
the language of prose and the language of poetry is
to the effect that the perfection of a language is to be
seen in its prose rather than in its poetry, that no
language or literature can be said to be perfect unless
it has a perfect prose, and that prose is the nurse of
the poetic language. The truth of this observation has
been since borne out by the growth and development
of the language of poetry not only in Italy, but also
elsewhere. "The ultimate end of criticism," said Coleridge, "is much more to establish the principles of
writing, than to furnish *rules* how to pass judgment
on what has been written by others; if indeed it were
possible that the two could be separated."[61] It was the
lack of such principles in his days that Leopardi
deplored—principles as applied to the creation of a
modern language as well as to the discussion of its
nature. Indeed, none in that age was more fully
aware of and more earnestly concerned about "that
scarcity of judgment, or rather that incapacity for any
right judgment and the lack of every critical art, of

which Alfieri complained . . . and which is so evident today whether because of the continuous experience of the great follies that are praised, or of the virtues (if someone by any chance happens to possess them) which are either unknown or neglected, denied or blamed."[62] As an example of this one may, of course, note that the Accademia della Crusca assigned its prize (for the best book published during the last forty years) in 1830 to Carlo Botta's *Storia d'Italia* in preference to Leopardi's *Operette morali.* No wonder Leopardi had to defend his art and his theory, as Cardarelli said, "against three-fourths of the Italian literary world."

One can therefore see very clearly that in the development of modern Italian—and not simply in the sphere of poetry, but also that of prose—Leopardi plays just as important a part as Manzoni. His parallel success in creating both a new prose style and a new poetic style—an idiom at once new and reminiscent of the best elements in the old and the classical language, whether Greek or Latin or Italian—has made him exercise a sober formative influence on the development of Italian. This influence may be compared with that of Manzoni, so far as prose is concerned, but with no other influence than that of Dante, in so far as poetry is concerned. "With Leopardi, and only with him," De Robertis observes, "after the instinctive genius of Dante, Italian poetry, as substance and as form, enters into a crisis and really renews itself." Acutely conscious of what he called "the hundred and fifty years of the immobility of our literature," Leopardi sought to revive literature by first revitalizing the language itself and by readjusting it to the needs of a modern writer. While Manzoni tried to bring standard Italian as near as possible to the language spoken in Florence, because of its having an illustrious literary tradition behind it, and wished that one and only one language were used all over Italy, Leopardi, long before Croce, definitely opposed the idea of restricting a nation's language to one province alone.[63] To insist that the literary and cultural richness of the Florentine speech gives it an unquestionable prerogative to influence and actually to determine the course of the successive development of Italian is the same, Leopardi thought, as to insist that the Italian people should write in a dead language. Dante himself did not want the language to be confined to a particular province or city, and the so-called court language itself of Dante's times was as full of variety as the courts and republics themselves. For all his admiration of the language and literature of the fourteenth century early in life, Leopardi would not have either the language of prose or that of poetry slavishly restricted to or exclusively influenced by it. He even went so far as to declare it to be the falsest notion that the poetic language in Italy was formed by Dante or Petrarch, and still more that the language of prose was formed by Boccaccio.[64] The linguistic ideal at which Leopardi aimed may be described in his own words: "to use the ancient and the modern and all the resources of the language in view and with the intention of creating a style and a manner which is neither familiar nor ancient, but, in general, elegant, noble, majestic, altogether distinct from the common and familiar discourse . . . as is precisely the style of Cicero in prose and of Virgil in poetry."[65]

"In spite of his classical education," therefore, as Emilio Bertana points out, "and his protestations of deference to tradition, in spite of the times, the friendships and the environment, and the idea that without an ancient tongue there cannot be elegant literature, Leopardi was, in point of language (and even more so in theory than in practice) a convinced liberal and modernist."[66] And he was so because he did not believe in the purity of language. Nor did he believe that there is any scope for a radical revolution in the relationship that there always has been between the language of prose and the language of poetry. While conceding with Wordsworth that the ultimate strength of the poetic diction depends on the proportion in which it draws on the real language of common men, he sided with Coleridge in upholding the essential difference that there is in the poet's use of that common language and that of a common man. Moreover, he went further than both Wordsworth and Coleridge in pleading for the use of true and, so to say, living archaisms, which are not archaisms at all, as one of the most effective modes of creating poetic elegance, by which he meant all those characteristics in the language of poetry that serve to distinguish it, and, so to say, elevate it, from the language of prose and familiar discourse. No poet, or theorist of poetry, looked so passionately and so consistently back to tradition and to ancient classicism, with Homer as its supreme poetic head, not simply for his own time, but also for later ages—"From Homer onwards everything has been perfected, except poetry";[67] and yet no poet or theorist of poetry has said, and what is more, has done, so much which has had such a profound and vital relevance to the development of poetry as well as language of poetry in Italy as Leopardi. His concept of language in general, and of the poetic language in particular, is at once conservative yet liberal, firm yet dynamic, all-inclusive yet eclectic. A language, Leopardi tells us, "always marches, naturally and reasonably, so long as it lives, and as it is absurd to wish that it stayed firm, so also it is prejudicial and detrimental to wish it to go further back than is necessary and to oblige it to retread the path that it had already trod duly and directly."[68]

In the development of the modern Italian language, therefore, Leopardi plays just as vital a part as Manzoni. In fact, he did for poetry what Manzoni did for prose. Each in his sphere—and Leopardi, to some extent, in prose as well as in poetry, that is to say, so far as philosophical and argumentative prose that has all the grace and elegance of literary style is concerned—succeeded in establishing a certain measure and in chalking out a definite course that Italian was to follow, and has, indeed, followed ever since.

To the creative writer's instinctive insight into the possibilities of a language to develop itself and to be molded into new and hitherto unexplored forms—an insight that Leopardi shared with Manzoni—Leopardi added his deep philological intimacy with Italian and other neo-Latin languages so as to be able to evolve a concept of language as a whole, and not simply as poetic language, which is at once progressive and traditional, elegant and familiar, a concept of a language borrowing not from one, but from all possible sources, in order to enrich itself and adapt itself to the ever-changing pattern and exigencies of life and thought. The cardinal point of Leopardi's whole attitude to the development of a language lies in his unqualified emphasis on the principle of liberty, involving, as it must, the principle of inclusiveness, rather than, as in the case of Manzoni, that of exclusiveness and limitation. And by linguistic liberty Leopardi for the most part means adaptability, which is, in the long run, the only source of the strength as of the richness of any language. With regard to this principle of liberty in the development of a language, Leopardi draws an illuminating contrast between Latin and Greek. "Of all the languages Latin is the least adaptable to modern things, because, in virtue of its having an ancient and markedly individual character, it is not free, unlike other ancient languages, like Greek, and therefore incapable of anything but what is ancient, and inadaptable to what is modern."[69] This lack of freedom and adaptability in Latin originates from the fact that it was used to perfection, in the heyday of its growth and richness, only in relation to a few genres of writing, and secondly from the fact that its real formation coincided "with the major growth and achievements of art," and that it had in Cicero "a writer and a *formator* too vast in himself, but too small for Latin, and too preeminent among other writers," so that "whosoever tried to restrict himself to his language, lost the liberty of the language, and whosoever rejected it, lost the purity, and having reconquered the liberty with violence degenerated it into anarchy," since, Leopardi acutely points out,

liberty, both among nations and among languages, is good only when it is enjoyed peacefully, legitimately, as a matter of right and without any contrast relating to it, but when it is acquired by violence it is not liberty, but lawlessness. For it is in the very nature of human things that after they have reached one extreme, they jump over to another, and then return again to the first, knowing not how to stop in the middle where nature during the primitive stage had placed them and where nature alone can reconduct them. Italian itself ran a similar risk in the sixteenth century when someone wanted to restrict it, not to the fourteenth century, as some pedants would like to do today, but only to the style and language of Dante, Petrarch, and Boccaccio, because of the eminence of these writers, or rather to restrict prose only to the language and style of Boccaccio, the lyric only to that of Petrarch, and so on—something against which Caro fought in his *Apologia*.[70]

Far from therefore accepting, with Manzoni, the principle of basing modern Italian on one speech—the Florentine because of its rich literary heritage—Leopardi went even to the length of denying that the credit of having formed Italian should go to Dante, Petrarch, and Boccaccio—the three supreme pillars of that heritage. In fact a language may not be considered to have been formed unless it has achieved a definite prose style as distinct from the language of poetry—prose being "the most natural, the most usual, and therefore the principal part of a language," and, therefore, "the perfection of a language consisting essentially in prose." The prose of Boccaccio, "the first and the only one who applied prose to literature in the fourteenth century,"[71] cannot be regarded as a model prose, because Boccaccio grossly mistook the nature and spirit of Italian. The clearcut difference between the language of prose and the language of poetry, as a matter of fact, could not possibly have existed in the fourteenth century, since Italian did not as yet possess enough of antiquity about it, and without this element of antiquity it is difficult to achieve the elegance of style and language which alone can distinguish the language of poetry from that of prose. Only in the eighteenth and the nineteenth centuries, Leopardi says,

the poetic language (and therefore also the poetic style) have been fully formed and perfected in Italian (I mean the poetic language and style, not, of course, poetry itself); it has come near to that of Virgil, the true, perfect, and sovereign model of the properly, absolutely, and distinctly poetic style; it has lost all airs of the familiar, and within certain limits it has considerably severed itself from the prose style. To say that the language of prose has detached itself from the poetic language is, of course, not true, though it is true that it has separated itself from the language of antiquity, as it always happens with the language of prose and that of common everyday speech which it cannot but resemble. . . . Hence, to tell the truth, it is the language of prose that separates itself from the language of poetry (and not the other way round), not so much because the latter is poetic, but because it is the follower of antiquity and attached (as far as possible) to antiquity, from which the language of prose detaches itself. Hence, the language and the style of the poems of Parini, Alfieri, Monti, and Foscolo is more appropriately and more perfectly poetic and distinct from prose than that of any other of our poets, including especially the greatest, the most classical, and the oldest.[72]

The principle of liberty—implying that of adaptability to new themes and material—therefore goes hand in hand with that of antiquity in Leopardi's theory of poetic language and of language in general. And in so far as he carried out an illuminatingly detailed analysis of the difference between the language of prose and that of poetry, and in so far as he himself was a consummate craftsman both in verse and prose, Leopardi's influence on the development, not only of Italian poetic style and diction, but also, what is less noted, on that of Italian prose has been by no means less, and in some fundamental respects, even more important than that of Manzoni or any other nineteenth century writer. "The accretions of time," Sir Walter Raleigh has said, "bring round a word many reputable meanings, of which the oldest is likely to be the deepest in grain. . . . It is a counsel of perfection—some will say, of vainglorious pedantry —but that shaft flies furthest which is drawn to the head, and who desires to be understood in the twenty-fourth century will not be careless of the meanings that his words inherit from the fourteenth."[73] Never was a poet so fully aware of these "reputable meanings," nor so much interested in probing into the deepest grain of words, so familiar with their literary history and etymological origin as Leopardi. He scrutinized the nature of prose and poetic style down to the single words and phrases on which style, in the last analysis, mainly depends. Other critics and theorists of poetry and style, both before and after Leopardi, may have given us a more convincing and more impressive interpretation of a particular poem or the entire output of a particular poet, a more subtle analysis of the aesthetic-cum-moral responses that a sound reading of a literary work produces, a more elaborate and more balanced evaluation of the historical setting and importance of a poem or an author. But none (in Italy, at any rate) has tackled the question of the nature of poetic style, of the essential difference between the language of prose and the language of poetry, and of the growth and development of the language itself, more patiently, with a greater wealth of interesting and relevant details as well as within an ampler range of context, and in the specific and mutually relevant terms of both modernity and antiquity, tradition and innovation, and at the same time with a more competent authority derived from first-hand knowledge of both ancient and modern languages and literatures and a life-long interest in the problems concerned, than Leopardi. His linguistic achievement alone, apart from his poetic greatness, is indeed so unique and its effect so far-reaching that not only the development of Italian has since been profoundly influenced by his thought and practice, but also the most significant evolutions and reforms in the idiom of modern Italian poetry, and, for that matter, of some aspects of prose too, have directly and indirectly owed much to him. Referring to the "two perfectly different manners" in which both Manzoni and Leopardi dealt with the problem of language of both prose and poetry, Francesco Flora remarks that "the task of those who came later seemed to consist, at a certain point, in finding an equilibrium, a new harmony between these two great experiences of modern prose."[74]

CHAPTER TEN

Leopardi and Ourselves

∽

Apart from his influence as a poet—and no poet, with the exception of Dante, has wielded a more powerful influence on the development of modern Italian poetry—Leopardi's influence as a poetic theorist on twentieth century poetic theory (in Italy) has also been of the utmost importance. In fact his influence as a poet and his influence as a poetic theorist are almost inseparable as were, indeed, his own experiences as a poet and as a theorist. Leopardi developed his ideas about poetry and noted them down in his *Zibaldone* (begun in July 1817, terminated in December 1832) at the same time as he was writing his poetry. But while one may speak of the mutual influence of the two activities—and, of course, such an influence was inevitable—it should not lead one to define that influence in terms of a cause-and-effect relationship. For, Leopardi did not first set out and develop his ideas about poetry, and then go on to apply and practice them in his creative experience. Nor, *vice versa*, did he confine himself, in the realm of poetic theory, to just what his own experience as a poet meant to him, even though that experience did somehow influence and even prejudice his total concept and theory of poetry. His insistence, for example, that the lyric is the highest, if not the only, form of poetic art may be clearly attributed to and closely connected with his own personal predilection for and his consummate ability in that form. Nevertheless there is much less of this organic cause-and-effect interdependence between Leopardi's poetry and poetic theory than is, for instance, the case with Tasso, of whose *Gerusalemme liberata* Ettore Mazzali rightly says that "the protagonist of the *Discorso dell'arte poetica*" has a triple role therein, that is to say, "as idea of the poem to be, as confirmation and justification of the poem accomplished, and as desire and aspiration to render the poem perfect."[1] To a certain extent, of course, one may say that the *Canti* too have a similar role to perform in Leopardi's poetic theory, or that this sort of relationship between one's actual work as a poet and one's theory of poetry is always more or less bound to be there. But it is at once less apparent, and what is more, less important, in so far as one's understanding of either the poetry or the theory of poetry of a given poet is concerned, in the case of Leopardi than in that of Tasso, or any other poet who also happens to be, at the same time, a poetic theorist. In other words there is something more impersonal and more independent about Leopardi's poetic theory than about Tasso's. Even when Leopardi exalted the lyric to be the highest and most genuine form of poetry, just as Tasso regarded the heroic poem to be the same, it was not merely a matter of personal taste and aptitude, confirmed and encouraged by his own practice and success in that form, but also the result of a long and critical study and pondering on the subject. Tasso, on the other hand, while theorizing about the nature of poetry, had, for the most part, his eye either on the sort of poem he had proposed himself to write or the one he was actually writing or the one he had already written, as well as on the poetic theories current in his days and the whole body of Aristotelian, post-Aristotelian, and Renaissance thought. Leopardi, too, for his part, is fully conversant with the theories of poetry from Aristotle down to his own day, and yet his attitude to them is more critical and more independent than that of Tasso. Much of what is indeed of fundamental importance in his theory is not something absolutely original in itself, but the rather original way in which he fits or explores the eternal verities of art in a new context and with a fresh emphasis. It does not, therefore, detract much from Leopardi's merit as a theorist of poetry to say that similar ideas are to be found in this or that writer, whether known or unknown to Leopardi. What really matters in Leopardi's theory is the way he regroups and correlates these ideas, sifting, analyzing, and interpreting them, not simply in the light of his poetic experience, but also in the light of his wide erudition and the critical tact and intuition it fostered. Thus even while borrowing ideas from others or unconsciously using the ideas of others, Leopardi works out new implications and new interpretations, in virtue of which he is not merely as a poet, but also, and above all, as a poetic theorist, much ahead of his times. "One has already seen," Professor N. Sapegno points out, "how, in the most intense of our romantic experience, Leopardi, with the poetics of the pure lyric and in spite of the residues of a predominantly humanistic education, independently arrived at theoretical positions substantially akin to those from which the European decadentism was to develop."[2]

But it is not merely the premises as well as the conclusions of decadentism that Leopardi largely anticipates, but also of much that was to come later on, both as a sequel of and as a reaction from that decadentism. In other words Leopardi's poetic theory as well as his poetry sums up not only the themes and the spirit of the decadent theory of art, but also those of the very reaction against it, and of much of what is called modernity, and what that reaction against decadentism brought about. The merit of Leopardi's theory of poetry as such, independently of his merit as a poet, is to be seen nowhere better than in the case of those modern poets and writers, who without sharing the devotion and enthusiasm of the Rondists, and of their leader Cardarelli, for Leopardi's work *in toto,* and without being even directly or indirectly influenced by his poetry at all, have yet been indebted to him for his ideas on poetry—ideas which have had a direct bearing and even influence on their attitude to and their conception of poetry. Very justly does Luciano Anceschi point out that "from this actuality of Leopardi's aesthetic reflection our most experienced poets (Montale, Ungaretti, and Quasimodo) derive the indication and the aspiration to 'a happy sentiment of time, which may prolong the cadences into a more flowing rhythm, into a truly and exclusive poetic discourse."[3]

In order to undertake a due evaluation of the influence of Leopardi's poetic theory on twentieth century poetics in general, one should start with some sort of description of the historical setting within which that influence worked, of the circumstances that delayed its working, and of the obstacles that acted against it. In a way, one should trace, however briefly, the history of Leopardi's fortune and influence after his death in 1837. Now, it is a well-known fact that whatever was written about Leopardi in Italy before Francesco De Sanctis—written, that is, by people like Tommaseo, Cantù, Mazzini, G. Scalvini, Orioli, Montani, and others—when it is not actually an impressive example of elaborate misunderstanding, either dictated by religious or moral prejudice, or simply by critical mediocrity often bordering on sheer obtuseness, has little or no critical pretentions about it. In its more inspired moments it manages at best to attain to a kind of uninspired and mechanical admiration of the inescapably obvious, but, by no means, the most important or the most typical qualities of Leopardi's art. The only critic who anticipates to some extent the acute, enlightened, and analytical judgments of the foreign critics of Leopardi—judgments and evaluations much superior in critical weight and originality to anything written about Leopardi in Italy before De Sanctis, and even to much of what was written after, until one comes to Carducci and Pascoli—is Gioberti who considered Leopardi's poems as "the most beautiful lyric poems written in Italy after those of Petrarch." With some critics it was Leopardi's pessimism, with others his echoes from classical poets, and with still others his complete and unswerving dedication to the pursuit of letters which was misunderstood as an indifference, on Leopardi's part, to the public and political issues of the day, that stood in their way of appreciating his art.

With De Sanctis interest in Leopardi's poetry, though not so much in his prose works, acquires a truly appreciative as well as critical character. Both in his lectures at the University of Naples and in his articles and essays as well as in his monumental history of Italian literature, De Sanctis succeeded, for the first time, in entering into the spirit of Leopardi's poetry and in interpreting it in terms of concepts and principles that would in a certain way form the basis of much of the literary and critical theory from Croce onwards. And what is more, Leopardi together with Dante and Manzoni, though in a greater degree than Manzoni, was one of those authors, the study and interpretations of whose works brought out the best and the most characteristic powers of De Sanctis, as critic and as the historian of literary history and taste, into play. De Sanctis starts with Leopardi's "superlative erudition" in which one can already note the development of "that criticism which still stands in the lower regions of the emendation and the illustration of the texts."[4] Even in Leopardi's translations of the *Idylls* of Moschus, undertaken when he was only seventeen De Sanctis sees "that living sentiment of nature which is so rare in the Italian poets." Referring to the translation of the fifth idyll he points out that "it is not a translation, but an original poem; I would rather say a prophetic poem," since it foreshadows so clearly the mature Leopardian style.[5] Leopardi's censure against Caro's translation of Virgil —Caro "considered inviolable by the purists, almost a divinity"—is rightly held by De Sanctis as an evidence of Leopardi's basically sound and sensible literary taste in so far as it justly points out that Caro has "travestied Virgil in toga into a Virgil in civilian dress."[6]

Coming to Leopardi's poetry, De Sanctis' criticism betrays both imaginative sympathy and psychological acumen, poetic sensibility and intellectual grasp and clarity. One of the places where it shows itself to be at its best—where it is what one usually means by creative criticism of the most authentic sort—is in his comments on "L'Infinito." The contemplation of the infinite is described as "really a religious contemplation," and this because there is in this poem "nothing philosophical as it would be in the subsequent poems." Before the poet, "there are no ideas, but only shadows of ideas, no concept of the infinite and the eternal, but only the sentiment thereof." The pleasure of the solitary contemplater, who "feels himself lost in that immensity," arises, "not from the things which he contemplates, but from the act of contemplating itself, from that act of imagining and forgetting oneself and losing oneself without one's will and one's conscience. It is the will of the Brahmin, who is also a poet, to merge his individuality in the universal life."[7] In so far as his interpretation of the psychological motives and spiritual contents of Leopardi's poetry is concerned, De Sanctis may be called the A. C. Bradley of Leopardian criticism. Sometimes, however, he indulges, like Bradley himself, to some extent, in giving vent to his excessive enthusiasm for his subject and his almost missionary zeal to bring out its greatness and originality. He institutes at times parallels and hyperboles, which ill accord with the generally serious and measured tone of his criticism. For instance, he calls Leopardi "the Italian Byron"—a comparison which does not say anything except that there is indeed so little to be compared between the two in so far as their art is concerned. The same comparison between Leopardi and Byron was also drawn by Matthew Arnold, though Arnold did not fail to notice, and rather emphasizes the essential difference between the two as well.

An equally, if not more, important part of De Sanctis' criticism concerns Leopardi's style and diction in which, perhaps more than in anything else, he finds, like Matthew Arnold himself, the secret of Leopardi's supreme genius. Believing that "it is easier to renovate ideas than the form,"[8] De Sanctis found in Leopardi precisely a new form, achieved by means of a diction with its "naked simplicity," and "chaste transparency," a form, that is to say, as far "from the negligence of the ones (the Manzonian school which aimed at reproducing reality in as realistic a way as possible and which sought after the simple and the natural) as from the affectation of the others (those writers, including Giordani himself, with their theatrical and conventional solemnity, who declared themselves to be classicists)."[9] It is above all from his experience of Leopardi's poetry as a supreme testimony that De Sanctis derives his new concept of form as in itself a concrete fact, as thought turned into art—something which both Dante and Leopardi illustrate in their own respective way as no other poet in Italian literature has ever done.

As to Leopardi's critical thoughts and observations, even though De Sanctis finds in them "diverse visible influences," he cannot but be impressed by "the liberty and originality of judgment." After quoting two passages from *Zibaldone,* the one concerning Leopardi's comments on Anacreon and the other Monti, De Sanctis notes in them "curiosity and exactness of observation, rectitude of impressions, soundness of judgment" which he describes as the "virile qualities of a penetrative genius."[10] Again, it is De Sanctis who gives once for all the answer to those who say that in Leopardi's philosophy there is nothing new. Commenting on one of the cardinal points of Leopardi's pessimism that either life has no scope at all, or it cannot have any other scope than that of human happiness, De Sanctis remarks that "this, which is a commonplace of the poets and philosophers, both ancient and modern, has in Leopardi the originality of a personal sentiment."[11] What constitutes the originality of thought in a poet is, therefore, not the thought in itself, but the degree of intensity with which he feels it and makes it his own.

Even in prose, De Sanctis is the first major critic to point out, Leopardi made a very notable contribution, inasmuch as he created, in his *Operette morali,* that skeleton "which was lacking in the Italian prose, and in the exact and solid formation of the skeleton are to be seen that intellectual virility, and that logical vigor, which, if not the only, are yet a very principal part of good prose."[12] Elsewhere, De Sanctis tells us that the *Operette morali* not only have a philosophical content which is important in itself, but also "a wealth of concepts and an originality of technique, as is the case with Galileo and Leibnitz, and hence they are a true work of art."[13]

After De Sanctis, there are two major names in Italian criticism—Carducci and Croce, though there are other Leopardi scholars like G. Chiarini, B. Zumbini, F. Colagrasso, G. Mestica, A. Graf, F. De Roberto, E. Donadoni who, whether under the direct or indirect influence of De Sanctis or independently of him, undertook the interpretation of one particular aspect of Leopardi's work or another. The publication of *Zibaldone* in 1898, however, marks an important landmark in the history of Leopardi criticism and also an important beginning. The very first critic to have studied the *Zibaldone,* Carducci was in a better position than De Sanctis or any other critic before him to be able to make a first-hand acquaintance with the gradual process of Leopardi's cultural and critical formation. What, however, impresses Carducci most in Leopardi is the romantic sentiment behind Leopardi's pessimism, in virtue of which he calls him the "Job of the thought and the poetry of Italy." Another thing that strikes him is the carthartic value of the form in Leopardi's poetry, in virtue of which "poetry is liberated not from every constriction, but from every rhythmical limit . . . ; it has carved out for itself, with the insistence of the assiduous, continuous, and corrosive thought, a form without form, almost the river-bed of a closed and subterraneous torrent, in which as it were to cast and disperse one's pain and be nothing."[14] The last thing worth mentioning about Carducci's criticism of Leopardi's poetry is his statement that "La ginestra" approaches socialism—a statement that throws as much light on Carducci himself as on Leopardi's poem.

It is when we come to Croce that we find the classical example of a great critic, or at least a great scholar and a considerable thinker, who, while he writes brilliant essays on other poets and writers, utterly fails to understand one single author. Whether this is due to prejudice, or deliberate misunderstanding, or sheer inability to see what is so obvious to others, or whether to all these things more or less, it is hard to say. Certain things, however, emerge rather clearly in this obscure and paradoxical (to say the least) aspect of Croce's work. Even though Croce used to describe philosophies such as that of optimism or pessimism as pseudophilosophies in so far as they are "philosophies for private use," his own Olympic idealism, which definitely tended towards optimism, could not, understandably enough, have much use for pessimism. What is, however, less understandable is that it led Croce to altogether condemn Leopardi as a thinker. And the fact that Leopardi was not, and neither wanted nor pretended to be, a systematic thinker because he was lacking in what Croce calls "speculative disposition and preparation" seems to lend support to another statement that Croce makes concerning Leopardi's theory of poetry and art, to the effect that "although he was led to meditate on the subject quite often, he could not say anything new or important, conceived in a rigorous way."[15] Now, for Croce, even in the realm of poetic theory and when it is a poet and not a philosopher as such who is in question, meditating and remarking about his own practical experience as poet, nothing could be really valid and important unless presented in the form of rigorously conceived and systematically built-up system—the sort of system, that is to say, that Croce himself was so dexterous in conceiving and building. It is not too unfair to suggest that perhaps it is, *inter alia,* the presence of too much of this "speculative disposition and preparation" and too much of a system "conceived in a rigorous way" that is responsible for the fact that, whatever might have been or still is Croce's influence on Italian letters, he has exercised so little influence elsewhere on the theory and practice of literary criticism. To take the example of English criticism alone, the two most influential exponents thereof in this century, namely T. S. Eliot and F. R. Leavis, in their replies to the present author's inquiry concerning Croce's influence in England generally and on them particularly, deny that it has been there at all either way. "Croce's name, of course," writes Leavis in a letter of November 13, 1963, "was in the modish currency in the 1920's; we were all prepared to be told that 'art is expression'; but Croce's aesthetic—Croce's 'influence'—made no difference at all in literary criticism or taste. There is nothing else I need say—or could say, so blank is my memory in respect of any Crocean influence." And T. S. Eliot, in a letter dated November 14, 1963, writes: "I, myself, have never looked at any of Croce's voluminous work which, for some reason or other, has quite failed to appeal to me as having anything to offer me. So far as I am aware none of the men you mention (F. R. Leavis, I. A. Richards, and William Empson) has undergone any influence at all from Croce, nor has any other critic whose name is at all associated with mine. . . . I seem to remember that Croce and other Italian philosophers were taken seriously by Prof. Smith at Oxford, but that was during the first world war when German philosophy was out of favour at Oxford and the Italians had to serve in their stead." But then have the great critics always, if ever, cared to build such systems? And we say critics, because a theorist of poetry is at bottom a critic, though not all critics may be called theorists. Nothing is, for instance, more unsystematic and less rigorously conceived than what goes under the name of Coleridge's theory and criticism in *Biographia Literaria,* or in Dr. Johnson's *Lives of the Poets.* As to the question of "speculative disposition and preparation" in which Leopardi was lacking, the answer may be found in the instructive irony with which Saintsbury chose to answer Croce's charge that he (Saintsbury) too was lacking in the same, when he said that he had studied philosophy at Oxford. For, is the systematic study of philosophy, the so-called "speculative disposition and preparation," after all, so essential to a poet or a critic, or for that matter, even to a true philosopher as distinguished from a professor, an exponent or a historian of others' philosophies, that he cannot say something of his own, supposing he has anything to say, without it?[16] Moreover, while it may be accepted that Leopardi was lacking in speculative preparation, this does not mean that he had no philosophical disposition whatsoever, for indeed these are two different things, and the presence or absence of one does not necessarily presuppose or preclude the other. Was it not Thoreau who had said very wisely that not all professors of philosophy are philosophers? One may not go as far as Giuseppe Rensi and call Leopardi "our great poet, and, at the same time . . . our major philosopher."[17] But there is no doubt that Leopardi, if any poet in Italy, had the speculative disposition, for the one irrefutable proof of this disposition is the very fact that Leopardi was habitually and spontaneously led to meditate and speculate, and continued to do so from a very early age till the very end of life. Moreover, his poetry itself is in the best sense of the term as much philosophical—philosophical, that is to say, in its inspiration and philosophical in its theme and treatment —as lyrical poetry can well be. In this connection it is apt to recall George Santayana's words:

In philosophy itself investigation and reasoning are only preparatory and servile parts, means to an end. They terminate in insight, or what in the noblest sense of the word may be called theory . . . a steady contemplation of all things in their order and worth. Such contemplation is imaginative. No one can reach it who has not enlarged his mind and tamed his heart. A philosopher who attains it is, for the moment a poet; and a poet who turns his practised and passionate imagination on the order of all things, or on anything in the light of the whole, is for the moment a philosopher.[18]

Leopardi himself insisted on the essential affinity between the poet and the philosopher as well as realized, like Coleridge, the need of a system for a thinker or a philosopher.

Since in order to be a true and great philosopher one requires the natural gifts of great imagination and great sensibility, it follows that the great philosophers are by nature the most antiphilosophical that one may imagine, in so far as the practice and the use of that philosophy in their life is concerned, and *vice versa* the most clumsy or the hardest, the coldest and the most antiphilosophical heads are by nature most disposed to the practical exercise of philosophy. . . . Truly, since nature always triumphs, it generally happens that those who are in theory the most philosophical are the least so in practice, and those who are the least disposed to the philosophical theory are the most philosophical in effect.[19]

Whatever merit we may or we may not attribute to the writer of this paragraph, we cannot deny that he had a certain philosophical disposition, and an awareness of his own position in this matter. Often what Leopardi wrote was written either in direct imitation of someone else's thought—an imitation that served him as a fillip to his own chain of thinking, which was something more than a mere paraphrase or elaboration of the original thought in question—or by unconsciously echoing something he had read and absorbed so well that it had become an integral part of his own mental furniture. But in a passage like the one just quoted there cannot be any doubt that what Leopardi is saying is not an echo or an elaboration of another writer's or philosopher's thought, but the very essence of what he himself thought and felt in this matter independently of any conscious or unconscious influence.

All this is not meant to prove that Leopardi was a systematic philosopher; Leopardi himself would be the first to deny that he was. Nor would it matter very much if one found that there is plenty of evidence to show that Leopardi had that very disposition, if not actually training or aptitude, for speculation which Croce denies to him. But the point is that Croce links up his statement concerning the lack of philosophical system and disposition in Leopardi with the lack of any utility, not to say originality and importance, in what he wrote about the theory and problems of the art of poetry. And this in turn determines—though one cannot well see why, even if all that were true—his mode of interpreting and evaluating Leopardi's poetry itself.

Nothing, however, would be more futile than to try to show that because in some respects Leopardi anticipated Croce, and, indeed, much of post-Crocian criticism and poetic theory, and because he managed to dispose of some fundamental themes of modern poetics just by means of a few laconic observations that have as much of pertinence and fruitfulness in them as the more elaborately developed systems of aesthetics or literary theory, Leopardi was far more original than, and therefore much superior to, Croce or other systematic theorists or philosophers. It is not the question of originality or superiority, or even that of temporal priority, that invests Leopardi's views with a certain authority and authenticity, and consequently with a degree of convincingness and persuasiveness, far superior to anything that one can possibly credit the ambitious schemes of poetic and literary theory with, but the simple fact that whatever Leopardi wrote about the art of poetry was firmly rooted in first-hand creative experience. Alluding to I. A. Richards' attempt to demolish the "revelation" theory held by the romantic poets and others, Middleton Murry observes that "we may with a good conscience retain the theory held by Goethe, Coleridge and Keats, and still believe that they, being at once great poets and subtle thinkers, were not wholly deluded."[20] In this list of great poets one may well put Leopardi—Leopardi not as against the demolishers of the "revelation" theory like I. A. Richards, but against the calculated neglect and indifference on the part of the upholders and promoters of that very theory—call it the theory of intuition or expression, or the theory of pure poetry or all of them more or less rolled into one—which his own unconnected but specifically lucid and telling observations so obviously point to and confirm. Hence one can say in respect of Croce what Cardarelli says in respect of Manzoni, that "if *Zibaldone* had come out in Manzoni's time . . . he would have saved himself the trouble of theorizing about the language, and that his polemics concerning taste and his poetics would have availed themselves of ampler and more solid views, if that were only for the sake of contrast."[21]

Now it is a well-known fact of the Italian literary history of this century that the merit of bringing out the importance, both historical and intrinsically literary, of Leopardi's poetic theory and its influence, direct or indirect, on, as well as its vital relevance to, twentieth-century poetry and poetics belongs mainly to the contributors of the literary periodical *La Ronda,* including Cardarelli, Cecchi, and Bacchelli. Considering Leopardi (roundabout 1920) as one of the major writers of modern times who have not been properly understood, they set out to demonstrate that though Leopardi pretended to appear to be the most ancient, he "was in effect the most modern of his contemporaries, the one who idolizes the past least." The keynote they struck in their special pleading for Leopardi the prose-writer and the poetic theorist is that of Leopardi's essential modernity—a modernity which he shared with and in which he even anticipated Baudelaire and Mallarmé and in virtue of which he profoundly influenced modern Italian (and not merely Italian) poetry, its several phases of development—the crepuscular, the futurist, the impressionist, and the hermetic.

It is, therefore, not for nothing that Montale, in many ways the very reverse of Leopardi in his poetry and in his poetic principles, asserted that after Leopardi it had become almost impossible to write poetry, that Thovez observed that Leopardi had exhausted the lyric blank verse form, that Ungaretti wondered —and wondered rightly—if there was another man "who saw the connection between form and inspiration with the human amplitude and acuteness of a Leopardi,"[22] that Cecchi called him "the only modern poet worthy of the *Greek Anthology*,"[23] that Valentino Piccoli found in him "a precursor, not only of the actual philological sciences, but also of the disvaluation of the theory of the literary genres which was, later on, to be practiced and accepted by the whole of contemporary criticism, from De Sanctis to Croce."[24] *Zibaldone*, Cardarelli points out, "has vigorously contributed to liberate Italian literature from too long and too sour an intervention of Crocianism."[25]

Not that the modern poets set out deliberately to imitate Leopardi; the really good poets knew better, and they understood perfectly well that it would be rash "to imitate a style which signs its name at every even pause." They chiefly looked upon Leopardi as a model in whose poetry not less than in whose personality the psychological-cum-poetic experience, with its characteristic depth and complexity, so typical of a modern poet, attains to a clear and concrete union with an infallibly appropriate form, as it has never done before or after, outside the work of Dante, and that too in a different way and in an altogether different context, let alone on a different scale. They found Leopardi's passionate adherence to the word, his incessant probing into its several meanings—historical, actual, etymological, and literary—and into the possibilities of its bearing an altogether new meaning as both an illuminating and inspiring guidance and an ever-present and ever relevant challenge.

The importance of Leopardi's poetry is, in a considerable degree, related to and determined by his importance as the originator of the philosophical lyric in Italy and as "the profoundest psychological poet" of our times. And the value of his observations on language is in just proportion to the soundness of his conviction that it is above all by a poet's language that you know him. Moreover, it is not the validity, originality, or depth of his philosophy as such that lends a tone of solemn universality to Leopardi's poetics or that entitles him to be considered as a philosophical poet, but the very fact that he exercised, with a habitual consistency, what Santayana calls "a steady contemplation of all things in their order and worth," and that he turned "his practised and passionate imagination on the order of all things, or on anything in the light of the whole."

Not only in his poetry, but also in his poetic

theory we see that fundamental union, operative and asserted at every step, between the aesthetic feeling and the moral feeling, which critics from Matthew Arnold, De Sanctis, and Croce down to F. R. Leavis and Yvor Winters have repeatedly asserted. To quote the last, "poetic morality and poetic feeling are inseparable, feeling and technique, or structure are inseparable. Technique has laws which govern poetic (and perhaps more general) morality than is commonly recognized." In the matter of pure technique, too, his mind, while theorizing, arrived at possibilities and conclusions, which have since been fully exploited.

The most important of Leopardi's technical explorations concerns prose-poems—poems in which the qualities of both prose and verse are so happily interfused without, however, losing their peculiar individuality or identity in that union, and without meriting the charge which Byron threw against Wordsworth that he "both by precept and example, shows that prose is verse, and verse is merely prose."

And yet whatever philosophy one may find in Leopardi, and whatever value or interpretation one may give to it, Leopardi demonstrates more effectively than any other critic or theorist of his time, or even of subsequent times, that literary criticism does not have to buttress itself against philosophical or aesthetic theories, that, first and foremost, it is sensibility on which it depends and from which it receives its sanction and impetus.

With all his philological learning and classical erudition, Leopardi's basic attitude to poetry—and especially to its medium, words—was far from being academic or pedantic; in fact all his efforts, both in his poetic theory and practice, were bent on liberating the language of poetry from academic rigor and literary fossilization. The modern antiliterary attitude owes much to Leopardi, whether directly or through the neoclassicist reaction of *La Ronda*. It was again Leopardi and his example that served as an effective antidote against the D'Annunzian current of poetry— a current in which Italian indulged in a kind of orgy and exhibitionism. As against the D'Annunzian exuberance Leopardi set the tone of essentiality and purity of his *Canti*. Hence much of what is existentialist in the poetry of Ungaretti, Quasimodo, and Montale, whether in the form of their poetry, in its content, or in their attitude to life, may be connected with that sort of influence which not only Leopardi's poetry, but also his poetic theory has exercised after the production of *Zibaldone,* and especially after the discussion by the Rondists of all the implications of that theory.

Again Leopardi's poetry and his repeated insistence that simplicity and clarity not only are the two fundamental virtues of good writing but also the two indispensable requisites of a good writer have served as a counterbalance to the fashionable obscurity of modern poetry—a counterbalance in reminding one that a modern attitude to life and the very essence of modernity with its multifarious complexity can, if the poet so choses, and makes a sincere effort in that direction, be expressed, as Leopardi himself expressed them, if not always, then certainly most of the time, in a language which is not so pronouncedly obscure as that of much of modern poetry.

Simplicity and clarity as applied to language do not, however, mean that the words should have no other meaning than the rationally plain and prosaic one. The language of poetry might be most simple, and yet in the hands of a true artist each word comes to acquire—and how well Leopardi's theory of poetic diction as well as his own poetry demonstrates this—unlimited and unpredictable properties of suggestion and evocation, an irreplaceable tone, an unmistakable identity, an inexhaustible richness. Whether these qualities one finds in the language of poetry are to be attributed to the poet's artistic skill and diligence; or whether they owe their existence to the visitation of poetic inspiration, which, however brief it might be in its duration, so transforms the poet's world of thought and feeling that he looks upon everything, including above all the language he uses, with altogether new eyes; or whether they depend on both these factors more or less—these are questions which Leopardi had exhaustively discussed in terms peculiarly relevant to modern poetic situation as well as to that of his own times. When, for instance, a modern poet, like Camillo Sbarbaro, says that he never "deliberately put [himself] before a blank paper" and that he "always wrote under a kind of dictatorship," he is consciously or unconsciously echoing what Leopardi himself had said concerning his own method of writing poetry, i.e., writing always under the influence of inspiration and never as a result of deliberate choice and intention. Similarly, when Sbarbaro observes that "it is easier to write than to cancel" and that "more than in what one manages to say, it is in what one manages to be silent about that the merit of the writer lies," he may have had Leopardi's own attitude in this question in mind—Leopardi who said, among other things, that "silence is the language of all strong passions, of love (even during its sweetest moments), of anger, of wonder, of fear. . . ."

Still, another way in which Leopardi exercised a vital influence on modern poets as well as on modern poetics is through his attitude to tradition and, at the same time, to modernity, and his ability to harmonize the two. No poet has effected this combination more successfully. Moreover, Leopardi's conception of tradition—poetic diction—as something dynamic and creative, something growing and changing, is precisely the same as that of a modern poet like Montale,[26] or Eliot—a conception which in practice amounts to a poet's being, as Sergio Solmi said in connection with Saba, "modern in an almost disconcerting way" and, at the same time, loyal to tradition. Loyalty to tradition served in Leopardi's case, as in the case of those who came after him and looked upon him as something like a spiritual guide, as an effective means of preventing one's modernity from lapsing into any form of decadence. In liberating the language from "the pompous dizzinesses of an oratory," and in attaining to a kind of primitivism which may be defined as "immediate and unveiled sentiment," Ungaretti, for instance—and together with Ungaretti other hermetic or para-hermetic poets—consciously derived stimulus and guidance from what Fubini has so happily called Leopardi's "classical primitivism."

Together with the formal and linguistic aspects, it was also the moral aspect of Leopardi's poetic theory that impressed twentieth-century poets and critics. "If any moral book could serve any purpose," Leopardi had said, "I think it would mostly be the poetic books, using the word 'poetic' in the widest sense of the term: that is to say books which are meant to move the imagination, and which may be written in prose no less than in verse. Now, I have little esteem for that poetry which, when read and meditated, does not leave in the reader's spirit such a noble sentiment that, for half an hour, it prevents him from harboring any vile thought or from doing any unworthy act."[27] Thus Leopardi is, if not the very first, yet among the most important names, in nineteenth-century poetry, who, in the course of their linguistic researches, betook themselves seriously to the discovery of forms in which, to quote Ungaretti, "an equilibrium of liberation, a moral equilibrium comes to be achieved in respect of the oppression of the material." Hence when Quasimodo observes that "only in the language is to be found the possibility of writing poetry," he intends to stress not merely the linguistic or formal aspect of poetry, but, above all, the inseparable connection between the aesthetic and the moral aspects that there is in poetry, the concept of poetic language as being not merely form, but also substance.

A modern poet, no less than Leopardi, and with the full consciousness of Leopardi's role and influence on the development of poetry, feels the contrast or conflict between truth and illusion—a conflict which he is even less able to resolve than Leopardi. For Leonardo Sinisgalli, for instance, "truth is injurious to poetry as sulphur is injurious to iron, and even its minimum doses debilitate it. . . . In art one must not ask for truth." And yet somehow, in his capacity as a philosophical poet, Leopardi made it his business to ask for truth; and one of the most noteworthy aspects of his poetic achievement is that he succeeded in realizing in practice, what he repeatedly denied in his poetic theory, namely, the combination, in one form or another, between truth and poetry. Another conflict that was so typical of Leopardi's poetic consciousness was the one between the finite and the infinite, between the sense or sentiment of temporality and that of eternity. The poetic significance of this conflict—Piero Bigongiari calls it "the infinite possible of time"—is to be found in the richness and extention of meaning each object or concept or experience that the poet happens to be dealing with comes to acquire, inasmuch as what is finite somehow comes to symbolize the infinite and what is infinite constantly reminds one of the finite, the particular, the limited.

This gives poetry a peculiar form of tension, apart from other forms or kinds of tension, which one usually considers as a prerequisite of most poetry.

Hence it is not for nothing that Cardarelli said—and he seems to have spoken not only for himself but for practically the whole generation of poets and readers of poetry to which he belonged—that "if I am not mistaken the two poets to whom I have so far been most profoundly indebted are Leopardi and Baudelaire." For no two poets have anticipated more clearly the spirit of modern literature, have helped, through their works, in bringing it about and in strengthening, enriching, and interpreting it, more efficaciously and more unequivocally than Leopardi and Baudelaire; and in so far as Leopardi, in some ways, anticipated by a few years even Baudelaire himself, he may be considered to be the very first to have done so. Nor is Leopardi's influence, and the impact of his ideas concerning the art of poetry, limited to Italy; it has had, at least since the publication of *Zibaldone,* echoes and repercussions even elsewhere, whenever the theory of poetry has been discussed. Yet, no doubt, his fame and influence (outside Italian literature) have not been so widely recognized as, say, that of Poe or Baudelaire, even though he not only anticipated them in many essential respects, but he was also, as we have seen, more deeply versed than they and, therefore, more competent and more authoritative in certain fields of knowledge that have bearing on the theory of poetry.

Moreover, Leopardi's vision of poetry had a richer historical and philosophical background than either Poe's or Baudelaire's; and consequently it is more comprehensive without being, on that account, the less specific, the less sharp, and the less persuasive.[28]

Further Observations on Poetry and Other Subjects

ↄↄ

EVEN THOUGH of all the subjects it was poetry that occupied Leopardi's mind most, it did not do so apart from other subjects which also interested him as a cultured man of his times. The passion for penetrating into the very core of matters that is manifest throughout the pages of *Zibaldone, Lettere,* and other writings so permeates various subjects that they become one well-nigh organic and integral whole, reflecting the multifaceted aspects of the same mind and personality. One of the profoundest observations concerning poetry and truth to be found in *Zibaldone* clearly explains how Leopardi's attitude to poetry was the attitude of an open-minded person—a person deeply aware of the subtle, sometimes apparently irrelevant and untenable, but germane issues concerning poetry. Whether it is the business of poetry to deal with truth more than with beauty or *vice versa,* and whether truth kills the illusions on which poetry is based is, in the last analysis, of the very essence of poetry, serving, in the form of a contrast, as the source of what is poetic about illusions—one thing is quite certain, that is, that the "spirit which is not open except to pure truth is capable of few truths, can discover but little truth, can know and feel but few truths in their true aspect, but few true and great connections among them and can hardly well apply the results of its own observations and reasonings."[1] It is this open-minded-ness that enables Leopardi to recognize, in spite of the repeated contrasts he draws between truth and illusions, reason and imagination, a possibility of their coexistence, if not reconciliation. And this he does not only by pointing out that illusions persist despite reason and knowledge, and that "man does not live except by religion and illusions"[2]—Leopardi's identifi-cation or juxtaposition as two alternatives of religion and illusions is characteristically significant—but also by asserting that "broadly speaking imagination and reason are not to be differentiated except by way of style or by the manner of saying the same things."[3]

Similarly Leopardi's contempt for most modern philosophers, whom he calls "philosophasters," is based neither on his lack of open-mindedness nor on his regard for philosophy as such, but on the clear as well as scientifically and philosophically precise and valid distinction he draws between philosophy properly so-called and the rest of knowledge and learning and above all of poetry and the fine arts in general. "No one is less of a philosopher than he who would like the whole world to be a philosopher and the whole of human life to be philosophical, which is tantamount to supposing that there were no more life in the world. And yet this is the desire of the philosophasters, or rather of the majority of the philosophers both past and present."[4] For however avid for knowledge and learning his mind may have been, Leopardi, like Housman, did not believe that man is really tormented by the desire to know, but by the desire for pleasure. "It is not true that man is by nature tormented by an infinite desire to know precisely. Not even the modern and corrupt man finds himself in this situation. . . . Man does not desire to know but to feel infinitely."[5]

This attitude to philosophy and to man's nature in general considerably influenced Leopardi's attitude to poetry. For, in so far as poetry is and ought to be written for the people in general—that it can be properly appreciated and judged only by a few is another matter—its aim should be to delight. And this applies even to the so-called philosophical poetry itself. Leopardi's own poetry is a very good example, for it very obviously is distinguished in that its philosophical character is not the result of Leopardi's stuffing it, as he himself criticized foreign poets for doing their poetry, with "technicalities, formulas, abstract and metaphysical notions, psychology, ideology, natural history, travel descriptions, geography, politics, erudition, science, art, and every other kind of trade."[6] It is in this sense that one can say with Leopardi that "the more philosophical poetry is, the less poetical it is," and that "literature, and especially poetry, has nothing to do with subtle, severe, and accurate philosophy, having, as it does, for its object the beautiful, which is, so to say, equivalent to falsehood since what is true (such is the sad destiny of man) can never be beautiful."[7]

Together with the relation between truth and poetry, it is the relation between language and poetry that formed the backbone of Leopardi's poetic theory. In discussing this relation he came to tackle and even pronounce his judgment upon questions which are typically modern. If, on the one hand, he admitted that the language of prose and the language of poetry are bound to be different and explained with analytical exhaustiveness wherein that difference consists and how a poet can achieve it, he warned, on the other hand, that this difference should not be carried beyond a certain point, otherwise it would defeat the very purpose for which it exists. In order to "remove from the vulgar use the common words and phrases" one should, Leopardi suggests, "bend and condition them in a manner not used at present, but which was used by people, poets, prose-writers, and others in the ancient times."[8] The formation of the poetic language depends basically on the use of this method. But so far as the individual quality of a poet's language is concerned, it requires something more than the use of this method; it requires that the poet should be fully aware of, manipulate and exploit to the utmost possible

the concomitant ideas connected with the meaning and also with the sound itself and other qualities of the words, ideas which play such an important part in the effect, especially the poetic and oratorical effect, of the writings, . . . [for] the effect of the same poem, oration, verse,

phrase, expression or any major or minor part whatsoever
of the writing, and especially of the poetical writing, is
bound to be infinitely various, according to the audience
or readers, and even according to the occasions and the
passing and changing circumstances in which each one
of them finds himself. For, those concomitant ideas, even
altogether independent of the word or the phrase in itself,
are very much different in a thousand respects, according
to the said differences of the persons (that is, the readers
or the hearers) concerned.[9]

It is because poetry, first and last, depends on the
inherent qualities of words and the ideas they communicate, directly or indirectly, through their logical
or symbolical meaning, through their suggestive power
or sound, as well as on that individual quality which
the poet himself puts in them, that not only rhyme,
but even verse is considered by Leopardi to be something nonessential to poetry. If a poet does use verse
as his medium, it is rather as a matter of habit—or
"assuefazione" as Leopardi calls it—than of necessity.
In discussing the nature of the relation between the
verse form and the intrinsic quality and essence of
poetry as such, Leopardi shows himself to be strikingly ahead of his times, and even more than
abreast of the modern notions and principles on
rhyme and verse. While recognizing the utility and
convenience of harmony, Leopardi, however, asserts
that "in substance and in itself poetry is not bound
with the verse. And yet outside the verse, it is necessary that what is daring and bold in expression—the
metaphors, the images, the concepts—all should assume
a milder character if one wants to escape the feeling

of disgust caused by affectation, and the sense of inconvenience from the too poetical quality of prose, although the notion of the poetic, in the widest sense of the term, does not at all include the idea or the necessity of verse or even of melody."[10] Thus, while Leopardi was, like Lamb—"Prose hath her cadences no less renowned than verse," said Lamb—well aware of prose melody as well as verse melody, he did not consider melody to be an essential factor either in prose or in verse.

It is in virtue of his perspicacious grasp of the problems connected with poetic language—and, consequently, with the very essence and nature of poetry itself—that Leopardi, even before Croce, and with a conviction backed by first-hand practical experience as a translator no less than as a poet, as was not the case with Croce, declared how difficult and well-nigh impossible it is to translate poetry from one language into another and also what a really good translation ought to be like. Since "every principal beauty in arts and in writing derives from nature and not from affectation and research," it follows that a translator "who endeavors to express the character and style of others and repeat what others have said in their manner and according to their taste"[11] must seem affected and therefore his translation must fail. An ideal translation would be one in which the author translated seems to belong both to the language in which he originally wrote and to the language into which he has been translated. "The perfection of a translation," says Leopardi, "consists in this, that the author translated may not be, for example, Greek in Italian, Greek or French in German, but as Italian or German as he is Greek or French."[12]

But as the translation of an author into a foreign language is difficult to the point of being almost impossible, so the mental translation of what one reads into terms of one's experience and understanding is no less difficult. This brings Leopardi face to face with the problem of reading and judging a work of art. While good poems, Leopardi thinks, are equally intelligible both to men endowed with imagination and sentiment and to men who are not, it is only the former who can enjoy poetry *as* poetry. And by the enjoyment of a poem Leopardi means the right sort of reading and evaluating the full effect and merit of a given poem, that is to say, comprehending something far beyond what the "material sense of the writing" is capable of conveying. Even though, as far as the material sense is concerned, the words say practically the same thing to a superficial man as to a profound man, not everybody can understand and appreciate a literary work properly. "Because the superficial man, that is to say, the man who cannot enter into the same state of mind as the author's, who cannot think more or less with the same profundity as the author, does materially understand what he reads, but does not see the connection between what the author writes and the truth of things as they are, . . . in brief he would understand the writing but not the truth of what is said therein, the truth that really exists. . . ."[13]

As to the poet's relation with his material and his manner of imitating nature, Leopardi very clearly foreshadows what has come to be regarded as the impersonal theory of poetry. "The more a poet talks in his own person and the more he adds something of his own to what he says, the less he imitates nature . . . and the sentimental is not produced by the sentimental, but by nature, *as she is,* and one must, indeed, imitate nature as she is in herself, as has been done by the ancients."[14] Poetic originality itself is more a matter of imitation, though of course imitation of a certain kind, than of anything else. "Is not *originality* what one contracts? and what one cannot possess unless one acquires it? . . . Hence what is originality? an acquired faculty, like any other faculty even though the adjunct of 'acquired' goes directly against the meaning and value of its name."[15] This is the only kind of originality possible in modern times, when "poetry has been reduced to an art in such a way that in order to be truly original [in the sense, for instance, in which the ancients were original] one must altogether break, violate, disdain, and depart from the customs, habits, and notions of the genres of poetry, accepted by all—something which is very difficult to do and which even the wise man rightly refrains from doing. . . ." But even if a good poet hazards the attempt to be original in this way and to depart from

every accepted idea, form, and custom, and tries to conceive of a poem in a manner all his own, without any regard [to other poems], he hardly succeeds in being truly original, or at least original like the ancient poets, because at every moment, even without his realizing it and much against his will, he would fall back on those forms, customs, parts, means, artifices, images, genres, etc., like a brooklet of water which runs through a place where other water has passed and which, however much you may try to prevent it, would always tend to fall into the rut which has been left by the preceding water. . . . Aeschylus, for example, while inventing now one and now another tragedy without established forms or customs and following his own nature, naturally varied every composition. So also Homer, while writing his poems, wandered freely through imaginary fields, choosing as he liked . . . since he had no precedents which circumscribed him and limited his vision. Thus the ancient poets seldom failed to be original, or rather they were always original, and it was just a matter of chance if they happened to be alike. But now with so many usages, examples, notions, definitions, rules, forms, and readings, however much a poet may wish to get away from the path that has been carved out, every now and then he returns to it, and while nature no longer works by herself, the poet's mind is always influenced by the ideas which he has acquired and which circumscribe the efficacy of nature and diminish the inventive faculty. . . ."[16]

In the same way his psychological interest in the nature and functioning of imagination, illusion, sensibility, and memory and in the period of childhood, while it lends his critique of poetry a new dimension, does not conflict with his purely literary and poetic interest in these subjects. In a word, a psychological interest in Leopardi, like the moral interest itself, sooner or later transforms itself into an artistic interest, and what strikes us in Leopardi's views on these subjects is not so much their psychological, philosophical, or moral value as such as it is the significance they have to the art of poetry. For example, the value of the period of childhood, whatever importance it may have from the purely psychological point of view, is seen to be closely connected with and indeed even dependent on the poetic purpose it serves, inasmuch as "the greatest number of the indefinite images and sensations that we experience after the period of childhood and in the rest of life are nothing but a memory of the childhood, depending on it and deriving from it. . . ."[17] And the poetic value of these memories and sensations is quite obviously stamped upon them in so far as they are indefinite, which in Leopardi's theory is almost synonymous with poetic. So also the detailed discussion of the nature and importance of illusions in man's life—a discussion carried out on the moral and psychological and even philosophical plane—is to be seen and interpreted in the light of the connection Leopardi sees between illusion and poetry. The importance of illusion in the making of poetry derives, for instance, from the fact that "in every sweet and sublime sentiment there is always an element of illusion,"[18] and the sign of a superior intelligence is not that it is free from illusions, but that it is "most easily capable of conceiving illusions and at the same time most readily capable of losing them."[19]

As Coleridge distinguishes between fancy and imagination, Leopardi too draws a distinction between the force and the fecundity of imagination, between the "profound, fervent, and tempestuous" imagination like that of Dante and Tasso—an imagination which Leopardi considers to be "a lamentable dowry, and the origin of the gravest and perpetual anguishes and solicitudes"—and the "rich, varied, light, instable, and childlike" imagination, which is "the most bountiful source of happy and pleasant thoughts, of sweet errors, and of various delights and comforts, and the greatest and the most fruitful gift which nature has kindly offered to living beings."[20] Elsewhere, he shows how the kind of imagination one possesses is related to one's character, how, for instance, the character of a man with a strong imagination, like Dante or Homer, is "grave, impassioned, ordinarily melancholy (at least in our times), profound in sentiments and passions, and apt to suffer greatly in life. The other, humorous, light, vagabond, inconstant in love, light-spirited, incapable of strong and durable passions and sufferings of the soul, easy to be consoled even in the greatest misfortunes. You may recognize in these two characters the truest portraits of Dante and Ovid, and you can see how the difference in their poetry corresponds exactly to the difference in their lives."[21]

Even in the consideration of the sentiment of melancholy as a poetic property, Leopardi brings all his interest in psychology and philosophy to bear upon the discussion of the theory and concept of poetry. While believing that "melancholy and sentimental poetry is breath of the spirit," he at the same time points out that "the oppression of the heart, whether due to some strong passion or despair or the profound feeling about the nothingness of things" is liable to choke this breath and consequently kill poetry. Thus the sort of melancholy that is conducive to poetry has nothing to do, except in a negative way, with utter despair and pessimism—an opinion which, coming as it does from Leopardi, would generally surprise many readers. Leopardi points out that "however little one who has never suffered any misfortune may know, one thing is certain that neither imagination nor melancholy sensibility has any strength without a breeze of prosperity and without the vigor of the spirit, that they cannot stay without a twilight, a ray, a glimmer of cheerfulness."[22]

Thus, in his attitude to poetry, and as a matter of fact to all the learning and scholarship that he brought to bear on the understanding and interpretation of the nature and meaning of poetry, Leopardi constantly shows himself to be pursuing a distinctly individual line of thought. Even where one can trace not merely the affinity between his thought and that of others whom he read, but also the acknowledged or unacknowledged influence of this or that writer or thinker, what chiefly strikes us is the unmistakably individual—one might even say, creative—way in which he assimilates that thought or that influence. Another thing that cannot fail to strike us is the presence of a sound critical mode and attitude behind whatever he writes. For even as regards his philological notes and comments, Leopardi was endowed with a power of writing and discussing even the most technical and abstruse problems of philology in a remarkably interesting and lively manner, usually denied to most philologists and classical scholars. And this also applies to much of what he wrote concerning the art and theory of poetry so that his style adds something to the persuasive power of the argument or thought in question. Often the most gnomic statements are used in order to cover an area of thinking and suggestion—for instance: "A great poet must have great defects"; "Silence is the language of all strong passions"; "A perfect man is never great: a great man is never perfect"; "Imagination is always drawn towards what does not fall within the range of the senses."[23]

As to the modernity of his thought, nothing can better illustrate it than the following quotations in each one of which he adumbrates, however sketchily or approximately the thought of three of the most influential thinkers of the last one hundred years. While explaining the relation between art and life and the very nature of artistic pleasure itself and its effect on man, Leopardi's thought comes quite near that of Schopenhauer:

Whatever poetry or writing or whatever part thereof expresses, either through style or through sentiments, the pleasure and the voluptuousness, also expresses, either by means of style or of the formal sentiments or of both, an abandonment, a carelessness, a negligence, and a kind of forgetfulness of everything. And generally speaking there is no other way of expressing the voluptuousness than this! So much so, that pleasure is nothing but an abandonment and an oblivion of life, a kind of sleep and death. Pleasure is rather a privation or a depression of sentiment than a sentiment itself, and still less a living sentiment. It is almost an imitation of insensibility and death, the greatest possible approach to a state contrary to the state

of life and to the privation of life, because life by its very
nature is pain.[24]

As to the importance of childhood not simply in the
poetic sense but also in the psychological or psycho-
analytical sense of the term, Leopardi writes in the
manner of one perfectly familiar with Freud's thought
in all its ramifications:

one must infer how important even the minimum impressions of childhood are, and how a large part of one's life
depends on that age; and how probable it is that people's
character, their inclinations, this or that action of theirs,
may quite often derive from the minutest circumstances
of their childhood; and how the character and most of all
the opinions (on which, in turn, depend the actions and
almost the whole of man's life) are often differentiated
because of the minimum circumstances and accidents and
differences belonging to childhood, even though the cause
or origin of such differences may be looked for, even by the
greatest connoisseurs of human nature, somewhere else.[25]

So also the various states of one's mind during sleep,
dreams, and wakefulness are described in terms not
too dissimilar from those of Freudian or modern
psychology. "It seems that the spirit, while falling
asleep, disposes of its thoughts and images of the
waking state, as we dispose of our clothes in a place
which is quite at hand, in order to be able to pick
them up as soon as it is awake. And this even without the operation of the willpower."[26]

Lastly, in the following passage one may detect
the germ and the very essence not only of certain
fundamental tenets of Darwinism, but even of those

of the more modern philosophy of Existentialism, as expounded especially by Sartre, Heidegger, and Unamuno. Regarding man's *summum bonum,* Leopardi tells us that it is always of necessity "willed, desired, and sought after . . . by man"; and yet in the course of

willing, seeking, and desiring it, man has never known nor shall ever know what it is . . . and that because his *summum bonum* does not exist at all. The purpose of man's nature may perhaps be found in Nature. But one must distinguish it from the end sought after by man's nature. This end does not exist in Nature and cannot exist by Nature. . . . Man (and the other animals as well) is not born to enjoy life, but only to perpetuate it, to communicate it to others who follow him, to conserve it. Neither he nor life itself nor any other object in the world is for himself, but on the contrary he is all for life. A frightful, but nevertheless a true proposition and conclusion of all metaphysics. Existence is not for him who exists, nor is it for his end and good; and if he finds therein any good, it is just a pure chance; the person who exists is for existence, and nothing but existence, and this is his real pure aim. The existing people exist so that one may continue existing, the existing individual is born and he exists so that one may continue to exist and so that existence may conserve itself in him and after him. All this is manifest if we see that the true and the only aim of Nature is the conservation of the species, and not the conservation or the happiness of the individuals; which happiness does not exist in the world at all, neither for the individuals nor for the species. Hence one must in the last stage come to the above-mentioned general, supreme, and terrible conclusion.[27]

From these passages it is sufficiently clear not only how much modern thought, if it does not directly owe to Leopardi's thought, yet resembles it and is foreshadowed by it, but also how it is directly and indirectly bound up with whatever else Leopardi wrote, and especially with what he wrote concerning the art and nature of poetry and allied themes. A document of singular interest and character, in which for about fifteen years Leopardi continued recording and ruminating the innermost thoughts and feelings and reactions of his spiritually, psychologically, and culturally rich and intense life, it would be difficult to find anywhere in literature a parallel even in the most approximative sense to Leopardi's *Zibaldone,* unless one were to imagine a kind of ideal combination into a single unified work of Coleridge's *Biographia Literaria,* La Rochefoucauld's *Maxims,* and Goethe's *Dichtung und Wahrheit.*

Some Remarks on the Nature of Beauty

∽

As with Keats, so also with Leopardi, under the shadow of personal sorrow and the presentiment of death—a presentiment which they both converted into a romantic gesture of desire or aspiration after death —the idea and the very contemplation of beauty played a very important part in their mental and artistic life. Apart from the classical question regarding the relation between beauty and virtue—and so far as Leopardi is concerned, "beauty is hardly ever to be found together with virtue, in spite of the fact that it seems to be its sister and companion"[1]—what interested and even obsessed both Keats and Leopardi more than anything else is the question: wherein does beauty consist and how can one best describe and characterize, if not define, its essence and its innumerable manifestations and applications? Of course, Leopardi is far more interested in and intellectually concerned with the artistic, rather than the moral, metaphysical, or mystical, aspect of beauty, even though in his ideal of beauty it is both the aesthetic and the moral elements that play a vital part. In his poem

"Al conte Carlo Pepoli," for instance, he refers to "the beautiful, which so rare, scarce, and fleeting, / Appears in the world." Artistic beauty, however, is not so rare, even if much of what passes under the name of artistic beauty would not meet Leopardi's approval either as art or as beauty. In another poem, "Sopra il ritratto di una bella donna," Leopardi comes very near to defining what his conception of beauty is—beauty as the "indescribable fount" of "excellent and immense thoughts and senses." The one word that Leopardi uses more than any other to characterize the essential quality of beauty is "convenience" or "harmony"; ugliness, therefore, is identified "inconvenience" or lack of harmony and proportion.

Our sense of beauty and our very idea and appreciation of beauty, however subjective and personal they might be, are not something inborn in us, but something acquired—acquired through the process of what Leopardi calls "assuefazione" or getting used to something. And in so far as this process, its meaning and its effect as well as its very functioning and operation, differs from person to person, from one place and country and epoch to another, beauty cannot be regarded as deriving from "primitive and universal nature."[2] In other words, the sense and the standard of beauty are not at all absolute, but relative. They depend, for the most part, on the custom, usage, and culture which a particular individual calls his own as well as on those individual differences and diversities in virtue of which one person is not quite the same as another.

Now, while habit and custom do generally help one develop a sense of beauty, they are more helpful in fostering one kind of beauty than another. In so far as music, architecture, and poetry, for instance, largely imitate invisible things, habit, training, and experience both cause and determine one's response to their beauty—response that without these things would be very poor, if not altogether meaningless. But in the case of painting and sculpture, which imitate "visible objects, whereof each and everyone can see the truth or falsity . . . the ideas of the pictorially and sculpturally beautiful are already formed in one before the (so-called process of) 'assuefazione' starts."[3]

Leopardi's use of the words "convenience" or "harmony" to indicate the essential quality of beauty may seem to suggest that beauty is to be found only in the coordination and interrelation of the parts of a single, but complex object. But beauty is also found in the object itself, even if it has no parts at all.

Many things can be so simple that they have almost no parts at all. Moral beauty and the kind of beauty that does not belong to the senses, has no parts. But the convenience of the thing in question is to be considered also in relation of the parts to the whole, or of the parts to the extrinsic [aspect thereof], to the use, the aim, the utility, time, and all sorts of circumstances and the effect which that object produces or must produce. A sword with a gem on its pointed end, even though it may agree with what is ornate, with the proportions, with the shape and the material of the rest, would be in any case ugly. This ugliness is not due to the lack of harmony among the parts or between one part and another, but to a lack of accord between one part and the aim or utility of the whole. There is an infinite number of such beauties or uglinesses as much sensuous as intellectual, moral, or literary.[4]

Thus, there is no purely aesthetic or artistic beauty in Leopardi: the moral or the utilitarian aspect or element is inseparably bound up with it. Moreover, beauty is not only something relative, but also something so subjective that unless a man perceives it for himself you cannot make him see it or tell him what it is.

It is while commenting on a remark of Montesquieu's, that pure beauty deriving from an exact or regular proportion rarely excites great passions, that Leopardi shows himself to be, *malgré lui,* a romantic in his attitude. One of the fundamental tenets of romanticism is, of course, the contrast between reason and imagination, art and nature, and the superiority of nature and imagination over art and reason. Order, regularity, and definiteness are associated with reason, and their opposites with imagination. That is why, says Leopardi, "a face or a person who is defective but vivacious, graceful, and full of a sensible and capricious spirit provokes, affects, and takes the fancy of one who looks at it or him, without there being any rule, reason, or exactness about it . . . similarly great passions arise for the most part, from caprice and from what is extraordinary and cannot be justified by means of reason."[5] Leopardi's view of beauty therefore touches on Pater's famous definition of the romantic as beauty mixed with strangeness as well as on Keats's identification of truth with beauty as seen by imagination.

Now, in our perception and judgment of beauty in a work of art or even in other things, we are influenced not merely by the habits or customs that we have acquired, but also by the opinions of others and by the reputation which a particular object has acquired in the course of time. For example, "the style of the fourteenth-century writers, (the *trecentisti*) is greatly appreciated by us because we know that it was proper to that age. If we see it most faithfully reproduced in a modern writer, even though it may not differ at all from the old style, it does not please us, or rather it disgusts us and seems to be extremely affected, because we know that it is not natural to the writer, even though one may not see it in the writing at all."[6]

Together with the idea of beauty, Leopardi discusses in considerable detail the ideas of the graceful. Leopardi distinguishes between beauty and grace as follows: "Grace ordinarily consists in movement: and let us say that beauty is in the instant, and grace is in time."[7] Elsewhere he defines grace as "the ugly in the beautiful" and observes that "the ugly in ugly and pure beauty are equally alien from grace."[8] And the element of the extraordinary, too, in the composition of beauty is a source of grace. However, the contrast between the beautiful and the ugly, the common and the ordinary should not be overdone, otherwise it produces ugliness instead of grace.

The connection between Leopardi's theory of beauty—if one may call it so—and his theory of poetry

is both direct and indirect. It is direct in so far as
Leopardi constantly exemplifies his remarks and ideas
concerning beauty by means of illustrations from
literature, and more specifically still, from poetry.
For instance, while asserting that "what is small is
graceful and what is big in itself in every respect,
. . . contrary to grace" Leopardi takes recourse to
poetry and observes that "a poet would not be appreciated if, for example, while personifying a moun-
tain, he should attribute to it delicate senses or qualities, or if he should attribute bigness to any subject
treated or described by him as being gracious or
delicate. . . ."[9] And the indirect relation between
Leopardi's view of beauty and his theory of poetry
can be seen in this, that even though Leopardi maintained that truth, not beauty, is the object of arts—
"Not the beautiful, but the true, that is to say, the
imitation of nature . . . is the object of the fine arts"[10]
—he applies much the same principles to the discussion
and definition of beauty—namely, the principles of
contrast, and at the same time of the harmonious
blending of incompatible qualities, and of "assuefazione" as he calls it through study, training, and the
cultivation of taste. Thus, for instance, while pointing
out the relationship between culture and the appreciation of beauty, he tells us:

Simple and natural people are much more delighted by
what is cultured, studied, and even affected and find it
much more graceful than what is simple and natural. On
the contrary, there is no quality or object more graceful
for cultured and civilized people than what is simple and

natural, words which in our languages and in our discussions are often synonymous with the graceful. . . . The graceful is nothing but the element of the extraordinary as extraordinary and as forming part of the beautiful, within the limits of "convenience" (or proportion and harmony). What is too simple is not graceful.[11]

Because of the circumstance that *Zibaldone* was published more than half a century after Leopardi's death and hence its influence, if at all, could have been felt only in this century, it has not been sufficiently well recognized that as in so many fields, including philology and poetic theory, so also in the field of aesthetics, Leopardi was a pioneer in Italy and jotted down in a simple and unpretentious way some of those ideas in his monumental diary which were to be discussed, elaborated, and paraded in the pages of such aestheticians as Ruskin, Bosanquet, Santayana, and Croce, not to mention Baurne and Hegel.

Notes

CHAPTER ONE

[1] Sir C. M. Bowra, *Inspiration and Poetry* (Cambridge, 1951), p. 32.

[2] Vincenzo Cardarelli, "La fortuna di Leopardi," *Opere complete* (Milan, 1962), p. 493.

[3] *Zibaldone*, I, 281. Unless otherwise stated, all quotations from Leopardi are from *Tutte le opere*, ed. Francesco Flora (Milan, 1949).

> Io compatisco tutti, ma in ispecie i poveri gramatici.

[4] *Zibaldone*, I, 163.

> Certamente ci vuole il buon gusto in una nazione, ma questo dev'essere negl'individui e nella nazione intiera, e non in un'adunanza cattedratica, e legislatrice, e in una dittatura.

[5] *Zibaldone*, I, 281.

> Omero che scriveva innanzi ad ogni regola, non si sognava certo d'esser gravido delle regole come Giove di Minerva o di Bacco, nè che la sua irregolarità sarebbe stata misurata, analizzata, definita, e ridotta in capi ordinati per servir di regola agli altri, e impedirli di esser liberi, irregolari, grandi e originali come lui.

[6] Samuel Taylor Coleridge, *Biographia Literaria*, ed. J. Shawcross (2 vols., Oxford, 1907), II, 65.

[7] *Le Poesie e le prose*, I, 894-95.

> Perchè quell'eccellenza non si conosce nè gustasi totalmente se non per mezzo dell'uso e dell'esercizio proprio, e quasi, per così dire, trasferita in se stesso.

[8] *Zibaldone*, I, 1531.

[9] "Shakespeare and the Stoicism of Seneca," *Selected Essays* (London, 1934), p. 135.

[10] Mario Fubini, "L'estetica e la critica letterarie nei *Pensieri* di Leopardi," *Giornale storico della letterature italiana*, XCVII (1931), 249.

¹¹ Leopardi's philosophy, both moral and aesthetic, as A. Momigliano justly observes, "is always kept very close to the daily experience, to his contacts with the world and to his solitudes" (*Elzeviri* [Florence, 1945], p. 139).

¹² Leopardi believed, with Coleridge, that a poet should be, to some extent, also a philosopher. "No man," says Coleridge, "was ever yet a great poet, without being at the same time a profound philosopher" (*Biographia*, II, 19). Leopardi defines his own position when he justifies one "who, in metaphysics, might love thinking more than reading, who might pretend to be a metaphysician without having read or understood Kant; who contents himself sometimes with knowing the results and conclusions of the speculations and reasonings of celebrated metaphysicians in order to find out for himself their truthfulness or convince himself of their unsubstantial character" (*Zibaldone,* II, 1138).

¹³ *Zibaldone*, I, 634.

> Egli cerca naturalmente e necessariamente un filo nella considerazione delle cose. E impossibile ch'egli si contenti delle nozioni e delle verità del tutto isolate. E se ne contentasse, la sua filosofia sarebbe trivialissima, e meschinissima, e non otterrebbe nessun risultato. Lo scopo della *filosofia* (in tutta l'estensione di questa parola) è il trovar le ragioni delle verità. Queste ragioni non si trovano se non se nelle relazioni di esse verità, e col mezzo del generalizzare. Non è ella, cosa notissima che la facoltà di generalizzare costituisce il pensatore? Non è confessato che la filosofia consiste nella speculazione de' rapporti?

¹⁴ *The Art of Poetry* (Oxford, 1923), p. 42.

¹⁵ *Zibaldone*, I, 826.

> E proprio ufficio de' poeti e degli scrittori ameni il coprire quanto si possa la nudità delle cose, come è ufficio degli scienziati e de' filosofi il rivelarla. Quindi le parole precise convengono a questi, e sconvengono per lo più a quelli; a dirittura l'uno e l'altro. Allo scienziato le parole più convenienti sono le più precise ed esprimenti un'idea più nuda. Al poeta e al letterato per lo contrario le parole più vaghe, ed esprimenti idee più incerte, o un maggior numero d'idee ec.

¹⁶ *Zibaldone*, I, 1264.

> L'uomo inesperto delle cose, è sempre di spirito e d'indole più o meno poetica.

¹⁷ *Zibaldone*, II, 330.

> Ma l'arte sua è di scegliere tra le cose note le più belle,

nuovamente e armoniosamente, cioè fra loro convenientemente, disporre le cose divulgate e adattate alla capacità dei più, nuovamente vestirle, adornarle, abbellirle coll'armonia del verso, colle metafore, con ogni altro splendore dello stile; dar lume e nobiltà alle cose oscure ed ignobili; novità alle comuni; cambiar aspetto, quasi per magico incanto, a che che sia che gli venga alle mani; pigliare verbigrazia i personaggi dalla natura, e farli naturalmente parlare, e nondimeno in modo che il lettore, riconoscendo in quel linguaggio il linguaggio ch'egli è solito di sentire dalle simili persone nelle simili circostanze, lo trovi pur nel medesimo tempo nuovo e più bello, senz'alcuna comparazione, dell'ordinario, per gli adornamenti poetici, e il nuovo stile, e insomma la nuova forma e il nuovo corpo di ch'egli è vestito.

[18] *Biographia,* II, 12.

[19] *Biographia,* II, 14.

[20] *Zibaldone,* I, 1169.

La più feconda e maravigliosa ritrovatrice de' rapporti e delle armonie le più nascoste.

[21] *Zibaldone,* I, 1239.

Vede tali rapporti, passa da una proposizione all'altra così rapidamente, ne comprende così vivamente e facilmente il legame, accumula in un momento tanti sillogismi, e così ben legati e ordinati, e così chiaramente concepiti, che fa d'un salto la strada di più secoli.

[22] *Zibaldone,* I, 1310-11.

Or questa facoltà appunto è quella che fa i grandi filosofi, e i grandi scopritori delle grandi verità. E si può dire che da una stessa sorgente, da una stessa qualità dell'animo, diversamente applicata, e diversamente modificata e determinata da diverse circostanze e abitudini, vennero i poemi di Omero e di Dante, e i Principii matematici della filosfia naturale di Newton.

[23] "L'estetica . . . di Leopardi," p. 249.

Piuttosto un ideale d'arte che un concetto dell'arte, piuttosto una commossa celebrazione del potere vivificatore della poesia che una soddisfacente definizione dell'attività estetica.

[24] *The Common Pursuit* (London, 1953), p. 114.

[25] Quoted in *Collected Essays* (London, 1938), p. 120.

[26] Vitaliano Brancati, Preface to *Società, lingua e letteratura d'Italia di Leopardi* (Milan, 1942), p. 17.

La pagina critica del Leopardi è ben più ferma di quella del De Sanctis . . . la ricchezza dei termini critici del

Leopardi (non formale ed estrinseca, ma tutta del sentire e del comprendere) è superiore a quella De Sanctis.

27 *Poesie e prose*, I, 894.

Ma bisogna saperlo fare quasi così perfettamente come lo scrittore medesimo che hassi a giudicare.

28 *Poesie e prose*, I, 895-96.

Piuttosto da consuetudine ciecamente abbracciata, che da giudizio proprio . . . dalle bellezze grosse e patenti, che dalle delicate e riposte; più dall'ardire che dalla verecondia; spesso eziandio dall'apparente più che dal sostanziale; e per l'ordinario più dal mediocre che dall'ottimo.

29 *Poesie e prose*, I, 898.

Seguono ogni menomo impulso della lettura, sentono vivamente ogni leggero tocco, e coll'occasione di ciò che leggono, creano in se mille moti e mille imaginazioni, errando talora in un delirio dolcissimo, e quasi rapiti fuori di se.

30 "Dante," *Selected Essays*, p. 251.

31 *Poesie e prose*, I, 899-900.

Ad essere gagliardamente mosso dal bello e dal grande immaginato.

32 *Poesie e prose*, I, 900.

L'eccessivo al moderato, il superbo o il vezzoso dei modi e degli ornamenti al semplice e al naturale, e le bellezze fallaci alle vere . . . la matura e compiuta bontà delle opere letterarie.

33 *Poesie e prose*, I, 575, 576-77.

In Teocrito piace la negligenza, in Mosco la delicatezza. Teocrito ha nascosto più accuratamente l'arte, di cui si è servito per dipingere la natura. Mosco l'ha lasciata trasparire un pocolino, ma in un modo che alletta, e non annoia, che fa gustare e non sazia, che mostrando solo una parte, e nascondendo l'altra, fa desiderare di vedere ancor questa.

Quanto a me, non ardisco anteporre Mosco a Teocrito, che ha bellezze inarrivabili, e che fra gli antichi è per eccellenza il poeta dei pastori e dei campi; ma non ho difficoltà di dire che a qualcuno dei suoi Idilli, nel quale domina quello stile austero, che ci pone innanzi agli occhi le genti di campagna con tutta la loro ruvidezza, io preferisco le graziose e colte poesie di Mosco.

34 *Poesie e prose*, I, 465, 467.

Ciò è verissimo, ma prova solo che Omero potè scrivere un poema giocoso, non che egli è in effetto l'autore della

Batracomiomachia. . . . Stefano Bergler conta fino ad otto parole della *Batracomiomachia,* che non sembrano essere state in uso al tempo di Omero, il quale non se ne servì mai nell'*Iliade* e nell'*Odissea,* benchè spesse volte avesse occasione di farlo.

[35] *Poesie e prose,* I, 467.

[36] *Poesie e prose,* II, 653-54.

Fu zelantissimo della purità del linguaggio, disputava a lungo sopra sole parole, esaminava a fondo le proprietà dei termini, pesava il valore particolare di ciascun sinonimo, e non isdegnava la qualità di Grammatico, persuaso che non basta pensare, ma che bisogna anche parlare, che l'Oratore non può far senza delle parole più che delle cose; che il pensiero langue ove non sia aiutato dai termini, e che alla corruzione della favella tien dietro quella della eloquenza.

[37] *Poesie e prose,* II, 654.

Non fu vago dell'inudito e del meraviglioso; serbò il suo stile esente dalla esagerazione, dalla squisitezza soverchia, dalla sublimità affettata; fuggì insomma con ogni cura possibile l'eccesso dell'artifizio.

[38] *Poesie e prose,* II, 665.

La forza e l'uso della parola *stile* sono oscuri e quasi fluttuanti, io non dico presso i più, ma eziandio presso i dotti e oculati i quali parimente l'adoprano nei modi specificati di sopra; e che dove è bisogno discernere le qualità delle forme dello stile dalle qualità della materia o sia delle parole e della favella.

[39] "La fortuna di Leopardi," p. 509.

CHAPTER TWO

[1] Leopardi had formed, quite early in life, a clear notion of what classicism in its essence means in so far as style and language are concerned and how "the propriety of concepts and expressions is just what distinguishes a classical writer from a mediocre one, and how the richer a language is, the more difficult it is to achieve the quality of propriety in one's expression" (*Lettere,* pp. 60-61). And even at the age of fourteen, we find him showing his preference for "the laconic style" as against "the defects of the Asiatic style" (*Lettere,* p. 7). Leopardi's poetry, especially the *Canti,* is an eloquent proof of his classical taste and sympathy, particularly in its stylistic, linguistic, and expressional aspects.

[2] *Poesie e prose*, II, 470.

> I romantici si sforzano di sviare il più che possono la poesia dal commercio coi sensi, per li quali è nata e vivrà finattantochè sarà poesia, e di farla praticare coll'intelletto, e strascinarla dal visibile all'invisibile e dalle cose alle idee, e trasmutarla di materiale e fantastica e corporale che era, in metafisica e ragionevole e spirituale.

[3] *Poesie e prose*, II, 473-74.

> L'intelletto in mezzo al delirio dell'immaginativa conosce benissimo ch'ella vaneggia, e onninamente e sempre tanto crede al meno falso quanto al più falso, tanto agli Angeli del Milton e alle sostanze allegoriche del Voltaire quanto agli Dei d'Omero, tanto agli spettri del Bürger e alle befane del Southey, quanto all'inferno di Virgilio . . . perchè in fatti sappiamo che il poeta sì come per cristiano e filosofo e moderno che sia in ogni cosa, non c'ingannerà mai l'intelletto, così per pagano e idiota e antico che si mostri, c'ingannerà l'immaginazione ogni volta che fingerà da vero poeta.

[4] *Poesie e prose*, II, 474.

> Dentro i confini del verisimile quelle migliori illusioni che gli pare, e quelle più grate a noi e meglio accomodate all'ufficio della poesia, ch'è imitar la natura, e al fine, ch'è dilettare.

[5] *Poesie e prose*, II, 477-78.

> E necessario che, non la natura a noi, ma noi ci adattiamo alla natura, e però la poesia non si venga mutando, come vogliono i moderni, ma ne' suoi caratteri principali, sia, come la natura, immutabile.

[6] *Poesie e prose*, II, 490-91.

> Appena s'accorgono dei tasti delicatissimi della natura: ci vogliono urtoni e picchiate e spuntonate romantiche per iscuoterle e svegliarle. . . . Nella fantasia di costoro fa molto più caso qualche lampada mezzo morta fra i colonnati d'un chieson gotico dipinta dal poeta, che non la luna su di un lago o in un bosco.

[7] Preface to *Lyrical Ballads* in *The Poetical Works of William Wordsworth*, ed. E. de Selincourt (5 vols., Oxford, 1940-1949), II, 389.

[8] Preface, *Lyrical Ballads*, p. 389.

[9] *Poesie e prose*, II, 497.

> E grandissima l'efficacia della poesia, quando l'imitazione è rara, l'oggetto comune.

[10] *Poesie e prose*, II, 508.

> Non solamente aguzzando gli occhi per iscorgere quello

che mentre abbiamo tuttora presente, non sogliamo vedere, impediti dall'uso, la quale è stata sempre necessarissima opera del poeta, ma rimovendo gli oggetti che la occultano, e scoprendola, e diseppellendo e spastando e nettando dalla mota dell'incivilimento e della corruzione umana quei celesti esemplari che si assume di ritrarre.

[11] *Poesie e prose*, II, 514.

Le cose ordinarissimamente, e in ispecie quando sono comuni, fanno al pensiero e alla fantasia nostra molto più forza imitate che reali . . . l'uomo nel leggere i poeti è meglio disposto che non suole a sentirla qualunque ella è.

[12] *Poesie e prose*, II, 516-17.

Questa sensibilità impurissima e snaturatissima . . . un mescuglio o una filza di rimembranze di storie di novelle di massime di sentenze di detti di frasi lette o sentite quella intima e spontanea, modestissima anzi ritrosa, pura dolcissima sublimissima, soprumana e fanciullesca, madre di gran diletti e di grandi affanni, cara e dolorosa come l'amore, ineffabile inesplicabile, donata dalla natura a pochi, ne' quali dove non sia viziata e corrotta, dove non sia malmenata e soppressata e pesta, tenerissima com'ella è, dove non sia soffocata e sterminata, dove in somma vinca pienamente i fierissimi e gagliardissimi nemici che la contrariano, al che riesce oh quanto di rado! e oltracciò non sia scompagnata da altre nobili e insigni qualità, produce cose che durano, certo son degne di durare nella memoria degli uomini.

[13] *Poesie e prose*, II, 524-25.

La molta scienza ci toglie la naturalezza e l'imitare non da filosofi ma da poeti, come faceano gli antichi, dove noi dimostriamo da per tutto il sapere ch'essendo troppo, è difficilissimo a ricoprirlo, e scriviamo trattati in versi, ne' quali non parlano le cose ma noi, non la natura ma la scienza.

[14] *Poesie e prose*, II, 525.

Gioviamocene pure, e poichè ci conosciamo bene, dipingiamoci al vivo; ma per Dio non mostriamo di conoscerci, se non vogliamo ammazzare la poesia. Lo schivare il qual male compiutamente, è difficilissimo, non impossibile: ben ci bisogna grandissimo studio di quei poeti che di scienza più scarsa fecero quell'uso, senza del quale è inutile ai poeti moderni la scienza più larga.

[15] Leopardi uses the word "illusion" to signify practically the same thing as, for example, William Empson's phrase

"fantasy-gratifications and a protective attitude towards one's inner life," which Empson considers "in some degree essential for the production of poetry" (*Seven Types of Ambiguity* [2nd ed., London, 1947], p. 21), or what Coleridge implied in his celebrated phrase "willing suspension of disbelief." "A half-philosopher," Leopardi acutely observes, "fights against the illusions just because he is deluded; a true philosopher loves them and preaches them because he is not" (*Zibaldone*, I, 1107-108).

16 *Poesie e prose*, II, 541.

> Non procede soltanto dalle qualità degli oggetti imitati, ma in oltre specialissimamente ed essenzialmente dalla maraviglia che nasce dal vedere quei tali oggetti quasi trasportati dove non pareva appena che si potesse, e rappresentati da cose che non pareano poterli rappresentare; di modo che infiniti oggetti i quali in natura non dilettano punto, imitati dal poeta o dal pittore o da altro tale artefice, dilettano estremamente, e altri che dilettavano anche reali, dilettano da vantaggio imitati.

17 *Poesie e prose*, II, 541.

> Credono i romantici che l'eccellenza della imitazione si debba stimare solamente secondoch'ella è vicina al vero, tanto che cercando lo stesso vero, si scordano quasi d'imitare, perchè il vero non può essere imitazione di se medesimo.

CHAPTER THREE

1 *Zibaldone*, I, 87.

2 *The Sacred Wood* (London, 1920), p. xiv.

3 *Zibaldone*, I, 24, 31.

4 Quoted by Karl Vossler, *Leopardi*, trans. into Italian by Tomasco Guoli (Naples, 1925), p. 81.

5 *English Traits and Representative Men* (London, 1906), p. 300.

6 Quoted by F. R. Leavis, *New Bearings in English Poetry* (London, 1942), p. 28.

7 Thomas Babbington Macaulay, *Critical and Historical Essays* (Everyman's Library), I, 153.

8 *Letters of Matthew Arnold to A. H. Clough*, ed. H. F. Lowry (Oxford, 1932), p. 126.

9 Quoted by Walter Bagehot, *Literary Studies* (Everyman's Library), II, 332.

[10] *Milton* (London, 1804), p. 43, ll. 2-7.

[11] Baudelaire pleaded for the necessity of "intoxication," be it of wine or music or love or money or poetry, as an antidote against "ennui"; and Nietzsche said that there is no art, no action, no aesthetic contemplation of any kind, unless it is preceded by the necessary condition of "drunkenness" (see his *Twilight of the Gods*).

[12] *Zibaldone*, I, 94.

> Che bel tempo era quello nel quale ogni cosa era viva secondo l'immaginazione umana e viva umanamente cioè abitata o formata di esseri uguali a noi! quando nei boschi desertissimi si giudicava per certo che abitassero le belle Amadriadi e i fauni e i silvani e Pane ec.

[13] *Zibaldone*, II, 1002.

> En métaphysique, en morale, les anciens ont tout dit. Nous nous rencontrons avec eux, ou nous les répétons. Tous les livres modernes de ce genre ne sont que des redites.

[14] *Zibaldone*, I, 263.

> Dalla natura e dalle vaghe idee proprie naturalmente della immaginazione primitiva.

[15] *Zibaldone*, I, 411.

> I fanciulli trovano il tutto nel nulla, gli uomini il nulla nel tutto.

[16] Quoted by Leavis, *New Bearings*, p. 50.

[17] *Zibaldone*, I, 1259.

> Il fanciullo sa talvolta assai più del filosofo, e vede chiaramente delle verità e delle cagioni, che il filosofo non vede se non confusamente, o non vede punto.

[18] *Zibaldone*, II, 341.

[19] *Zibaldone*, II, 203.

> Quei campi fertilissimi per natura, ma non mai lavorati, i quali, sottoposti che sono all'industria umana, rendono ne' primi anni due e tre volte più, e producono messi molto più rigogliose e vivide che non fanno negli anni susseguenti malgrado di qualsivoglia studio, diligenza ed efficacia di coltura.

[20] *Zibaldone*, I, 163.

> In rigor di termini, poeti non erano se non gli antichi, e non sono ora se non i fanciulli, o giovanetti, e i moderni che hanno questo nome, non sono altro che filosofi.

[21] *Zibaldone*, I, 514.

> La poesia sentimentale è unicamente ed esclusivamente propria di questo secolo, come la vera e semplice

(voglio dire non mista) poesia imaginativa fu unicamente ed esclusivamente propria de' secoli Omerici, o simili a quelli in altre nazioni.

22 *Oxford Addresses on Poetry* (London, 1961), p. 10.

23 *Zibaldone*, I, 32.

La Natura vuol essere illuminata dalla ragione non incendiata.

24 *Zibaldone*, I, 470.

Le intimità, i secreti, le parti delle cose rimote e segregate dai sensi e dal pensiero dei più.

25 *Zibaldone*, II, 182.

Non penetra ella fino all'essenza delle cose che esistono, ed anche di se medesima?

26 *Zibaldone*, II, 182.

Ella è dannosa, ella rende impotente colui che l'usa, e tanto più quanto maggiore uso ei ne fa, e a proporzione che cresce il suo potere, scema quello di chi l'esercita e la possiede, e più ella si perfeziona, più l'essere ragionante diviene imperfetto: ella rende piccoli e vili e da nulla tutti gli oggetti sopra i quali ella si esercita, annulla il grande, il bello, e per così dir la stessa esistenza, è vera madre e cagione del nulla, e le cose tanto più impiccoliscono quanto ella cresce; e quanto è maggiore la sua esistenza in intensità e in estensione, tanto l'esser delle cose si scema e restringe ed accosta verso il nulla.

27 *Zibaldone*, II, 340.

La natura così analizzata non differisce punto da un corpo morto.

28 *Zibaldone*, II, 183.

Ella tanto meno vede quanto più vede.

29 This bringing together, at a certain point, of reason and imagination in his poetic theory—where they are, more often than not, contrasted with each other—is the result not only of an acute critical sensibility, but also of a deep speculative power—the sort of bringing together that occurs also in a modern critic, F. R. Leavis. Criticizing Milton's "dominating sense of righteousness and a complete incapacity to question or explore its significance and conditions," Leavis observes: "This defect of intelligence is a defect of imagination" (*Revaluation* [London, 1953], p. 58).

30 *Zibaldone*, I, 1171.

La ragione ha bisogno dell'immaginazione e delle illusioni ch'ella distrugge; il vero del falso; il sostanziale dell'apparente; l'insensibilità la più perfetta della sensibilità la più viva; il ghiaccio del fuoco; la pazienza dell'impazienza; l'impotenza della somma potenza; il piccolissimo del grandissimo; la geometria e l'algebra, della poesia ec.

31 *Zibaldone*, I, 1021.

Omero non credeva certo a quello ch'egli immaginava.

32 *Zibaldone*, I, 1021.

L'immaginazione, eccetto ne' fanciulli, non ha, e non abbisogna di fondamento nella persuasione. . . . La scienza può dunque sommamente indebolire l'immaginazione; pur non è incompatibile seco lei. Per l'opposto, il sentimento se non è fondato sulla persuasione è nullo.

33 *Zibaldone*, II, 1068.

Volevano spiegare e non mistificare, e scoprire; tendevano a dichiarar colle cose sensibili quelle che non cadono sotto i sensi, a render ragione a lor modo e meglio che potevano, di quelle cose che l'uomo non può comprendere, o che essi non compredevano ancora. Gl'inventori delle ultime mitologie, i platonici, e massime gli uomini dei primi secoli della nostra era, decisamente cercavano l'oscuro nel chiaro, volevano spiegare le cose sensibili e intelligibili colle non intelligibili e non sensibili; si compiacevano delle tenebre; rendevano ragione delle cose chiare e manifeste, con dei misteri e dei secreti. Le prime mitologie non avevano misteri, anzi erano trovate per ispiegare, e far chiari a tutti, i misteri della natura; le ultime sono state trovate per farci creder mistero e superiore alla intelligenza nostra anche quello che noi tocchiamo con mano, quello dove, altrimenti, non avremmo sospettato nessuno arcano.

34 *Zibaldone*, I, 106.

Impedimenti e contrasti a quella felicità che agli antichi non pareva un sogno come a noi pare . . . come mali evitabili e non evitati.

35 *Zibaldone*, II, 808.

Non è propria de' tempi nostri altra poesia che la malinconica, nè altro tuono di poesia che questo, sopra qualunque subbietto ella possa essere. . . . Fra gli antichi avveniva tutto il contrario, il tuono naturale che rendeva la loro cetra era quello della gioia o della forza della solennità ec. La poesia loro era tutta vestita a festa, anche, in certo modo, quando il subbietto l'obbligava ad esser trista. Che vuol dir ciò? O che gli antichi avevano meno sventure reali di noi, (e questo non è forse vero), o che meno le sentivano e meno le conoscevano, il che viene a esser lo stesso, e a dare il medesimo risultato, cioè che gli antichi erano dunque meno infelici de' moderni. E tra gli antichi metto anche, proporzionatamente, l'Ariosto ec.

[36] *Zibaldone*, I, 399.

Sempre più grandi, magnanimi e forti di noi, nell'eccesso delle sventure, e nella considerazione della necessità di esse, e della forza invincibile che li rendeva infelici e gli stringeva e legava alla loro miseria senza che potessero rimediarvi e sottrarsene, concepivano odio e furore contro il fato, e bestemmiavano gli Dei, dichiarandosi in certo modo nemici del cielo, impotenti bensì, e incapaci di vittoria o di vendetta, ma non perciò domati, nè ammansati, nè meno, anzi tanto più desiderosi di vendicarsi, quanto la miseria era la necessità era maggiore. . . . Noi che non riconosciamo nè forza alcuna di necessità personificata che ci costringa, non abbiamo altra persona da rivolger l'odio e il furore (se siamo magnanimi, e costanti, e incapaci di cedere) fuori di noi stressi.

[37] *Zibaldone*, I, 481.

Perchè non ci sono più spettatori, tutti recitano, e la virtù e le buone qualità che si fingono, nessuno le ha, e *nessuno le crede negli altri.*

[38] *The Philosophy of Nietzsche* (New York, 1927), pp. 1063, 1065.

CHAPTER FOUR

[1] *Zibaldone*, I, 829.

[2] *Zibaldone*, I, 1094.

L'amica della verità, la luce per discoprirla, la meno soggetta ad errare . . . il vero filosofo nello stato di allegria non può far altro che persuadersi, non che il vero sia bello o buono, ma che il male cioè il vero si debba dimenticare, e consolarsene, o che sia conveniente di dar qualche sostanza alle cose, che veramente non l'hanno.

[3] *Zibaldone*, II, 420.

Il vero poeta è sommamente disposto ad esser gran filosofo, e il vero filosofo ad esser gran poeta, anzi nè l'uno nè l'altro non può esser nel gener suo nè perfetto nè grande, s'ei non partecipa più che mediocremente dell'altro genere.

4 *Zibaldone,* II, 293.

Poco ai tempi d'Omero valeva ed operava quello che negli uomini si chiama cuore, moltissimo l'immaginazione. Oggi per lo contrario (e così a' tempi di Virgilio), l'immaginazione è generalmente sopita, agghiacciata, intorpidita, estinta. . . . Se l'animo degli uomini colti è ancor capace d'alcuna impressione, d'alcun sentimento vivo, sublime e poetico, questo appartien propriamente al cuore. . . . I poeti d'immaginazione oggidì manifestano sempre lo stento e lo sforzo e la ricerca, e siccome non fu la immaginazione che li mosse a poetare, ma essi che si espressero dal cervello e dall'*ingegno,* e si crearono e fabbricarono una immaginazione artefatta, così di rado o non mai riescono a risuscitare e riaccendere la vera immaginazione, già morta, nell'animo de' lettori, e non fanno alcun buono effetto.

5 *Zibaldone,* I, 186.

Immergono l'anima in un abisso di pensieri indeterminati, de' quali non sa vedere il fondo nè i contorni.

6 *Zibaldone,* I, 1323.

Lo stato di disperazione rassegnata, ch'è l'ultimo passo dell'uomo sensibile, e il finale sepolcro della sua sensibilità . . . mortale alla sensibilità, ed alla poesia (in tutti i sensi, ed estensione di questo termine).

7 *Zibaldone,* II, 380.

Piuttosto che versarsi al di fuori ama anzi per lo contrario di rannicchiarsi, concentrarsi e restringe, per così dire, l'animo in se stesso quanto più può.

8 Dedication, *Canti* (Florence, 1830).

9 *Sacred Wood,* p. 48.

10 *Pope and Human Nature* (Oxford, 1958), p. 59.

11 *Lettere,* p. 271.

Il mio travaglio deriva più dal sentimento dell'infelicità mia particolare, che dalla certezza dell'infelicità universale e necessaria.

12 *Lettere,* p. 1033.

L'on a voulu considérer mes opinions philosophiques comme le résultat de mes souffrances particulières, et que l'on s'obstine à attribuer à mes circonstances matérielles ce qu'on ne doit qu'à mon entendement. Avant de mourir, je vais protester contre cette invention de la faiblesse et de la vulgarité, et prier mes lecteurs de s'attacher à détruire mes observations et mes raisonnements plutôt que d'accuser mes maladies.

¹³ *Zibaldone*, I, 565-66.

Un'invenzione venuta dall'ingegno e meditazione di un uomo profondo, non si considera come accidentale. Ma quante circostanze accidentalissime sono bisognate perchè quell'uomo arrivasse a quella capacità. Circostanze relative alla coltura dell'ingegno suo; relative alla nascita, agli studi, ai mezzi estrinseci d'infiniti generi, che colla loro combinazione l'han fatto tale, e mancando lo avrebbero reso diversissimo.

¹⁴ *Zibaldone*, II, 1190-91.

Il piacer fino, intimo e squisito delle arti, o vogliamo dire il piacere delle arti perfezionate (e fra le arti comprendo la letteratura e la poesia), non può esser sentito se non dagl'intendenti, perch'esso è uno di que' tanti di cui la natura non ci dà il sensorio; ce lo dà l'assuefazione, che qui consiste in istudio ed esercizio. Perchè il popolo, che non potrà mai aver tale studio ed esercizio, gusti il piacer delle lettere, bisogna che queste sieno meno perfette. Tal piacere sarà sempre minore assai di quello che gl'intendenti riceverebbero dalle lettere perfezionate.

¹⁵ *Lettere*, pp. 477-78.

Non avete avuto il torto promettendo per me, perchè avete dovuto credere che io fossi come sono tutti gli altri che fanno versi. Ma sappiate che in questa e in ogni altra cosa io sono molto dissimile e molto inferiore a tutti. E quanto ai versi, l'intendere la mia natura vi potrà servire da ora innanzi per qualunque simile occasione. Io non ho scritto in mia vita se non pochissime e brevi poesie. Nello scriverle non ho mai seguito altro che un'ispirazione (o frenesia), sopraggiungendo la quale, in due minuti io formava il disegno e la distribuzione di tutto il componimento. Fatto questo, soglio sempre aspettare che mi torni un altro momento, e tornandomi (che ordinariamente non succede se non di là a qualche mese), mi pongo allora a comporre, ma con tanta lentezza, che non mi è possibile di terminare una poesia, benchè brevissima, in meno di due o tre settimane. Questo è il mio metodo, e se l'ispirazione non mi nasce da sè, più facilmente uscirebbe acqua da un tronco, che un solo verso dal mio cervello. Gli altri possono poetare sempre che vogliono, ma io non ho questa facoltà in nessun modo, e per quanto mi pregaste, sarebbe inutile, non perch'io non volessi compiacervi, ma perchè non potrei. . . . I miei versi farebbero piuttosto l'effetto contrario . . . il certo è che chieder versi a una natura difficile e infeconda come la mia, è

> lo stesso che chiedermi un vescovato: questo non posso
> dare, e quelli non so comporre se non per caso.

[16] As to the actual output, if we consider sheer quantity,
Leopardi's is by no means so small. Besides the *Canti*, he wrote,
among other things, two long poems, *Appressamento della
morte* and *I Paralipomeni della Batracomiomachia*, which,
though they do not witness to the presence of the same poetic
inspiration behind them as the deservingly more celebrated
Canti, have yet a certain interest of their own, and in any case
they go to prove that Leopardi's occupation with poetic
theories did not actually prevent him from attempting that
sort of poetry which he considered, in theory, to be much
inferior to the lyric.

[17] *Lettere*, p. 253.

> Mi domandi che cosa io pensi e che scriva. Ma io da
> gran tempo non penso nè scrivo nè leggo cosa veruna,
> per l'ostinata imbecillità de' nervi degli occhi e della
> testa: e forse non lascerò altro che gli schizzi delle
> opere ch'io vo meditando, e ne' quali sono andato
> esercitando alla meglio la facoltà dell'invenzione che
> ora è spenta negl'ingegni italiani.

[18] In other words, the creative process, of which the poem
is the result and the inspiration is the starting point as well as,
together with conscious artistry, the guiding spirit, does not
altogether cease with the poem. In a different form, it continues in a well-trained and attentive reader, whose first and
last business it is to make what he is reading imaginatively,
and, perhaps, even more than imaginatively, his own, to transfer
that work, as Leopardi puts it, within himself. This is what
T. S. Eliot means when he says that "the poem's existence is
somewhere between the writer and the reader" (*The Use of
Poetry and the Use of Criticism*, p. 30); for, as Empson justly
points out, "the process of getting to understand a poet is
precisely that of constructing his poems in one's mind" (*Seven
Types of Ambiguity*, p. 62).

[19] *Zibaldone*, II, 1195.

> L'entusiasmo l'ispirazione, essenziali alla poesia, non
> sono cose durevoli. Nè si possono troppo a lungo
> mantenere in chi legge.

[20] *Zibaldone*, II, 1181.

> La poesia sta essenzialmente in un impeto.

[21] *Zibaldone*, I, 1020; 788.

> L'epoca della perfezione e quindi della possibile felicità

sì dell'uomo che delle altre cose . . . l'apice, la perfezione, l'*akmē* della natura umana.

22 *Zibaldone*, II, 357.

Lunghissime e pazientissime ed esattissime ricerche, esperienze, confronti, studi, ragionamenti, meditazioni, esercizi della mente, dell'ingegno, della facoltà di pensare di riflettere di osservare di ragionare.

23 *Zibaldone*, II, 357.

Il poeta lirico nell'ispirazione, il filosofo nella sublimità della speculazione, l'uomo d'immaginativa e di sentimento nel tempo del suo entusiasmo, l'uomo qualunque nel punto di una forte passione, nell'entusiasmo del pianto; ardisco anche soggiungere, mezzanamente riscaldato dal vino, vede e guarda le cose come da un luogo alto e superiore a quello in che la mente degli uomini suole ordinariamente consistere. Quindi è che scoprendo in un sol tratto molte più cose ch'egli non è usato di scorgere a un tempo, e d'un sol colpo d'occhio discernendo e mirando una moltitudine di oggetti, ben da lui veduti più volte ciascuno, ma non mai tutti insieme . . . egli è in grado di scorger con essi i loro rapporti scambievoli, e per la novità di quella moltitudine di oggetti tutti insieme rappresentantisegli, egli è attirato e a considerare, benchè rapidamente, i detti oggetti meglio che per l'innanzi non avea fatto, e ch'egli non suole.

24 Keats, on the contrary, considered a long poem to be "a test of Invention which I take to be the Polar Star of poetry, as Fancy is the Sails, and Imagination the Rudder" (*The Letters of John Keats,* ed. M. B. Forman [Oxford, 1948], p. 53).

25 *Zibaldone*, II, 1181.

Il poema epico è contro la natura della poesia: 1. domanda un piano concepito e ordinato con tutta freddezza; 2. che può aver a fare colla poesia un lavoro che domanda più e più anni d'esecuzione? la poesia sta essenzialmente in un impeto. E anche contro natura assolutamente. Impossibile che l'immaginazione, la vena, gli spiriti poetici, durino, bastino, non vengano meno in sì lungo lavoro sopra un medesimo argomento. E famosa non meno che manifesta, la stanchezza e lo sforzo di Virgilio negli ultimi sei libri dell'*Eneide* scritti veramente per proposito, e non per impulso dell'animo, nè con voglia.

26 *Zibaldone*, II, 1063.

Primogenito di tutti . . . un'amplificazione del lirico, o vogliam dire il genere lirico che tra gli altri suoi mezzi e

subbietti ha assunta principalmente e scelta la narra-
zione, poeticamente modificata.

27 *Zibaldone,* II, 550.

L'*Iliade,* oltre all'essere il più perfetto poema epico
quanto al disegno . . . lo è ancora quanto ai caratteri
principali, perchè questi sono più interessanti che negli
altri poemi.

28 *Zibaldone,* II, 1064, 1182.

Esso non è un'ispirazione, ma un'invenzione; figlio della
civiltà, non della natura; poesia per convenzione e per
volontà degli autori suoi, più che per la essenza sua. . . .
Il poeta è spinto a poetare dall'intimo sentimento suo
proprio, non dagli altrui. Il fingere di avere una passione,
un carattere ch'ei non ha (cosa necessaria al drammatico) è cosa alienissima dal poeta. . . . L'estro del
drammatico è finto, perch'ei dee fingere.

CHAPTER FIVE

1 Giovanni Pascoli, "Il Fanciullino," *Pensieri e discorsi*
(Bologna, 1914), p. 15.

2 "Il Fanciullino," p. 86.

3 *Zibaldone,* I, 251.

Bisogna distinguere in fatto di belle arti, entusiasmo,
immaginazione, calore, ec., da invenzione massimamente
di soggetti. La vista della bella natura desta entusiasmo.
Se questo entusiasmo sopraggiunge ad uno che abbia
già per le mani un soggetto, gli gioverà per la forza
della esecuzione, ed anche per la invenzione ed originalità secondaria, cioè delle parti, dello stile, delle
immagini, in somma di tutto ciò che spetta all'esecuzione,
ma difficilmente, o non mai, giova all'invenzione del
soggetto. Perchè l'entusiasmo giovi a questo, bisogna
che si aggiri appunto e sia cagionato dallo stesso
soggetto, come l'entusiasmo di una passione. Ma
l'entusiasmo astratto, vago, indefinito, che provano spesse
volte gli uomini di genio, all'udire una musica, allo
spettacolo della natura, ec., non è favorevole in nessun
modo all'invenzione del soggetto, anzi appena delle
parti, perchè in quei momenti l'uomo è quasi fuor di
se, si abbandona come ad una forza estranea che lo
trasporta, non è capace di raccogliere nè di fissare le
sue idee, tutto quello che vede, è infinito, indeterminato,
sfuggevole, e così vario e copioso, che non ammette nè
ordine nè regola nè facoltà di annoverare, o disporre,

o scegliere, o solamente di concepire in modo chiaro e
completo, e molto meno di *saisir* un punto (vale a dire
un soggetto) intorno al quale possa ridurre tutte le
sensazioni e immaginazioni che prova, le quali non
hanno nessun centro.

4 *Zibaldone*, I, 505-506.

Il poeta nel colmo dell'entusiasmo, della passione ec. non
è poeta, cioè non è in grado di poetare. All'aspetto della
natura, mentre tutta l'anima sua è occupata dall'immagine dell'infinito, mentre le idee se gli affollano al
pensiero, egli non è capace di distinguere, di scegliere,
di afferrarne veruna. . . . L'infinito non si può esprimere
se non quando non si sente: bensì dopo sentito: e
quando i sommi poeti scrivevano quelle cose che ci
destano le ammirabili sensazioni dell'infinito, l'animo
loro non era occupato da veruna sensazione infinita; e
dipingendo l'infinito non lo sentiva.

5 *Zibaldone*, I, 252.

Ci vuole un tempo di forza, ma tranquilla; un tempo di
genio attuale piuttosto che di entusiasmo attuale (o sia,
piuttosto un atto di genio che di entusiasmo); un influsso
dell'entusiasmo passato o futuro o abituale, piuttosto che
la sua presenza, e possiamo dire il suo crepuscolo, piuttosto che il mezzogiorno. Spesso e adattatissimo un
momento in cui dopo un entusiasmo, o un sentimento
provato, l'anima sebbene in calma, pure ritorna come a
mareggiare dopo la tempesta, e richiama con piacere la
sensazione passata. Quello forse è il tempo più atto, il
più frequente della concezione di un soggetto originale,
o delle parti originali di esso. E generalmente si può
dire che nelle belle arti e poesia, le dimostrazioni di
entusiasmo d'immaginazione e di sensibilità, sono il
frutto immediato piuttosto della memoria dell'entusiasmo,
che dello stesso entusiasmo, riguardo all'autore.

6 *The Name and Nature of Poetry* (Cambridge, 1945), pp.
49-50.

7 *Zibaldone*, I, 952.

8 *The Principles of Literary Criticism* (London, 1947), p.
181.

9 *Zibaldone*, I, 253.

Quello che veduto nella realtà delle cose, accora e
uccide l'anima, veduto nell'imitazione . . . apre il cuore
e ravviva.

10 *Zibaldone*, I, 4-5.

Non il Bello ma il Vero o sia l'imitazione della Natura
qualunque si è l'oggetto delle Belle arti. Se fosse il

Bello, piacerebbe più quello che fosse più bello e così si andrebbe alla perfezione metafisica, la quale in vece di piacere fa stomaco nelle arti. . . . E che non sia il solo bello naturale lo scopo delle Belle Arti vedesi in tutti i poeti specialmente in Omero, perchè se questo fosse, avrebbe dovuto ogni gran poeta cercare il più gran bello naturale che si potesse, dove Omero ha fatto Achille infinitamente men bello di quello che potea farlo, e così gli Dei ec. e sarebbe maggior poeta Anacreonte che Omero. . . . La perfezione di un'opera di Belle Arti non si misura dal più bello ma dalla più perfetta imitazione della natura.

[11] *Leopardi,* p. 9.

[12] Edgar Allan Poe, "The Poetic Principle," *Edgar Allan Poe, Representative Selections,* ed. Margaret Alterton and Hardin Craig, American Writers Series (New York, 1935), p. 386.

[13] *Zibaldone,* I, 5-6.

L'utile non è il fine della poesia benchè questa possa giovare. E può anche il poeta mirare espressamente all'utile e ottenerlo (come forse avrà fatto Omero) senza che però l'utile sia il fine della poesia, come può l'agricoltore servirsi della scure a segar biade o altro senza che il segare sia il fine della scure. La poesia può esser utile indirettamente, come la scure può segare, ma l'utile non è il suo fine naturale, senza il quale essa non possa stare, come non può senza il dilettevole, imperocchè il dilettare è l'ufficio naturale della poesia.

[14] *Zibaldone,* I, 104.

Degli orrori e dell'eccessivo terribile tanto caro ai romantici, dal quale l'immaginazione e il sentimento, invece d'esser scosso, è oppresso e schiacciato, e non trova altro partito a prendere che la fuga, cioè chiuder gli occhi della fantasia e schivar quell'immagine che tu gli presenti.

[15] *Zibaldone,* I, 80.

Altrimenti la natura non è imitata naturalmente.

[16] *Zibaldone,* I, 1106.

[17] *Zibaldone,* II, 779.

Il buono imitatore deve aver come raccolto e immedesimato in se stesso quello che imita, sicchè la vera imitazione non sia propriamente imitazione, facendosi d'appresso se medesimo, ma espressione.

[18] Benedetto Croce, *Breviario di estetica* (Bari, 1952), p. 31.

[19] *Breviario,* p. 32.

20 *Zibaldone*, I, 514.

Più esatta corrispondenza alla natura ed al vero. . . .
Prontissimo e acutissimo e rigoroso giudice della verità
o falsità, della proprietà o improprietà, della naturalezza,
o forzatura, della efficacia o languidezza ec. delle
invenzioni, delle situazioni, de' sentimenti, delle sentenze,
delle espressioni.

21 Torquato Tasso, *Gerusalemme liberata*, Canto XX, stanza
30.

22 *Zibaldone*, II, 552.

Ogni sensazion viva è gradevole perciocchè viva,
benchè d'altronde, e pure per se, dolorosa o paurosa ec.

23 *Lettere*, p. 74.

Senza stringente necessità della storia (e anche allora
con buon giudizio e garbo) non si dee mai figurare il
brutto. . . . Omero Virgilio e gli altri grandi avrebbero
errato infinite volte, e Dante sopra tutti che ha figurato
il brutto così sovente. . . . Certamente le arti hanno da
dilettare, ma chi può negare che il piagnere il palpitare
l'inorridire alla lettura di un poeta non sia dilettoso?

24 *Zibaldone*, I, 1098.

La memoria non è che un'imitazione della sensazione
passata, e le ricordanze successive, imitazioni delle
ricordanze passate. La memoria (cioè insomma l'intelletto) è quasi imitatrice di se stessa. . . . L'uomo imita
anche inventando, ma in maniera più larga, cioè imita
le invenzioni con altre invenzioni, e non acquista la
facoltà inventiva (che par tutto l'opposto della imitativa)
se non a forza d'imitazioni, ed imita nel tempo stesso
che esercita detta facoltà inventiva, ed essa stessa è
veramente imitativa.

25 *Biographia*, II, 12.

26 *Biographia*, II, 14.

27 *Zibaldone*, I, 231.

Come le persone di poca immaginazione e sentimento
non sono atte a giudicare di poesia, o scritture di tal
genere, e leggendole, e sapendo che sono famose, non
capiscono il perchè, a motivo che non si sentono
trasportare, e non s'immedesimano in verun modo collo
scrittore, e questo, quando anche siano di buon gusto e
giudizio, così vi sono molte ore, giorni, mesi, stagioni,
anni, in cui le stesse persone di entusiasmo ec. non
sono atte a sentire, e ad esser trasportate, e però a
giudicare rettamente di tali scritture.

28 *An Experiment in Criticism* (Cambridge, 1961), pp. 88-
89.

[29] *Zibaldone*, II, 339.

> Chiunque esamina la natura delle cose colla pura ragione, senz'aiutarsi dell'immaginazione nè del sentimento . . . potrà . . . *analizzare*, cioè risolvere e disfar la natura, ma e' non potrà mai ricomporla, voglio dire e' non potrà mai dalle sue osservazioni e dalla sua analisi tirare una grande e generale consequenza.

[30] Ugo Foscolo, *Opere edite e postume*, ed. E. Mayer and L. S. Orlandini (11 vols., Florence, 1939), IV, 297.

[31] *Zibaldone*, I, 1209.

> Dall'unione di cose o qualità che paiono incompatibili ec.

[32] *Zibaldone*, I, 1209.

> Sottilissime, minutissime, sfuggevolissime sono le cause e la natura de' più grandi piaceri umani. E la maggior parte di essi si trova in ultima analisi derivare da quello che non è ordinario, e da ciò appunto, ch'esso non è ordinario ec. La maraviglia, principal fonte di piacere nelle arti belle, poesia, ec. da che cosa deriva ed a qual teoria spetta, se non a quella dello straordinario?

[33] *Zibaldone*, II, 341.

> La natura . . . composta, conformata, e ordinata ad un effetto poetico.

[34] *Zibaldone*, II, 1230-31.

> All'uomo sensibile e immaginoso, che viva, come io sono vissuto gran tempo, sentendo di continuo ed immaginando, il mondo e gli oggetti sono in certo modo doppi. Egli vedrà cogli occhi una torre, una campagna; udrà cogli orecchi un suono d'una campagna; e nel tempo stesso coll'immaginazione vedrà un'altra torre, un'altra campagna, udrà un altro suono. In questo secondo genere di obbietti sta tutto il bello e il piacevole delle cose. Trista quella vita (ed è pur tale la vita comunemente) che non vede, non ode, non sente se non che oggetti semplici, quelli soli di cui gli occhi, gli orecchi e gli altri sentimenti ricevono la sensazione.

CHAPTER SIX

[1] Concerning the French influence on Leopardi, and in particular that of the eighteenth century, Francesco Flora observes that "one may say, without excessive paradox, that the themes of philosophical meditation in Leopardi are stimulated by his reading of a few French authors, some of whom he

knew only through a few selected pages of their writings; he could, nevertheless, divine their thought in virtue of his penetration and his capacity to deduce" (*Leopardi e la letteratura francese* [Milan, 1947], p. 21). The so-called French influence on Leopardi, such as that of writers and thinkers like Rousseau, Voltaire, Madame de Staël, Chateaubriand, Descartes, Bossuet, and others, was, like most influences, the result of a predisposition for which he wanted some sort of confirmation and echo in others. Later on, Leopardi rebelled against French culture. He considered France as "the most corrupt nation of the world and the one farthest removed from nature." Part of the reason for this reaction was, of course, his desire to liberate Italy from the domination of what he called "the immense Gallicism which overfloods the customs, the literature, and the language of the Italians and other Europeans."

2 *Zibaldone*, I, 234-35.

L'origine del sentimento profondo dell'infelicità, ossia lo sviluppo di quella che si chiama sensibilità, ordinariamente procede dalla mancanza o perdita delle grandi e vive illusioni. . . . La sensibilità che si trova nei giovani ancora inesperti del mondo e dei mali, sebbene tinto di malinconia, è diverso da questo sentimento e promette e dà a chi lo prova non dolore ma piacere e felicità.

3 *Zibaldone*, I, 161-62.

Nella carriera poetica il mio spirito ha percorso lo stesso stadio che lo spirito umano in generale. Da principio il mio forte era la fantasia, e i miei versi erano pieni d'immagini, e delle mie letture poetiche io cercava sempre di profittare riguardo alla immaginazione. Io era bensì sensibilissimo anche agli affetti, ma esprimerli in poesia non sapeva. Non aveva ancora meditato intorno alle cose, e della filosofia non avea che un barlume . . . e con quella solita illusione che noi ci facciamo, cioè che nel mondo e nella vita ci debba esser sempre un'eccezione a favor nostro. Sono stato sempre sventurato, ma le mie sventure d'allora erano piene di vita, e mi disperavano perchè mi pareva (non veramente alla ragione, ma ad una saldissima immaginazione) che m'impedissero la felicità, della quale gli altri credea che godessero. . . . La mutazione totale in me, e il passaggio dallo stato antico al moderno, seguì si può dire dentro un anno, cioè nel 1819 dove privato dell'uso della vista, e della continua distrazione della lettura, cominciai a sentire la mia infelicità in un modo assai più tenebroso, cominciai ad abbandonar la speranza, a riflettere profondamente sopra le cose . . . a divenir filosofo di professione (di poeta ch'io era), a sentire l'infelicità certa del mondo, in luogo di conoscerla. . . . Allora l'immaginazione in me fu sommamente infiacchita, e quantunque la facoltà dell'invenzione allora appunto crescesse in me grandemente, anzi quasi cominciasse, verteva però principalmente, o sopra affari di prosa, o sopra poesie sentimentali. E s'io mi metteva a far versi, le immagini mi venivano a sommo stento, anzi la fantasia era quasi disseccata.

4 *Zibaldone*, I, 1036.

Una scontentezza, una malinconia viva ed energica, un desiderio non si sa di che, una specie di disperazione che piace, una propensione ad una vita più vitale, a sensazioni più sensibili . . . l'energia delle facoltà dell'anima . . . compagna della scontentezza e del desiderio, e quindi dell'infelicità, specialmente quando nulla corrisponde all'attività interna.

5 *Zibaldone*, II, 14.

Le sensazioni o fisiche o massimamente morali che l'uomo può provare, sono, niuna di vero piacere, ma indifferenti o dolorose.

6 *Zibaldone*, II, 14.

Disposta indifferentemente a sentire ogni sorta di sensazioni, in sostanza però non viene a esser altro che una maggior capacità di dolore.

7 *Zibaldone*, I, 1238.

Se mancassero altre prove che il vero è tutto infelice, non basterebbe il vedere che gli uomini sensibili, di carattere e d'immaginazione profonda, incapaci di pigliare le cose per la superficie, ed avvezzi a ruminare sopra ogni accidente della vita loro, sono irresistibilmente e sempre strascinati verso la infelicità? Onde ad un giovane sensibile, per quanto le sue circostanze paiano prospere, si può senz'alcun dubbio predire che sarà presto o tardi infelice, o indovinare ch'egli è tale.

8 *Poesie e prose*, I, 875-77.

Sappi che dal vero al sognato, non corre altra differenza, se non che questo può qualche volta essere molto più bello e più dolce, che quello non può mai . . . piacere è un subbietto speculativo, e non reale; un desiderio, non un fatto; un sentimento che l'uomo concepisce col pensiero, e non prova; o per dir meglio, un concetto, e non un sentimento. Non vi accorgete voi che nel tempo stesso di qualunque vostro diletto, ancorchè desiderato infinitamente, e procacciato con fatiche e molestie indicibili; non potendovi contentare il goder che fate in ciascuno di quei momenti, state sempre aspettando un goder maggiore e più vero, nel quale consista in somma quel tal piacere; e andate quasi riportandovi di continuo agl'istanti futuri di quel medesimo diletto? . . . Ma narrami tu se in alcun istante della tua vita, ti ricordi aver detto con piena sincerità ed opinione: io godo. Ben tutto giorno dicesti e dici sinceramente: io godrò; e parecchie volte, ma con sincerità minore: ho goduto. Di modo che il piacere è sempre o passato o futuro, e non mai presente.

9 *Zibaldone*, I, 32.

Le illusioni sono in natura, inerenti al sistema del mondo, tolte via affatto o quasi affatto, l'uomo è snaturato; ogni popolo snaturato è barbaro.

10 *Zibaldone*, I, 126.

Pare un assurdo, e pure è esattamente vero, che, tutto il reale essendo un nulla, non v'è altro di reale nè altro di sostanza al mondo che le illusioni.

11 *Leopardi*, p. 102.

12 The sense of harmony between nature and oneself is the basis of such attitudes as the pantheistic or the idealistic attitude to nature—or to the universe—an attitude that results in one's possessing and becoming one with the whole world around, or as Vossler calls it, subduing the whole world and the history of humanity to one's own sentiment of life. This is a typically classical attitude, as defined by Goethe—an attitude in which man feels himself "one with nature and consequently looks upon the outside world not as something strange, but as something which he recognizes as answering to his own feelings." Now Leopardi looked upon nature as something not only strange, mysterious, and inscrutable, but as something positively hostile.

13 *Zibaldone*, I, 91.

Gli ardiri rispetto a certi modi epiteti frasi metafore, tanto commendati in poesia e anche nel resto della letteratura e tanto usati da Orazio non sono bene spesso altro che un bell'uso di quel vago e in certo modo quanto alla costruzione, irragionevole, che tanto è necessario al poeta. Come in Orazio dove chiama mano di bronzo quella della necessità (ode alla fortuna) ch'è un'idea chiara, ma espressa vagamente (errantemente) così tirando l'epiteto come a caso a quello di cui gli avvien di parlare senza badare se gli convenga bene cioè se le due idee che gli si affacciano l'una sostantiva e l'altra di qualità ossia aggettiva si possano così subito mettere insieme, come chi chiama *duro* il vento perchè difficilmente si rompe la sua piena quando se gli va incontro.

14 *Zibaldone*, I, 244-45.

La matematica la quale misura quando il piacer nostro non vuol misura, definisce e circoscrive quando il piacer nostro non vuol confini (sieno pure vastissimi, anzi *sia pur vinta l'immaginazione dalla verità*), analizza quando il piacer nostro non vuole analisi nè cognizione intima ed esatta della cosa piacevole (*quando anche questa cognizione non riveli nessun difetto nella cosa, anzi ce la faccia giudicare più perfetta di quello che credevamo, come accade nell'esame delle opere di genio, che scoprendo tutte le bellezze, le fa sparire*), la matematica, dico, dev'esser necessariamente l'opposto del piacere.

15 One reason why "vagueness" is poetically so fruitful is that it is the source of one of those types of ambiguity, which, according to Empson, characterizes much good poetry—"ambiguity by vagueness," as he calls it, "such as was used to excess by the Pre-Raphaelites" (*Seven Types of Ambiguity,* p. 26). Some sort of vagueness is inherent in the nature of poetry itself, for while most poetry manages to say what it means— and most poetry does mean something, whether we regard its being and its meaning to be one and the same or two different but complementary things—it does not and need not say all. In attempting to say all, poetry often ceases to be poetry.

16 *Education and the University* (London, 1943), p. 70.

17 *Poesie e prose*, I, 894-95.

A conoscere perfettamente i pregi di un'opera perfetta o vicina alla perfezione . . . non basta essere assuefatto a scrivere, ma bisogna saperlo fare quasi così perfettamente come lo scrittore medesimo che hassi a giudicare . . . perchè quell'eccellenza non si conosce nè gustasi totalmente se non per mezzo dell'uso e dell'esercizio proprio, e quasi, per così dire, trasferita in se stesso.

18 Quoted by Cleanth Brooks, *Modern Poetry and the Tradition* (London, 1948), p. 19.

19 Brooks, *Modern Poetry,* p. 17.

20 *Zibaldone,* I, 260.

Tutti i piaceri da lontano sono grandi, e da vicino minimi, aridi, voti e nulli.

21 *Zibaldone,* I, 135.

Le parole . . . non presentano la sola idea dell'oggetto

significato, ma quando più quando meno, immagini
accessorie.

22 *Zibaldone*, I, 126.

Errare nel vago e indeterminato di quelle idee fan-
ciullesche, che nascono dall'ignoranza dell'intiero.

23 *Zibaldone*, II, 484.

Le idee sono per lo più definibili, ma i sentimenti quasi
mai.

24 Not all philosophy and all truths discovered by reason
and intellect, however, were ruled out by Leopardi from the
sphere of literature and poetry. "The philosophy of Socrates,"
he said, "could be used and shall always be used in literature
and poetry; but not the philosophy of Locke or Leibnitz. . . .
The philosophy of Socrates partook much of nature, but the
latter does not do so at all, and it is all reason" (*Zibaldone*,
I, 914).

25 *Zibaldone*, I, 392.

L'ultimo grado del sapere, consiste in conoscere che
tutto quello che noi cercavamo era davanti a noi, ci
stava tra' piedi, l'avressimo saputo, e lo sapevamo già,
senza studio: anzi lo studio solo e il voler sapere, ci ha
impedito di saperlo e di vederlo; il cercarlo ci ha
impedito di trovarlo.

26 *Zibaldone*, I, 733.

Tutte le verità e tutte le cose esistenti, sono legate fra
loro assai più strettamente ed intimamente ed essenzialmente, di quello che creda o possa credere e concepire
il comune degli stessi filosofi.

27 *Lettere*, p. 72.

28 *Principles of Literary Criticism*, p. 276.

29 *Zibaldone*, I, 971.

L'animo umano è così fatto ch'egli prova molto maggior
soddisfazione di un piacer piccolo, di un'idea di una
sensazione piccola, ma di cui non conosca i limiti, che
di una grande, di cui veda o senta i confini. . . . La
scienza distrugge i principali piaceri dell'animo nostro,
perchè determina le cose e ce ne mostra i confini, benchè
in moltissime cose, abbia materialmente ingrandito
d'assaissimo le nostre idee. Dico materialmente e non
già spiritualmente, giacchè, per esempio, la distanza dal
sole alla terra, era assai maggiore nella mente umana
quando si credeva di poche miglia, nè si sapeva quante,
di quello che ora che si sa essere di tante precise
migliaia di miglia. Così la scienza è nemica della
grandezza delle idee, benchè abbia smisuratamente

ingrandito le opinioni naturali. Le ha ingrandite come idee chiare, ma una piccolissima *idea confusa* è sempre maggiore di una grandissima, affatto *chiara*. L'incertezza se una cosa sia o non sia del tutto, è pur fonte di una grandezza, che vien distrutta dalla certezza che la cosa realmente è.

30 *Zibaldone*, I, 234.

Quella è necessaria alla fecondità e varietà dell'immaginativa, alla proprietà verità evidenza ed efficacia dell'imitazione. Questa non può fare che non pregiudichi al poeta. Allora giova sommamente al poeta l'erudizione, quando l'ignoranza delle cause, concede al poeta, non solamente rispetto agli altri ma anche a se stesso, l'attribuire gli effetti che vede o conosce, alle cagioni che si figura la sua fantasia.

31 *Zibaldone*, I, 234.

Omero e Dante per l'età loro seppero moltissime cose e più di quelle che sappiano la massima parte degli uomini colti d'oggidì, non solo in proporzione dei tempi, ma anche assolutamente.

32 *Zibaldone*, I, 1361.

L'idea di una cosa *terminata*, cioè al di là di cui non v'è più *nulla;* di una cosa terminata *per sempre,* e che non tornerà *mai più.*

33 *Zibaldone*, I, 382.

Non solo la facoltà conoscitiva, o quella di amare, ma neanche l'immaginativa è capace dell'infinito, o di concepire infinitamente, ma solo dell'indefinito, e di concepire indefinitamente . . . l'anima non vedendo i confini, riceve l'impressione di una specie d'infinità, e confonde l'indefinito coll'infinito.

34 *Zibaldone*, I, 506.

Quando i sommi poeti scrivevano quelle cose che ci destano le ammirabili sensazioni dell'infinito, l'animo loro non era occupato da veruna sensazione infinita; e dipingendo l'infinito non lo sentiva.

35 *New Bearings*, p. 119.

CHAPTER SEVEN

1 *Zibaldone*, I, 38.
2 *Zibaldone*, I, 38-39.

Il senso è chiaro, e quel *si frange* non ha che far niente con *sul tuo sasso,* e n'è distinto quanto meglio si può dire. Ma la collocazione casuale delle parole è tale, che io metto pegno che quanti leggono la Canzone del Chiabrera colla mente così sull'aspettare immagini, a prima giunta si figurano Firenze personificata . . . che percuota la testa e si franga il crine sul sasso del Zanchini; quantunque immediatamente poi venga a ravvedersi e a comprendere senza fatica l'intenzione del poeta ch'è manifesta. Ora, lasciando se l'immagine ch'io dico sia conveniente o no, certo è che non è voluta dal poeta, e ch'egli perciò deve schivare questa illusione quantunque momentanea . . . eccetto s'ella non gli piacesse come forse si potrebbe dare il caso, ma questo non dev'essere se non quando l'immagine illusoria non nocia alla vera e non ci sia bisogno di ravvedimento per veder questa seconda, giacchè due immagini in una volta non si possono vedere, ma bensì una dopo l'altra.

3 *Zibaldone*, I, 39.

Il lettore stia sempre tra le immagini.

4 *Zibaldone*, I, 39.

Di una grand'arte e di un grandissimo effetto procurando quel vago e quell'incerto ch'è tanto propriamente e sommamente poetico.

5 *Zibaldone*, I, 39.

Ma quasi ispirate da cosa invisibile e incomprensibile e da quell'ineffabile ondeggiamento del poeta che quando è veramente inspirato dalla natura dalla campagna e da checchessia, non sa veramente com'esprimere quello che sente, se non in modo vago e incerto, ed è perciò naturalissimo che le immagini che destano le sue parole appariscano accidentali.

6 Quoted by Leo Spitzer, *A Method of Interpreting Literature*, Smith College Lectures (Northampton, Mass., 1949), p. 1.

7 *Zibaldone*, I, 229-30.

Lord Byron nelle annotazioni al *Corsaro* (forse anche ad altre sue opere) cita esempi storici di quegli effetti delle passioni, e di quei caratteri ch'egli descrive. Male. Il lettore deve sentire e non imparare la conformità che ha la tua descrizione ec. colla verità e colla natura, e che quei tali caratteri e passioni in quelle tali circostanze producono quel tale effetto; altrimenti il diletto poetico è svanito, e la imitazione, cadendo sopra cose ignote, non produce maraviglia, ancorchè esattissima. . . . E la poesia si trasforma in un trattato, e l'azione sua dall'immaginazione e dal cuore passa all'intelletto. Effettivamente la poesia di Lord Byron sebbene caldissima, tuttavia per la detta ragione, la quale fa che quel calore non sia communicabile, è nella massima parte un trattato oscurissimo di psicologia, ed anche non molto utile, perchè i caratteri e passioni ch'egli descrive sono così strani che non combaciano in verun modo col cuore di chi legge, ma ci cascano sopra disadattamente, come per angoli e spicoli, e l'impressione che ci fanno è molto più esterna che interna. . . . La sola cosa che deve mostrare il poeta è di non capire l'effetto che dovranno produrre in chi legge, le sue immagini, descrizioni, affetti ec.

8 *Lettere*, p. 72.

9 *Zibaldone*, I, 1124.

Il potersi perciò spaziare coll'immaginazione, riguardo a ciò che non si vede.

10 *Zibaldone*, I, 1162.

Quanto una lingua è più ricca e vasta, tanto ha bisogno di meno parole per esprimersi.

11 *Zibaldone*, I, 1269.

Un fedelissimo pittore degli oggetti, ed un ostinatissimo e acutissimo cacciatore d'immagini . . . una copia di parole e di versi, che non destano l'immagine senza lungo circuito, e così poco o nulla v'ha di simultaneo, giacchè anzi lo spirito è condotto a veder gli oggetti appoco appoco per le loro parti.

12 *Zibaldone*, I, 1269.

Perchè ogni parola presso lui è un'immagine.

13 *Zibaldone*, I, 86.

Ovidio, il cui modo di dipingere è l'enumerare . . . non lascia quasi niente a fare al lettore, laddove Dante che con due parole desta un'immagine lascia molto a fare alla fantasia, ma dico fare non già faticare, giacchè ella spontaneamente concepisce quell'immagine e aggiunge quello che manca ai tratti del poeta che son tali da richiamar quasi necessariamente l'idea del tutto.

14 *Zibaldone*, I, 1509.

Ovidio descrive, Virgilio dipinge, Dante . . . non solo dipinge da maestro in due colpi, e vi fa una figura con un tratto di pennello; non solo dipinge senza descrivere (come fa anche Virgilio ed Omero), ma intaglia e scolpisce dinanzi agli occhi del lettore le proprie idee, concetti, immagini, sentimenti.

15 *Zibaldone*, I, 1275.

(Talvolta comprese in una brevissima frase, in una sola parola ec.) debbano essere solamente accennate; e così pure solamente accennate le connessioni e relazioni loro col soggetto, o colle altre immagini, idee, sentenze ec. a cui son vicine, a cui spettano, a cui si riferiscono ec. E questo ancora piace, perchè obbliga l'anima ad una continua azione, per supplire a ciò che il poeta non dice, per terminare ciò ch'egli solamente comincia, colorire ciò ch'egli accenna, scoprire quelle lontane relazioni, che il poeta appena indica. . . . Ecco come la soppressione stessa di parole, di frasi, di concetti, riesca bellezza, perchè obbliga l'anima piacevolmente all'azione, e non la lascia in ozio.

16 *Principles of Literary Criticism*, p. 120.

17 *Zibaldone*, I, 1424.

L'uomo odia l'inattività, e di questa vuol esser liberato dalle arti belle.

18 *Name and Nature of Poetry*, p. 42.

19 *Zibaldone*, II, 611-12.

Una continua e non mai interrotta azione, vivacità e freschezza d'immaginazione . . . sia pure immaginosissima e poetichissima l'invenzione e la qualità delle cose in esso trattate ed espresse . . . per il contrasto e sconvenienza ec. che sarà tanto maggiore, quanto quelle e l'invenzione ec. saranno più immaginose e poetiche.

20 Leopardi's conception of the nature and function of a poetic image (and by implication of the nature and function of poetry itself), of which it is both an integral part and an indispensable medium, is not dissimilar to that of C. Day Lewis. "Poetry's truth," says Lewis, "comes from the perception of a unity underlying and relating all phenomena, and . . . poetry's task is the perpetual discovery, through its imaging, metaphor-making faculty, of new relationships within this pattern, and the rediscovery and renovation of old ones" (*The Poetic Image* [London, 1947], p. 34).

21 *Zibaldone*, II, 610-11.

A poter *saisir* i rapporti, le affinità, le somiglianze ec. ec. o vere, o apparenti, poetiche ec. degli oggetti e delle cose tra loro, o a scoprire questi rapporti, o ad inventarli.

22 *Name and Nature of Poetry*, p. 14.

C HAPTER EIGHT

1 "A Talk on Dante," delivered at the Italian Institute, London, July 4, 1950. Also in T. S. Eliot, *Selected Prose*, ed. John Hayward (London, 1953), p. 100.

2 Francesco De Sanctis, *La Critica*, XIV (1916), 23.

3 Apropos of stylistic and poetic fastidiousness, Leopardi quotes Cicero to the effect that "men with a taste in eloquence are never fully satisfied either with their own works or with those of others, and that their mind *semper divinum aliquid atque infinitum desiderat*, to which the powers of eloquence can never attain. This saying is to be noted most of all in connection with art, criticism, and taste" (*Zibaldone*, I, 1030).

4 *Zibaldone*, II, 315.

> Una filosofia ed una letteratura moderna e filosofica, le quali finora non ebbe mai.

5 *Lettere*, p. 174.

> Dopo essermi annoiato parecchi giorni colla lettura de' nostri lirici più famosi . . . questo genere capitalissimo di componimento abbia tuttavia da nascere in Italia.

6 See G. Mestica, "La conversione letteraria e la cantica giovanile," *Studi leopardiani* (Florence, 1901).

7 "L'estetica . . . di Leopardi," p. 265.

8 *Leopardi*, p. 63.

9 *Zibaldone*, II, 1063.

> Espressione libera e schietta di qualunque affetto vivo e ben sentito dell'uomo.

10 *Zibaldone*, I, 1180.

> Infiammato del più pazzo fuoco, l'uomo la cui anima è in totale disordine, l'uomo posto in uno stato di vigor febbrile e straordinario (principalmente, anzi quasi indispensabilmente corporale) e quasi di ubbriachezza?

11 A similar distinction between ancient and modern poetry —the one so superb in stylistic richness and felicity of expression, the other basing its chief strength and charm on the content, on the superabundance of the inner life, on the dialogue of the mind with itself—was drawn by Matthew Arnold in a letter to Clough: "Keats and Shelley were on a false track when they set themselves to reproduce the exuberance of expression, the charm, the richness of images, and the felicity, of the Elizabethan poets, Yet critics cannot get to learn this. . . . Modern poetry can only subsist by its contents" (*Letters to Clough*, p. 124).

12 *Zibaldone*, I, 29.

> Chi non ha studiato e non ha letto, e insomma come costoro dicono è immune dai pregiudizi dell'arte, è innocente ec. non iscrive mica con semplicità, ma tutto all'opposto.

13 Leopardi's emphasis on a diligent study of the classics is

motivated, at least in part, by the recognition of the importance of tradition as being something not passively and half-consciously accepted, but consciously and deliberately acquired, or obtained, in Eliot's phrase, "by great labour."

[14] As to the effect, on the development of sensibility and on the education of the sentiments as distinguished from the necessity (with a view to cultivating style), of the study of the classics in the case of the great majority of people, Leopardi is one with Housman, who said: "I do not believe that the proportion of the human race whose inner nature the study of the classics will specially transform and beautify is large; and I am quite sure that the proportion of the human race on whom the classics will confer that benefit can attain the desired end without that minute and accurate study of the classical tongues which affords Latin professors their only excuse for existing (*Selected Prose* [Cambridge, 1961], p. 97). It is strange, and at the same time characteristically significant, that both Leopardi and Housman, erudite classicists as they were, should have said so.

[15] *Zibaldone*, I, 94.

> Nemico mortalissimo dell'affettazione massimamente in tutto quello che spetta agli affetti dell'animo e del cuore . . . ho sempre cercato di lasciare la natura al tutto libera e spontanea operatrice ec. A ogni modo mi sono avveduto che la lettura de' libri non ha veramente prodotto in me nè affetti o sentimenti che non avessi.

[16] *Complete Works* (3 vols., London, 1913), III, 182.

[17] *Zibaldone*, I, 77.

> Anche la stessa negligenza e noncuranza e sprezzatura e la stessa inaffettazione può essere affettata, risaltare.

[18] *Zibaldone*, I, 1536.

> Nelle parole si chiudono e quasi si legano le idee, come negli anelli le gemme, anzi s'incarnano come l'anima nel corpo, facendo seco loro come una persona, in modo che le idee sono inseparabili dalle parole, e divise non sono più quelle, sfuggono all'intelletto e alla concezione, e non si ravvisano, come accadrebbe all'animo nostro disgiunto dal corpo.

[19] This identification of body and form, word and meaning is a central argument in Leopardi's theory of poetry and anticipates Croce's identification of poetic intuition and its expression—"body and spirit, internal and external, divided as they are in naturalistic abstraction, are all one in reality, in which the verb is incarnated" (*La Poesia* [Bari, 1953], p. 5).

[20] *New Bearings,* p. 13.

[21] *Zibaldone,* I, 34.

> Una semplicità e candidezza sua propria, che però si piega e si accomoda mirabilmente alla nobiltà e magnificenza del dire . . . si piega ottimamente alle immagini, delle quali le tre canzoni abbondano e sono innestate nello stile e formanti il sangue di esso.

[22] *Zibaldone,* I, 138; 35.

> Egli versa il suo cuore, e gli altri l'anatomizzano (anche i più eccellenti) ed egli lo fa parlare, e gli altri ne parlano.
>
> La mollezza e quasi untuosità come d'olio soavissimo delle sue Canzoni.

[23] *Zibaldone,* II, 218-19.

> Lo stile e il linguaggio poetico in una letteratura già formata, e che n'abbia uno, non si distingue solamente dal prosaico nè si divide e allontana solamente dal volgo per l'uso di voci e frasi che, sebbene intese, non sono però adoperate nel discorso familiare nè nella prosa, le quali voci e frasi non sono per lo più altro che dizioni e locuzioni antiche, andate, fuor che ne' poemi, in disuso; ma esso linguaggio si distingue eziandio grandemente dal prosaico e volgare per la diversa inflessione materiale di quelle stesse voci e frasi che il volgo e la prosa adoprano ancora. . . . Perocchè non è da credere che la inflessione d'una voce sia stimata, e quindi veramente sia, più elegante o per la prosa o pel verso, perchè e quanto ella è più conforme all'etimologia, ma solamente perchè e quanto ella è meno trita dall'uso familiare, essendo però bene intesa e non riuscendo ricercata. (Anzi bene spesso è trivialissima l'inflessione regolare ed etimologica, ed elegantissima e tutta poetica le medesima voce storpiata. . . .)

[24] *Zibaldone,* II, 439.

> Molto più propriamente e più perfettamente poetico e distinto dal prosaico, che non è quello di verun altro de' nostri poeti, inclusi nominatamente i più classici e sommi antichi.

[25] *Zibaldone,* I, 499. Thus Leopardi himself draws the same distinction between "poetry" and "literature" as Croce was to do later on—a distinction that assumes the form and character of a veritable contrast.

> Piuttosto letterati di finissimo giudizio, che poeti.

[26] *Zibaldone,* I, 513.

> Uno squisitissimo traduttore . . . uno avvedutissimo e

finissimo rimodernatore del vecchio stile e della vecchia
lingua.

27 *Zibaldone*, I, 1425.

Bastante foza di passione e sentimento, per esser vero
poeta.

28 *A History of Modern Criticism* (2 vols., London, 1955),
II, 272.

29 *Zibaldone*, I, 499.

Tanto è vero che la poesia migliore è la più antica,
all'opposto della prosa, dove l'arte può aver più luogo.

30 *Lettere*, p. 63.

Se io vorrò seguir Dante, forse mi riuscirà di farmi
proprio quel linguaggio e vestirne i pensiere miei a far
versi de' quali non si possa dire, almeno non così
subito, questa è imitazione, ma se vorrò mettermi a
emulare una lettera del Caro, non sarà così.

31 Quoted by Norman Marlow, *A. E. Housman: Scholar and
Poet* (London, 1958), p. 133.

32 *Lettere*, pp. 62-63.

Non credo che si possa citare esempio di vero poeta il
quale non abbia cominciato a poetare da giovanetto;
nè che molti poeti si possano addurre i quali siano
giunti all'eccellenza, anche nella prosa, e in questi
pochissimi, mi par di vedere che prima sono stati poeti
e poi prosatori. E in fatti a me parea che quanto alle
parole e alla lingua, fosse più difficile assai il conservare
quella proprietà senza affettazione e con piena scioltezza
e disinvoltura nella prosa che nel verso, perchè nella
prosa l'affettazione e lo stento si vedono . . . come un
bufalo nella neve, e nella poesia non così facilmente,
primo, perchè moltissime cose sono affettazioni e stirac-
chiature nella prosa, e nella poesia no, e pochissime che
nella prosa nol sono, lo sono in poesia, secondo, perchè
anche quelle che in poesia sono veramente affettazioni,
dall'armonia e dal linguaggio poetico son celate facilmente, tanto che appena si travedono.

33 *Zibaldone*, I, 36.

Robusto nelle immagini, sufficientemente fecondo nell'invenzione e nelle novità, facile appunto come Pindaro a
riscaldarsi infiammarsi sublimarsi anche per le cose
tenui, e dar loro al primo tocco un'aria grande ed
eccelsa. . . . Imitò anche bene i greci e Pindaro e
Orazio nell'economia del componimento.

34 In this Leopardi comes very near to the position of those,
like Housman and Yvor Winters, for example, who maintain

that poetry can be written about nothing, as, indeed, some very good poems (Housman cites the song from *Measure for Measure*, "Take, O take, those lips away" as an illustration) have been. Virtually an opposite view has been expressed by T. S. Eliot: "Style alone cannot preserve; only good style in conjunction with permanently interesting content can preserve." (*The Use of Poetry and the Use of Criticism*)

35 *Zibaldone*, I, 1272.

Prova quella sensazione di vigore . . . che si prova nel far un rapido cammino, o nell'esser trasportato da veloci cavalli, o nel trovarsi in un'energica azione, ed in un punto di attività.

36 *Oxford Addresses*, p. 34.

37 *Zibaldone*, I, 1530.

In ultima analisi la forza dell'arte nelle cose umane è maggiore assai che non è quella della natura.

38 *Zibaldone*, II, 1181.

Il poema epico è contro la natura della poesia.

39 *Zibaldone*, II, 1230.

La *Divina Commedia* non è che una *lunga Lirica*.

40 *Zibaldone*, I, 1269.

La rapidità e la concisione dello stile, piace perchè presenta all'anima una folla d'idee simultanee, o così rapidamente succedentisi, che paiono simultanee . . . non ha tempo di restare in ozio.

41 *Zibaldone*, I, 1359-60.

A quello che altrove dico delle cause per cui piace la rapidità ec. dello stile, massime poetico, ec. aggiungi che da quella forma di scrivere, nasce necessariamente a ogni tratto l'inaspettato, il quale deriva dalla collocazione e ordine delle parole, dai sensi metaforici, i quali ti obbligano, seguendo innanzi colla lettura a dare alle parole già lette un senso bene spesso diverso da quello che avevi creduto; dalla stessa novità dei traslati, e dalla naturale lontananza delle idee, ravvicinate dall'autore ec. Tutte cose, che oltre il piacere della sorpresa, dilettano perchè lo stesso trovar sempre cose inaspettate tien l'animo in continuo esercizio ed attività; e di più lo pasce colla novità, colla materiale e parziale maraviglia derivante da questa o quella parola, frase, ardire.

42 *Zibaldone*, II, 422-23.

Disprezzano affatto, anzi neppur concepiscono, la novità de' pensieri, delle immagini, de' sentimenti; e non avendo nè pensieri, nè immagini, nè sentimenti, tuttavia per riguardo del loro stile si credono poeti, e poeti perfetti e classici: questi tali sarebbero forse ben sorpresi se loro si dicesse, non solamente che chi non è buono alle immagini, ai sentimenti, ai pensieri non è poeta . . . ma che chiunque non sa immaginare, pensare, sentire, inventare, non può nè possedere un buono stile poetico . . . nè giudicarlo nelle opere proprie nè nelle altrui; che l'arte e la facoltà e l'uso dell'immaginazione e dell'invenzione è tanto indispensabile allo stile poetico, quanto e forse ancor più ch'al ritrovamento, alla scelta, e alla disposizione della materia, alle sentenze e a tutte l'altre parti della poesia.

[43] *Zibaldone*, II, 611-12.

Una continua e non mai interrotta azione, vivacità e freschezza d'immaginazione . . . il più poetico di quanti si conoscono, e forse il non plus ultra della poetichità . . . per il contrasto e sconvenienza ec. che sarà tanto maggiore, quanto quelle e l'invenzione ec. saranno più immaginose e poetiche.

[44] *Zibaldone*, II, 4-5.

Non basta che lo scrittore sia padrone del proprio stile. Bisogna che il suo stile sia padrone delle cose: e in ciò consiste la perfezion dell'arte, e la somma qualità dell'artefice. Alcuni de' pochissimi che meritano nell'Italia moderna il nome di scrittori (anzi tutti questi pochissimi), danno a vedere di esser padroni dello stile: vale a dir che il loro stile è fermo, uguale, non traballante, non sempre sull'orlo di precipizi, non incerto . . . ma libero e sciolto e facile, e che si sa spandere e distendere e dispiegare e scorrere, sicuro di non dir quello che lo scrittore non vuole intendere, sicuro di non dir nulla in quel modo che lo scrittore non lo vuol dire, sicuro di non dare in un altro stile, di non cadere in una qualità che lo scrittore voglia evitare. . . . Questi tali son padroni del loro stile. Ma il loro stile non è padrone delle cose, vale a dir che lo scrittore non è padrone di dir nel suo stile tutto ciò che vuole . . . molte cose che farebbero all'argomento, al tempo ec. che sarebbero utili o necessarie in proposito, e ch'essi desidererebbero dire, e concepiscono perfettamente, e forse anche originalmente . . . tuttavia le fuggono, o le toccano di fianco, e di traverso, e se ne spacciano pel generale, o ne dicono sola una parte, sapendo ben che tralasciano l'altra, e che sarebbe bene il dirla, o in somma non confidano o disperano di poterle dire o dirle pienamente nel loro stile. La qual cosa non è mai accaduta ai veri grandi scrittori, ed è mortifera alla letteratura.

⁴⁵ *Zibaldone*, II, 1104.

Les ouvrages bien écrits seront les seuls qui passeront à la postérité; la quantité des connaissances, la singularité des faits, la nouveauté même des découvertes ne sont pas de sûrs garants de l'immortalitè . . . le style est l'homme même. . . . S'il est élevé, noble, sublime, l'auteur sera également admiré dans tous les temps.

⁴⁶ *Le problème du style* (2nd ed., Paris, 1938), p. 154.

CHAPTER NINE

¹ *Zibaldone*, II, 162.

In tutte le lingue tanto gran parte dello stile appartiene ad essa lingua, che in veruno scrittore l'uno senza l'altra non si può considerare. La magnificenza, la forza, la nobiltà, l'eleganza, la semplicità, la naturalezza, la grazia, la varietà, tutte o quasi tutte le qualità dello stile, sono così legate alle corrispondenti qualità della lingua, che nel considerarle in qualsivoglia scrittura è ben difficile il conoscere e distinguere e determinare quanta e qual parte di esse (e così delle qualità contrarie) sia propria del solo stile, e quanta e quale della sola lingua.

² *Zibaldone*, II, 162.

Ma tanta è la forza e l'autorità delle voci nello stile, che mutate quelle, o le loro forme, il loro ordine ec. tutte o ciascuna delle predette qualità si mutano, o si perdono, e lo stile di qualsivoglia autore o scritto, cangia natura in modo che più non è quello nè si riconosce.

³ *Zibaldone*, II, 1070. The connection between language (including style) and character was recognized even by Ben Jonson when he pointed out that "the excess of Feasts and apparell are the notes of a sick State, and the wantonnes of language, of a sick mind" (*Timber, or Discoveries* in *Critical Essays of the Seventeenth Century*, ed. J. E. Spingarn [2 vols., Bloomington, Ind., 1957], I, 28). And in our own day William Empson, too, observes that "it might . . . be possible to relate a poet's attitude to life with his attitude to words, as apart from what he said with them" (*Seven Types of Ambiguity*, p. 87).

Quella franchezza e libertà di pensare . . . decorosa sprezzatura del suo stile . . . una certa magnanimità, una fiducia ed estimazion lodevole di se stesso, una generosità d'animo.

⁴ *Zibaldone*, I, 1519. One of the reasons why a common

and uncultivated reader would not be able to appreciate the beauties of literary masterpieces is simply that most readers, as Wordsworth pointed out, are "unacquainted with the various stages through which words have passed."

> Uomini semplici e naturali sono molto più dilettati e trovano molto più grazioso il colto, lo studiato, e anche l'affettato che il semplice e il naturale.

5 *Zibaldone*, II, 238-39.

> Quei pregi fondamentali d'ogni qualunque scrittura, quelle qualità indispensabili anzi di primissima necessità, senza cui gli altri pregi a nulla valgono . . . queste non sono mai altro che il frutto dell'arte.

6 *Zibaldone*, I, 241-42.

> L'universalità di una lingua deriva principalmente dalla regolarità geometrica e facilità della sua struttura, dall'esattezza, chiarezza materiale, precisione, certezza de' suoi significati ec. cose che si fanno apprezzare da tutti, essendo fondate nella secca ragione, e nel puro senso comune, ma non hanno che far niente colla bellezza, ricchezza (anzi la ricchezza confonde, difficulta e pregiudica), dignità, varietà, armonia, grazia, forza, evidenza, le quali tanto meno conferiscono o importano alla universalità di una lingua, quanto: 1. non possono esser sentite intimamente, e pregiate, se non dai nazionali.

7 *Zibaldone*, I, 135-36.

> Le parole, come osserva il Beccaria (*Trattato dello stile*) non presentano la sola idea dell'oggetto significato, ma quando più quando meno, immagini accessorie. Ed è pregio sommo della lingua l'aver di queste parole. Le voci scientifiche presentano la nuda e circoscritta idea di quel tale oggetto, e perciò si chiamano termini perchè determinano e definiscono la cosa da tutte le parti. Quanto più una lingua abbonda di parole, tanto più è adattata alla letteratura e alla bellezza.

8 *Zibaldone*, I, 826.

> E proprio ufficio de' poeti e degli scrittori ameni il coprire quanto si possa la nudità delle cose, come è ufficio degli scienziati e de' filosofi il rivelarla. Quindi le parole precise convengono a questi, e sconvengono per lo più a quelli; a dirittura l'uno e l'altro. Allo scienziato le parole più convenienti sono le più precise ed esprimenti un'idea più nuda. Al poeta e al letterato per lo contrario le parole più vaghe, ed esprimenti idee più incerte, o un maggior numero d'idee.

9 *Zibaldone*, I, 1228.

> La libertà, il più bello ed util pregio di una lingua.

[10] *Zibaldone*, II, 130.

Il genio e lo spirito di qualsivoglia altra lingua, e di qualunque autore di essa.

[11] *Zibaldone*, II, 132.

Contiene in se stessa, per dir così, tutte le lingue virtualmente. . . . Ella ha quello che equivale a ciò che le altre hanno, ma non già quello stesso precisamente che le altre hanno. Ella può dunque colle sue forme rappresentare e imitare l'andamento dell'altre, restando però sempre la stessa, e sempre una, e conservando il suo carattere ben distinto da tutte.

[12] *Zibaldone*, I, 706.

Legata di tutte quante le lingue antiche e moderne, colte o incolte.

[13] *Zibaldone*, I, 471.

La migliore di tutte le lingue è quella che può esser l'uno e l'altro, e racchiudere eziandio tutti i gradi che corrono fra questi due estremi.

[14] *Zibaldone*, II, 222.

Prodigiosamente ricca, tragga e formi la sua ricchezza da sole pochissime radici, col mezzo del grand'uso ch'ella fa della composizione e derivazione de' vocaboli.

[15] *Zibaldone*, I, 323.

La poesia e la prosa francese si confondono insieme, e la Francia non ha vera distinzione di prosa e di poesia, non solamente perchè il suo stile poetico non è distinto dal prosaico, e perch'ella non ha vera lingua poetica . . . i suoi poeti (massime moderni) sono più scrittori, e pensatori e filosofi che poeti, e perchè Voltaire, per esempio, nell'*Enriade,* scrive con quello stesso *enjouement,* con quello stesso *esprit,* con quella stess'aria di conversazione, con quello stesso *tour* e giuoco di parole di frasi di maniere e di sentimenti e sentenze, che adopra nelle sue prose: non solamente, dico, per tutto questo, ma anche perchè la prosa francese, oramai è una specie di poesia.

[16] *Zibaldone*, I, 1273.

La *vivezza* e il pregio di tutto ciò . . . non consiste in altro che nella *frequenza,* e nella *lunghezza* dei salti da un luogo, da un'idea all'altra. Le quali cose derivano dall'*arditezza* dell'elocuzione materiale. Della quale arditezza essendo incapace la lingua francese, è incapace di stile poetico, e le mille miglia separata dal *lirico.*

[17] *Zibaldone*, I, 1202.

Non solo l'eleganza, ma la nobiltà la grandezza, tutte

le qualità del linguaggio poetico, anzi il linguaggio poetico esso stesso, consiste, se ben l'osservi, in un modo di parlare indefinito, o non ben definito, o sempre meno definito del parlar prosaico o volgare. . . . Tutto ciò ch'è precisamente definito, potrà bene aver luogo talvolta nel linguaggio poetico, giacchè non bisogna considerare la sua natura che nell'insieme, ma certo propriamente parlando, e per se stesso, non è poetico. Lo stesso effetto e la stessa natura si osserva in una prosa che senza esser poetica, sia però sublime, elevata, magnifica, grandiloquente. La vera nobiltà dello stile prosaico, consiste essa pure costantemente in non so che d'indefinito. . . . E v'è non pertanto assai notabile diversità fra l'indefinito del linguaggio poetico, e quello del prosaico, oratorio.

[18] *Biographia*, II, 25 n.

[19] *Zibaldone*, I, 1196.

La lingua italiana non ha mai sofferto, come la francese, una riforma, venuta da un solo fonte ed autorità, cioè da un'Accademia, e riconosciuta dalla nazione, la quale la ristringesse alle sole parole comunemente usitate al tempo della riforma, o che poi fossero per venire in uso, togliendole affatto la libertà di adoperare quanto di buono d'intelligibile ed inaffettato si potesse trovare nel capitale della lingua non più solito ad usarsi, ma usato dagli antichi.

[20] *Zibaldone*, I, 1198.

Ripugna alla natura di lingua viva.

[21] *Zibaldone*, I, 492.

Cadere nell'arido, nel monotono, nel matematico.

[22] *Littérature et philosophie mêlées* (Paris, 1864), I, 17.

[23] *Zibaldone*, I, 1490.

I francesi non hanno poesia che non sia prosaica, e non hanno oramai prosa che non sia poetica. Il che confondendo due linguaggi distintissimi per natura loro, e tutti due proprie dell'uomo per natura sua, nuoce essenzialmente all'espressione de' nostri pensieri, e contrasta alla natura dello spirito umano: il quale non parla mai poeticamente quando ragiona coll'animo riposato ec. come par che sieno obbligati di fare i francesi, se vogliono scrivere in prose che sia per loro elegante e spiritosa ed ornata.

[24] *La poesia e la poetica di Leopardi* (Milan, 1949), p. 158.

[25] *Zibaldone*, I, 1205.

Ne' versi rimati, per quanto la rima paia spontanea, e sia lungi dal parere stiracchiata, possiamo dire per esperienza di chi compone, che il concetto è mezzo del poeta, mezzo della rima, e talvolta un terzo di quello e due di questa, talvolta tutto della sola rima. Ma ben pochi son quelli che appartengono interamente al solo poeta, quantunque non paiano stentati, anzi nati dalla cosa.

[26] Quoted by Cardarelli, *Opere complete* (Milan, 1962), p. 939.

[27] *Zibaldone*, I, 833.

Scompagnata, solitaria e circoscritta . . . fare errare la nostra mente nella moltitudine delle concezioni, e nel loro vago, confuso, indeterminato, incircoscritto.

[28] Geoffrey Tillotson, *Augustan Studies* (London, 1961), pp. 49-50.

[29] *Zibaldone*, I, 1041.

La forza dell'opinione, dell'assuefazione ec. e come tutto sia relativo, si può anche vedere nelle parole, ne' modi, ne' concetti, nelle immagini della poesia e della prosa comparativamente. Paragone il quale si può facilmente istituire, mostrando per esempio come una parola, una sentenza non insolita, che non fa verun effetto nella prosa perchè vi siamo assuefatti, lo faccia nel verso.

[30] *Zibaldone*, I, 1100.

Le idee concomitanti . . . sono spessissimo legate alla parola (che nella mente umana è inseparabile dalla cosa, è la sua immagine, il suo corpo, ancorchè la cosa sia materiale, anzi è un tutto con lei, e si può dir che la lingua, riguardo alla mente di chi l'adopra, contenga non solo i segni delle cose, ma quasi le cose stesse) sono dico legate alla parola più che alla cosa, o legate a tutte due in modo che divisa la cosa dalla parola (giacchè la parola non si può staccar dalla cosa), la cosa non produce più le stesse idee.

[31] *Zibaldone*, I, 1102.

Una folla d'idee concomitanti, derivate dalla vivacità delle impressioni che accompagnavano quelle parole in quella età, e dalla fecondità dell'immaginazione fanciullesca.

[32] *Zibaldone*, I, 1103-104.

Non c'è forse un uomo a cui una parola medesima . . . produca una concezione precisamente identica a quella di un altro . . . forse nessun individuo (come nessuna nazione rispetto alle altre) ha precisamente le idee di un altro, circa la più identica cosa. . . . Così gli uomini concepiscono diversissime idee di una stessa cosa, ma esprimendo questa con una medesima parola, e variando anche nell'intender la parola, questa seconda differenza nasconde la prima: essi credono di esser d'accordo, e non lo sono.

[33] *Augustan Studies,* p. 81.

[34] *Zibaldone,* I, 1216-17.

Posteri, posterità (e questo più perchè *più generale*), *futuro, passato, eterno, lungo,* in fatto di tempo, *morte, mortale, immortale* e cento simili, son parole di senso o di significazione quanto indefinita, tanto poetica e nobile, e perciò cagione di nobiltà, di bellezza ec. a tutti gli stili.

[35] *Zibaldone,* I, 1146.

"Il pin che *di lontan* veder *soleva"*: Dove l'effetto delle parole *di lontano* si unisce a quello del *soleva,* parola di significato egualmente vasto per la copia delle rimembranze che contiene. Togliete queste due parole ed idee; l'effetto di quel verso si perde, e si scema se togliete l'una delle due.

[36] *Zibaldone,* I, 1150.

La notte confondendo gli oggetti, l'animo non ne concepisce che un'immagine vaga, indistinta, incompleta, sì di essa che quanto ella contiene. Così *oscurità, profondo* ec. ec.

[37] *Zibaldone,* I, 1164.

Le parole che indicano moltitudine, copia, grandezza, lunghezza, larghezza, altezza, vastità ec. ec. sia in estensione, o in forza, intensità ec. ec. sono pure poeticissime, e così le immagini corrispondenti. Come nel Petrarca:

Te solo aspetto, e quel che *tanto* AMASTI,
E laggiuso è rimasto, il mio bel velo.

E in Ippolito Pindemonte:

Fermossi alfine il cor che BALZO *tanto.*

Dove notate che il *tanto* essendo indefinito, fa maggiore effetto che non farebbe *molto, moltissimo, eccessivamente, sommamente.* Così pure le parole e le idee *ultimo, mai più, l'ultima volta,* ec. ec. sono di grand'effetto poetico, per l'infinità.

[38] *Zibaldone,* I, 827.

I diversi stili domandano diverse parole, e come quello ch'è nobile per la prosa, e ignobile bene spesso per la poesia, così quello ch'è nobile ed ottimo per un genere di prosa, è ignobilissimo per un altro.

[39] Sir Walter Raleigh, *Style* (London, 1904), p. 21.

[40] George Saintsbury, *The Peace of the Augustans* (London, 1946), p. 10.

[41] *Zibaldone*, II, 1236.

Conservare la purità della lingua è un'immaginazione, un sogno, un ipotesi astratta, un'idea, non mai riducibile ad atto, se non solamente nel caso di una nazione che, sia riguardo alla letteratura e alle dottrine, sia riguardo alla vita, non abbia ricevuto nulla da alcuna nazione straniera.

[42] *Augustan Studies*, p. 101.

[43] *Biographia*, II, 56-57.

[44] *Zibaldone*, I, 738.

Odio gli arcaismi, e quelle parole antiche, ancorchè chiarissime, ancorchè espressivissime, bellissime, utilissime, riescono sempre affettate, ricercate, stentate, massime nella prosa. Ma i nostri scrittori antichi, ed antichissimi, abbondano di parole e modi oggi disusati, che oltre all'essere di significato apertissimo a chicchessia, cadono così naturalmente, mollemente, facilmente nel discorso, sono così lontani da ogni senso di affettazione o di studio ad usarli, e in somma così freschi (e al tempo stesso bellissimi ec.), che il lettore il quale non sa da che parte vengano, non si può accorgere che sieno antichi, ma deve stimarli modernissimi e di zecca: parole e modi dove l'antichità si può conoscere, ma per nessun conto sentire. E laddove quegli altri si possono paragonare alle cose stantivite, rancidite, ammuffite col tempo; questi rassomigliano a quelle frutta che intonacate di cera si conservano per mangiarle fuor di stagione, e allora si cavano dalla intonacatura vivide e fresche e belle e colorite, come si cogliessero dalla pianta. E sebbene dismessi, e ciò da lunghissimo tempo, o nello scrivere, o nel parlare, o in ambedue, non paiono dimenticati, ma come riposti in disparte, e custoditi, per poi ripigliarli.

[45] *Timber*, p. 38.

[46] *Correspondence of Thomas Gray*, ed. Paget Toynbee and Leonard Whibley (3 vols., Oxford, 1935), I, 192.

[47] *Poetic Diction* (2nd ed., London, 1952), p. 163.

[48] *Zibaldone*, I, 912.

Quelle qualità loro che giovano per l'una parte alla ragione, e per l'altra da lei dipendono, si accrescono e perfezionano col tempo; quelle che dipendono dalla natura, decadono, si corrompono, e si perdono. Quindi le lingue guadagnano in precisione, allontanandosi dal

primitivo, guadagnano in chiarezza, ordine, regola ec.
Ma in efficacia, varietà ec. e in tutto ciò ch'è bellezza,
perdono sempre quanto più s'allontanano, da quello
stato che costituisce la loro primitiva forma. La
combinazione della ragione colla natura accade quando
elle sono applicate alla letteratura. Allora l'arte corregge
la rozzezza della natura, e la natura la secchezza dell'arte.
Allora le lingue sono in uno stato di perfezione relativa.
Ma qui non si fermano. La ragione avanza e, avanzando
la ragione, la natura retrocede. L'arte non è più
contrabbilanciata. La precisione predomina, la bellezza
soccombe.

[49] Cf. Sir Herbert Read: "Poetry is a more primitive mode
of expression than prose, and that is why the language of
primitive peoples often seems poetic to us" (*Collected Essays,*
p. 42). Though this statement openly begs the question—poetry
is more primitive; therefore the language of primitive peoples
is more poetic—it means to imply or demonstrate the same
point as Leopardi makes with greater analytical lucidity.

[50] *Zibaldone*, I, 982.

Piccole e sfuggevoli differenze fra i significati di parole,
che tuttavia non furono inventate per lusso, ma per
vera utilità.

[51] *Style*, p. 47.

[52] *Zibaldone*, I, 1455.

Ciascuna bellezza, sì di una lingua in genere (eccetto
l'armonia e la ricchezza delle parole, o delle loro inflessioni), sì di un modo di dire in ispecie, è un dispetto
alla grammatica universale, e una espressa (benchè or
più grave or più leggera) infrazione delle sue leggi.

[53] Even Robert Bridges with all his classical conservatism
and with his unswerving devotion to the principle of "continuous literary decorum"—a devotion that prevented him from
doing justice to, and even from perceiving or recognizing, the
genius and originality manifest in Gerard Manley Hopkins'
poetry—pleaded against forbidding what he calls "apt and
desirable grammatical forms merely because they are not read
in the newspapers or heard at the dinner-table" ("Poetic Diction in English," *English Critical Essays, Twentieth Century,*
ed. P. M. Jones [Oxford, 1950], p. 8).

[54] *Zibaldone*, I, 1382.

Egli è pienissimo di locuzioni, modi, forme figuratissime,
irregolarissime . . . non sieno meno contrarie alle regole
della sintassi greca, che all'ordine logico universale del
discorso.

55 *Zibaldone*, I, 892.

Il pellegrino delle voci e dei modi, se è eccessivamente pellegrino, o eccessivo per frequenza ec. distrugge l'ordine, la regola, la convenienza, ed è fonte di bruttezza.

56 *Biographia*, II, 49.

57 *Zibaldone*, II, 218-19.

Lo stile e il linguaggio poetico in una letteratura già formata, e che n'abbia uno, non si distingue solamente dal prosaico nè si divide e allontana solamente dal volgo per l'uso di voci e frasi che, sebbene intese, non sono però adoperate nel discorso familiare nè nella prosa, le quali voci e frasi non sono per lo più altro che dizioni e locuzioni antiche, andate, fuor che ne' poemi, in disuso; ma esso linguaggio si distingue eziandio grandemente dal prosaico e volgare per la diversa inflessione materiale di quelle stesse voci e frasi che il volgo e la prosa adoprano ancora. Ond'è che spessissimo una tal voce o frase è poetica pronunziata o scritta in un tal modo, e prosaica, anzi talora affatto impoetica, anzi pure ignobilissima e volgarissima in un altro modo. . . . Questo mezzo di distinguere e separare il linguaggio d'un poema da quello della prosa e del volgo inflettendo o condizionando diversamente dall'uso la forma estrinseca d'una voce o frase prosaica e familiare, è frequentissimamente adoperato in ogni lingua che ha linguaggio poetico distinto, lo fu da' greci sempre, lo è dagl'italiani: anzi, parlando puramente del linguaggio, e non dello stile, poetico, il detto mezzo è l'uno de' più frequenti che s'adoprino a conseguire il detto fine, e più frequente forse di quello delle voci o frasi inusitate.

58 *Zibaldone*, II, 1042.

E senza l'antico non vi può esser *lingua* poetica.

59 *Zibaldone*, I, 1459.

Ora che cosa vuol dire una lingua che abbia proprietà? Non altro, se non una lingua ardita, cioè capace di scostarsi nelle forme, nei modi ec. dall'ordine e dalla ragion dialettica del discorso, giacchè dentro i limiti di quest'ordine e di questa ragione, nulla è proprio di nessuna lingua in particolare, ma tutto è comune di tutte (parlo in quanto alle forme, facoltà ec. e non in quanto alle nude parole, o alle inflessioni della medesime, isolatamente considerate). Dunque se non è, nè può esser bella la forma di una lingua che non ha proprietà, non è nè può esser bella una lingua che nella forma sia tutta o quasi tutta matematica, e conforme alla grammatica universale. E così di nuovo si viene a concludere che la bellezza delle forme di una lingua (tanto delle forme in genere, quanto di ciascuna in particolare) non può non trovarsi in opposizione colla grammatica generale, nè esser altro che una maggiore o minor violazione delle sue leggi.

[60] *Zibaldone,* II, 629.

Fra le lingue illustri moderne, la più separata e meno dominata dall'uso, è, cred'io, l'italiana, massime oggi, perchè l'Italia ha men società d'ogni altra colta nazione, e perchè la letteratura fra noi è molto più esclusivamente che altrove, propria de' letterati, e perchè l'Italia non ha lingua illustre moderna.

[61] *Biographia,* II, 63.

[62] *Zibaldone,* I, 580.

Quella miseria di giudizio, o piuttosto quella incapacità d'ogni retto giudizio, e mancanza d'ogni arte critica, di cui lagnavasi l'Alfieri . . . e che oggidì è così evidente per la continua esperienza sì della grandi scempiaggini lodate, sì dei pregi (se qualcuno per miracolo ne occorre) o sconosciuti, o trascurati, o negati, o biasimati.

[63] Croce's criticism of Manzoni's theory of language ("since the nine-tenths or ninety-nine one-hundredths of the common Italian language coincides with the language of Florence, even the tenth part, which is different, should conform itself to the language of Florence") as being "arbitrary and absurd" since "neither is the Florentine use something fixed and unique, nor is there any rational motive to impose it, there being no rationality in the arithmetic of the nine-tenths or the ninety-nine one-hundredths" (*A. Manzoni* [Bari, 1952], pp. 83-84).

[64] *Zibaldone,* I, 928.

Se in questi tre sommi (Dante, Petrarca, Boccaccio) . . . si volesse anche riporre il perfezionamente ec. della lingua italiana poetica (che è falsissimo), non si può nel trecento riporre, a cagione de tre sommi, quello della lingua italiana prosaica.

[65] *Zibaldone,* II, 897.

Usar l'antico e il moderno e tutte le risorse della lingua, in vista e con intenzione di fare uno stile e una maniera nè familiare nè antica, ma elegante in generale, nobile, maestosa, distinta affatto dal dir comune . . . quale è appunto quello di Cicerone nella prosa e di Virgilio nella poesia.

[66] "La mente di G. Leopardi," *Giornale storico della letteratura italiana,* XLI (1903), 214.

67 *Zibaldone*, I, 87.

Tutto si è perfezionato da Omero in poi, ma non la poesia.

68 *Zibaldone*, I, 523-24.

Perchè la lingua e naturalmente e ragionevolmente cammina sempre finch'è viva, e come è assurdissimo il voler ch'ella stia ferma, contra la natura delle cose, così è pregiudizievole e porta discapito il volerla riporre più indietro che non bisogna, e obbligarla a rifare quel cammino che avea già fatto dirittamente e debitamente.

69 *Zibaldone*, I, 1253.

La lingua latina è fra tutte quante la meno adattabile alle cose moderne, perch'essendo di carattere antico, e *proprissimo* e marcatissimo, è priva di libertà, al contrario delle altre antiche, e quindi incapace d'altro che dell'antico, e inadattabile al moderno, a differenza della greca.

70 *Zibaldone*, I, 1256-57.

Ai maggiori incrementi dell'arte che si vedessero tra gli antichi ec. ec.; o dall'aver ella avuto in Cicerone uno scrittore e un *formatore* troppo vasto per se, troppo poco per lei, troppo eminente sopra gli altri, alla cui lingua chi si restrinse, perdette la libertà della lingua, chi ricusolla, perdette la purità, ed avendo riconquistata la libertà colla violenza, degenerolla in anarchia. Perocchè la libertà e ne' popoli e nelle lingue è buona quando ella è goduta pacificamente e senza contrasto relativo ad essa, e come legittimamente e per diritto, ma quando ella è conquistata colla violenza, è piuttosto mancanza di leggi, che libertà. *Essendo proprio delle cose umane da poi che son giunte ad una estremità, saltare alla contraria, poi risaltare alla prima, e non sapersi mai più fermare nel mezzo, dove la natura sola nel primitivo loro andamento le aveva condotte, e sola potrebbe ricondurle.* Un simile pericolo corse la lingua italiana nel cinquecento, quando alcuni volevano restringerla, non al trecento, come oggi i pedanti, ma alla sola lingua e stile di Dante, Petrarca e Boccaccio, per la eminenza di questi scrittori, anzi la prosa alla sola lingua e stile del Boccaccio, la lirica a quello del solo Petrarca ec. contro i quali combatte il Caro nell'*Apologia*.

71 *Zibaldone*, I, 928-29.

La prosa è la parte più naturale, usuale, e quindi principale di una lingua, e la perfezione di una lingua consiste essenzialmente nella prosa. Ma il Boccaccio primo ed unico che applicasse nel trecento la prosa italiana alla letteratura, senza la quale applicazione la lingua non si forma, non può servir di modello alla prosa.

[72] *Zibaldone*, II, 438-39.

Si è formato pienamente e perfezionato il linguaggio (e quindi anche lo stile) poetico italiano (dico il linguaggio e lo stile poetico, non già la poesia); s'è accostato al Virgiliano, vero, perfetto e sovrano modello dello stile propriamente e totalmente e distintissimamente poetico; ha perduto ogni aria di familiare; e si è con ben certi limiti, e ben certo, nè scarso, intervallo, distinto dal prosaico. O vogliamo dir che il linguaggio prosaico si è diviso esso medesimo dal poetico. Il che propriamente non sarebbe vero; ma e' s'è diviso dall'antico; e così sempre accade che il linguaggio prosaico, insieme coll'ordinario uso della lingua parlata, al quale ei non può fare a meno di somigliarsi, si vada di mano in mano cambiando e allontanando dall'antichità. . . . Ond'è che il linguaggio prosaico si scosti per vero dire esso stesso dal poetico (piuttosto che questo da quello), ma non in quanto poetico, solo in quanto seguace dell'antico, e fermo (quanto più si può) all'antico, da cui il prosaico s'allontana. Del resto, il linguaggio e lo stile delle poesie di Parini, Alfieri, Monti, Foscolo è molto più propriamente e più perfettamente poetico e distinto dal prosaico, che non è quello di verun altro de' nostri poeti, inclusi nominatamente i più classici e sommi antichi.

[73] *Style*, pp. 32-33.

[74] *La poesia e la poetica di G. Leopardi* (Milan, 1949), p. 201.

CHAPTER TEN

[1] See Introduction, *Le Prose di Tasso* Mondadori edition Milan.

[2] *Compendio di storia della letteratura italiana* (3 vols., Florence, 1957), III, 459.

[3] *Saggi di poetica e di poesia* (Florence, 1942), p. 64.

[4] Francesco De Sanctis, *La Letteratura italiana nel secolo XIX*, Vol. III, *Giacomo Leopardi*, ed. Walter Binni (Bari, 1961), p. 16.

[5] De Sanctis, pp. 44-45.

[6] De Sanctis, p. 59.

[7] De Sanctis, p. 117.

[8] De Sanctis, p. 159.

[9] De Sanctis, p. 228.

10 De Sanctis, p. 253.

11 De Sanctis, p. 258.

12 De Sanctis, p. 273.

13 De Sanctis, p. 287.

14 Quoted by G. Goffis, *Leopardi,* Storia della critica Series (Palermo, 1961), p. 41.

15 See his essay on Leopardi in *Poesia e non poesia* (4th ed., Bari, 1946).

16 In this connection it is apt to recall what F. R. Leavis says, while answering René Wellek's criticism that in his dealings with English poetry he should have "made [his] assumptions more explicitly and defended them systematically." "Literary criticism and philosophy," says Leavis, "seem to me to be quite distinct and different kinds of discipline. . . . The reading demanded by poetry is of a different kind from that demanded by philosophy. . . . The business of a literary critic is to attain a peculiar completeness of response and to observe a peculiarly strict relevance in developing his response into commentary; he must be on his guard against abstracting improperly from what is in front of him and against any premature or irrelevant generalizing—of it or from it" (*The Common Pursuit,* pp. 211-13).

17 "Lo scetticismo estetico del Leopardi," *Rivista d'Italia,* XXII (1919), 318-29.

18 *The Philosophy of Santayana,* ed. Irwin Edman (New York, 1936).

19 *Zibaldone,* II, 987.

> Siccome ad essere vero e grande filosofo si richiedono i naturali doni di grande immaginativa e gran sensibilità, quindi segue che i grandi filosofi sono di natura la più antifilosofica che dar si possa quanto alla pratica e all'uso della filosofia nella vita loro, e per lo contrario le più goffe o dure, fredde e antifilosofiche teste sono di natura le più disposte all'esercizio pratico della filosofia. . . . Veramente, siccome la natura trionfa sempre, accade generalmente che i più filosofi per teoria, sono in pratica i meno filosofi, e che i meno disposti alla filosofia teorica, sono i più filosofi nell'effetto.

20 *Selected Criticism,* ed. Richard Rees (Oxford, 1960), p. 210.

21 *La Ronda,* III (1921), 130.

22 "Immagini del Leopardi e nostre," *Nuova antologia,* Feb. 16, 1943, p. 221.

23 "Attualità di Leopardi," *Corriere della sera,* May 30, 1937, p. 3.

[24] *Attraverso lo 'Zibaldone'* (2 vols., Turin, 1944), I, xxx.

[25] In *Attraverso*, I, 944.

[26] For Montale's conception of tradition and diction see, among other writings of his, one of his earliest articles on "Stile e tradizione" in *Il Baretti*, Jan. 15, 1925.

[27] *Poesie e prose*, I, 979.

> Se alcun libro morale potesse giovare, io penso che gioverebbero massimamente i poetici: dico poetici, prendendo questo vocabolo largamente; cioè libri destinati a mouvere la immaginazione; e intendo non meno di prose che di versi. Ora io fo poca stima di quella poesia che letta e meditata, non lascia al lettore nell'animo un tal sentimento nobile, che per mezz'ora, gl'impedisca di ammettere un pensier vile, e di fare un'azione indegna.

[28] Leopardi's view of poetry is historical in a particular way —historical, that is to say, in the sense that it is based on a contrast between ancient and modern times, which makes him classify the whole of poetry into two broad categories, the imaginative and the sentimental. While one may well find details that are questionable in Leopardi's observations on the transition from the imaginative poetry of ancient times to the sentimental poetry of his own time—in the differing poetics that may be discerned as one moves from Homer to Virgil, to Tasso, and on down to Alfieri and Manzoni—yet one may find in his overview a clear picture, adequate for the poet and for the critic, not only of the progress of poetry from Homer onwards during some of its most interesting phases, but also some sort of account, more stimulating and illuminating than systematical or exhaustive, of "the poetics, the currents, the taste, and the sensibility" of different epochs, an account of the sort which as Mario Praz observes may very well replace conventional literary history.

Appendix a

[1] *Zibaldone*, I, 1232.

> Quell'anima che non è aperta se non al vero puro, è capace di poche verità, poco può scoprir di vero, poche verità può conoscere e sentire nel loro vero aspetto, pochi veri e grandi rapporti delle medesime, poco bene può applicare i risultati delle sue osservazioni e ragionamenti.

[2] *Zibaldone*, I, 223.

> L'uomo non vive d'altro che di religione o d'illusioni.

3 *Zibaldone*, I, 1276.

L'immaginazione in gran parte non si diversifica dalla ragione, che pel solo stile, o modo, dicendo le stesse cose.

4 *Zibaldone*, I, 843.

Nessuno è meno filosofo di chi vorrebbe tutto il mondo filosofo, e filosofica tutta la vita umana, che è quanto dire, che non vi fosse più vita al mondo. E pur questo è il desiderio ec. de' filosofastri, anzi della maggior parte de' filosofi presenti e passati.

5 *Zibaldone*, I, 330.

Non è vero che l'uomo naturale sia tormentato da un desiderio infinito precisamente di conoscere. Neanche l'uomo corrotto e moderno si trova in questo caso. . . . L'uomo non desidera di conoscere, ma di sentire infinitamente.

6 *Zibaldone*, I, 219.

Di tecnicismi, di formole, di nozioni astratte e metafisiche, di psicologia, d'ideologia, di storia naturale, di scienza di viaggi, di geografia, di politica, e d'erudizione, scienza, arte, mestiero d'ogni sorta.

7 *Zibaldone*, I, 828.

La poesia, quanto è più filosofica, tanto meno è poesia. . . . La bella letteratura, e massime la poesia, non hanno che fare colla filosofia sottile, severa ed accurata; avendo per oggetto il bello, ch'è quanto dire il falso, perchè il vero (così volendo il tristo fato dell'uomo) non fu mai bello.

8 *Zibaldone*, II, 221-22.

Allontanar dall'uso volgare le voci e frasi comuni, l'infletterle e condizionarle in maniere inusitate al presente, ma dagli antichi nazionali, parlatori, prosatori o poeti usitate.

9 *Zibaldone*, II, 787.

Le idee concomitanti annesse alla significazione o anche al suono stesso e ad altre qualità delle parole, le quali idee hanno tanta parte nell'effetto, massimamente poetico ovvero oratorio ec., delle scritture, ne risulta che necessariamente l'effetto d'una stessa poesia, orazione, verso, frase, espressione, parte qualunque, maggiore o minore, di scrittura, è, massime quanto al poetico, infinitamente vario, secondo gli uditori o lettori, e secondo le occasioni e circostanze anche passeggere e mutabili in cui ciascuno di questi si trova. Perocchè quelle idee concomitanti, indipendentemente ancora affatto dalla parola o frase per se, sono differentissime per mille rispetti, secondo le dette differenze apparte- nenti alle persone.

10 *Zibaldone*, I, 1097.

In sostanza, e per se stessa, la poesia non è legata al verso. E pure fuor del verso, gli ardimenti, le metafore, le immagini, i concetti, tutto bisogna che prenda un carattere più piano, se si vuole sfuggire il disgusto dell'affettazione, e il senso della sconvenienza di ciò che si chiama troppo poetico per la prosa, benchè il poetico, in tutta l'estensione del termine, non includa punto l'idea nè la necessità del verso, nè di veruna melodia.

11 *Zibaldone*, I, 288.

Ogni bellezza principale nelle arti e nello scrivere deriva dalla natura e non dall'affettazione o ricerca . . . si sforza di esprimere il carattere e lo stile altrui, e ripetere il detto di un altro alla maniera e gusto del medesimo.

12 *Zibaldone*, I, 1311.

La perfezion della traduzione consiste in questo, che l'autore tradotto, non sia, per esempio, greco in italiano, greco o francese in tedesco, ma tale in italiano o in tedesco, quale egli è in greco o in francese.

13 *Zibaldone*, I, 305-306.

Perchè l'uomo superficiale, l'uomo che non sa mettere la sua mente nello stato in cui era quella dell'autore; insomma l'uomo che appresso a poco non è capace di pensare colla stessa profondità dell'autore, intende mate- rialmente quello che legge, ma non vede i rapporti che hanno quei detti col vero . . . brevemente, intenderanno appuntino lo scritto, e non capiranno la verità di quello che dice, verità che esisterà realmente.

14 *Zibaldone*, I, 23.

Il poeta quanto più parla in persona propria e quanto più aggiunge di suo, tanto meno imita . . . e . . . il sentimentale non è prodotto dal sentimentale, ma dalla natura, *qual ella è*, e la natura *qual ella è* bisogna imitare, ed hanno imitata gli antichi.

15 *Zibaldone*, I, 1335.

Moltiplicare i modelli, le riflessioni ec. quella specie di maniera o di facoltà, *che si chiama originalità (origi- nalità* quella che si contrae? e che infatti non si possiede mai se non s'è acquistata? . . . Che cosa è dunque l'originalità? facoltà acquisita, come tutte le altre, benchè questo aggiunto di acquisita ripugna dirittamente al significato e valore del suo nome).

16 *Zibaldone*, I, 60-61.

La poesia si sia già ridotta ad arte, in maniera che per essere veramente originale bisogna rompere violare disprezzare lasciare da parte intieramente i costumi e le abitudini e le nozioni di nomi di generi ec. ricevute da tutti, cosa difficile a fare . . . ogni idea ricevuta da ogni forma da ogni consuetudine, e si metta a immaginare una poesia tutta sua propria, senza nessun rispetto, difficilissimamente riesce ad essere veramente originale, o almeno ad esserlo come gli antichi, perchè a ogni momento anche senz'avvedersene, senza volerlo, sdegnandosene ancora, ricadrebbe in quelle forme, in quegli usi, in quelle parti, in quei mezzi, in quegli artifizi, in quelle immagini, in quei generi ec. ec. come un riozzolo d'acqua che corra per un luogo dov'è passata altr'acqua, avete bel distornarlo, sempre tenderà e ricadrà nella strada ch'è restata bagnata dall'acqua precedente. . . . Eschilo per esempio inventando ora una ora un'altra tragedia senza forme senza usi stabiliti, e seguendo la sua natura, variava naturalmente a ogni composizione. Così Omero scrivendo i suoi poemi, vagava liberamente per li campi immaginabili, e sceglieva quello che gli pareva giacchè . . . non avendoci esempi anteriori che glieli circoscrivessero e gliene chiudessero la vista. In questo modo i poeti antichi difficilmente *s'imbattevano a non essere originali,* o piuttosto erano sempre originali, e s'erano simili era caso. Ma ora con tanti usi con tanti esempi, con tante nozioni, definizioni, regole, forme, con tante letture ec. per quanto un poeta si voglia allontanare dalla strada segnata a ogni poco ci ritorna, mentre la natura non opera più da se, sempre naturalmente e necessariamente influiscono sulla mente del poeta le idee acquistate che circoscrivono l'efficacia e della natura e scemano la facoltà inventiva.

17 *Zibaldone,* I, 405.

La massima parte delle immagini e sensazioni indefinite che noi proviamo pure dopo la fanciullezza e nel resto della vita, non sono altro che una rimembranza della fanciullezza, si riferiscono a lei, dipendono e derivano da lei.

18 *Zibaldone,* I, 127.

Perchè in ogni sentimento dolce e sublime entra sempre l'illusione.

[19] *Zibaldone*, I, 156.

Facilissime a concepire illusioni, e facilissime e prontissime a perderle.

[20] *Poesie e prose*, I, 965.

Profonda, fervida e tempestosa . . . funestissima dote, e principio di sollecitudini e angosce gravissime e perpetue . . . ricca, varia, leggera, instabile e fanciullesca; la quale si è larghissima fonte di pensieri ameni e lieti, di errori dolci, di vari diletti e conforti; e il maggiore e più fruttuoso dono di cui la natura sia cortese ad anime vive.

[21] *Zibaldone*, I, 170.

Grave, passionato, ordinariamente (ai nostri tempi) malinconico, profondo nel sentimento e nelle passioni, e tutto proprio a soffrir grandemente della vita. L'altro scherzevole, leggiero, vagabondo, incostante nell'amore, bello spirito, incapace di forti e durevoli passioni e dolori d'animo, facile a consolarsi anche nelle più grandi sventure ec. Riconoscete in questi due caratteri i verissimi ritratti di Dante e di Ovidio, e vedete come la differenza della loro poesia corrisponda appuntino alla differenza della vita.

[22] *Zibaldone*, I, 156.

Quantunque chi non ha provato la sventura non sappia nulla, è certo che l'immaginazione e anche la sensibilità malinconica non ha forza senza un'aura di prosperità, e senza un vigor d'animo che non può stare senza un crepuscolo un raggio un barlume di allegrezza.

[23] *Zibaldone*, I, 38, 160, 381; II, 449.

Un gran poeta deve aver grandi difetti.

Il silenzio è il linguaggio di tutte le forti passioni.

Un uomo perfetto non è mai grande. Un uomo grande non è mai perfetto.

L'immaginazione spinge sempre verso quello che non cade sotto i sensi.

[24] *Zibaldone*, II, 903.

Qualunque poesia o scrittura, o qualunque parte di esse esprime o collo stile o co' sentimenti, il piacere e la voluttà, esprime ancora o collo stile o co' sentimenti formali o con ambedue un abbandono una noncuranza una negligenza una specie di dimenticanza d'ogni cosa. E generalmente non v'ha altro mezzo che questo ad esprimere la voluttà! Tant'è, il piacere non è che un abbandono e un oblio della vita, e una specie di sonno e di morte. Il piacere è piuttosto una privazione o una depressione di sentimento che un sentimento, e molto meno un sentimento vivo. Egli è quasi un'imitazione della insensibilità e della morte, un accostarsi più che si possa allo stato contrario alla vita ed alla privazione di essa, perchè la vita per sua natura è dolore.

25 *Zibaldone*, I, 483.

Si deve inferire quanto sieno importanti le benchè minime impressioni della fanciullezza, e quanto gran parte della vita dipenda da quell'età; e quanto sia probabile che i caratteri degli uomini, le loro inclinazioni, questa o quell'altra azione ec. derivino bene spesso da minutissime circostanze della loro fanciullezza; e come i caratteri ec. e le opinioni massimamente (dalle quali poi dipendono le azioni e quasi tutta la vita) si diversifichino bene spesso per quelle minime circostanze, e accidenti, e differenze appartenenti alla fanciullezza, mentre se ne cercherà la cagione e l'origine in tutt'altro, anche dai maggiori conoscitori dell'uomo.

26 *Zibaldone*, I, 198.

Pare che l'anima nell'addormentarsi deponga i suoi pensieri e immagini d'allora, come deponiamo i vestimenti, in un luogo alla mano e vicinissimo, affine di ripigliarli, subito svegliata.

27 *Zibaldone*, II, 998-99.

Il sommo bene è voluto, desiderato, cercato di necessità . . . ma egli nel volerlo, cercarlo, desiderarlo, non ha mai saputo nè mai saprà che cosa esso sia . . . e ciò perchè il suo sommo bene non esiste in niun modo. Il fine della natura dell'uomo esisterà forse in natura. Ma bisogna ben distinguerlo dal fine cercato dalla natura dell'uomo. Questo fine non esiste in natura, e non può esistere per natura. . . . L'uomo (e così gli altri animali) non nasce per goder della vita, ma solo per perpetuare la vita, per comunicarla ad altri che gli succedano, per conservarla. Nè esso, nè la vita, nè oggetto alcuno di questo mondo è propriamente per lui, ma al contrario esso è tutto per la vita. Spaventevole, ma vera proposizione e conchiusione di tutta la metafisica. L'esistenza non è per l'esistente, non ha per suo fine l'esistente, nè il bene dell'esistente; se anche egli vi prova alcun bene, ciò è un puro caso: l'esistente è per l'esistenza, tutto per l'esistenza, questa è il suo puro fine reale. Gli esistenti esistono perchè si esista, l'individuo esistente nasce ed esiste perchè si continui ad esistere e l'esistenza si conservi in lui e dopo di lui. Tutto ciò è manifesto dal vedere che il vero e solo fine della natura è la conservazione delle specie, e non la conservazione nè la felicità degl'individui; la qual felicità non esiste neppur punto al mondo, nè per gl'individui nè per le specie. Da ciò necessariamente si dee venire in ultimo grado alla generale, sommaria, suprema e terribile conclusione detta di sopra.

Appendix B

1 *Lettere*, p. 197.

La bellezza appena è mai che si trovi insieme colla virtù, non ostante che sembri compagna e sorella.

2 *Zibaldone*, II, 334.

3 *Zibaldone*, II, 335.

Oggetti visibili, della quale ognun vede la verità o la falsità, onde le idee del bello e del brutto pittorico e scultorio, in quanto queste arti sono imitative, è già determinata in ciascheduno prima dell'assuefazione.

4 *Zibaldone*, I, 263-64.

Molte cose possono esser così semplici che quasi non abbiano parti. E il bello morale, e tutto quel bello che non appartiene ai sensi, non ha parti. Ma la convenienza della cosa si considera anche rispetto alle relazioni del tutto, o delle parti coll'estrinseco: per esempio, coll'uso, col fine, coll'utilità, col luogo, col tempo, con ogni sorta di circostanza, coll'effetto che produce o deve produrre ec. Una spada con una gemma sulla punta, la qual gemma corrispondesse perfettamente all'ornato, alle proporzioni, alla configurazione, alla materia del resto, a ogni modo sarebbe brutta. Questa bruttezza non è scovenienza di parti, non di una parte coll'altre, ma di una parte col suo uso o fine. Di questo genere sono infinite bruttezze o bellezze tanto sensibili, che intelligibili, morali, letterarie ec.

5 *Zibaldone*, I, 259.

Un volto o una persona difettosa ma viva, graziosa ec. o fornita di un animo capriccioso, sensibili ec. sorprende, riscalda, affetta e tocca il capriccio di chi la riguarda, senza regola, senza esattezza, senza ragione ec. ec. e così le grandi passioni nascono per lo più dal capriccio, dallo straordinario ec. e non si ponno giustificare colla ragione.

6 *Zibaldone*, I, 890-91.

Lo stile dei trecentisti ci piace sommamente perchè sappiamo ch'era proprio di quell'età. Se lo vediamo fedelissimamente ritratto in uno scrittore moderno, ancorchè non differisca punto dall'antico, non ci piace, anzi ci disgusta, e ci pare affettatissimo, perchè sappiamo che non è naturale allo scrittore, sebben ciò dallo scritto non apparisca per nulla.

7 *Zibaldone*, I, 209.

La grazia ordinariamente consiste nel movimento: e diremo così, la bellezza è nell'istante, e la grazia nel tempo.

8 *Zibaldone*, II, 1229.

Il brutto nel bello. Il brutto nel brutto, e il bello puro, sono medesimamente alieni dalla grazia.

9 *Zibaldone*, I, 1211.

E mal sarebbe accolto quel poeta che personificando, per esempio, un monte gli attribuisse qualità o sensi delicati ec. o che attribuisse della grandezza a qualunque soggetto da lui descritto o trattato come grazioso o delicato.

10 *Zibaldone*, I, 4.

Non il Bello ma il Vero o sia l'imitazione della Natura qualunque si è l'oggetto delle Belle arti.

11 *Zibaldone*, I, 1519-20.

Gli uomini semplici e naturali sono molto più dilettati e trovano molto più grazioso il colto, lo studiato, e anche l'affettato che il semplice e il naturale. Per lo contrario non v'è qualità nè cosa più graziosa per gli uomini civili e colti che il semplice e il naturale, voci che nelle nostre lingue e ne' nostri discorsi sono bene spesso sinonime di grazioso. . . . Grazioso non è altro che lo straordinario in quanto straordinario, appartenente al bello, dentro i termini della convenienza. Il troppo semplice non è grazioso.

Bibliographical Essay

IN PROPORTION to the total amount of what has been written on Leopardi as a poet, what has been written on him as a critic and as a theorist of poetry is conspicuously meager. What follows is the essential—the word "essential" has to be remembered—bibliography of things written on Leopardi—both in Italy and, even though to a very limited extent, elsewhere—exclusively or mainly as a critic and as a theorist of poetry. And in so far as Leopardi's poetic theory is largely to be found in *Zibaldone* whatever concerns this work directly or indirectly also concerns that theory, and as such, it justifies its place in the specialized kind of bibliography that the present one is. When not quoted, the place of publication is Florence.

Bibliographies

The following are the chief bibliographic studies of Leopardi and his work: *Bibliografia leopardiana,* vol. I (to 1898), ed. G. Mazzatinti and M. Menghini (1931), vol. II (1898-1930), ed. G. Natali (1932), vol. III (1931-1951), ed. G. Natali and G. Musumarra (1953); E. Bigi, "G. Leopardi," *I classici italiani nella storia della critica,* ed. W. Binni (1955); Umberto

Bosco, *Repertorio bibliografico della letteratura italiana,* vol. I (1948-1949) (1953), vol. II (1950-1953) (1960); Lanfranco Caretti, *Avviamento allo studio della letteratura italiana* (1953); *Catalogo del fondo leopardiano* of the Biblioteca Comunale of Milan (Milan, 1958); G. Doro, "Bibliografia leopardiana (1928-1929)," *Aevum,* IV (1930); N. D. Evola, "Bibliografia leopardiana (1935-1939)," *Aevum,* XV (1941); R. Frattarolo, *Studi leopardiani (1940-1949)* (Rome, 1950); Alberto Frattini, "Studi leopardiani del dopoguerra," *Convivium,* no. 1 (January-February, 1952); G. Fucilla, *Retrospettiva: pagine dimenticate di bibliografia leopardiana* (Catanzaro, 1937); *Notizie introduttive e sussidi bibliografici,* vol. 2 (Milan, 2nd ed., 1958); *Bibliografia analitica leopardiana (1952-1960),* ed. A. Torotoreto (1963).

Editions of Leopardi's Works

The most up-to-date and authoritative edition of Leopardi's complete works is *Tutte le opere di Giacomo Leopardi,* edited in five volumes by Francesco Flora and published in Milan: Vol. I-II, *Le poesie e le prose* (1940); Vol. III-IV, *Zibaldone di pensieri* (1937-1938); Vol. V, *Lettere* (1949). Other editions of Leopardi's works are: *Opere di Giacomo Leopardi,* ed. Antonio Ranieri, 2 vols. (1845); *Epistolario di Giacomo Leopardi,* ed. F. Moroncini (1934-1942); *Pensieri di varia filosofia e di bella letteratura,* 7 vols. (1898-1900); *Zibaldone,* ed. Giuseppe De Robertis (1922); selections from *Zibaldone,* ed. Vitaliano Brancati, *Società,*

lingua e letteratura d'Italia (1816-1832) (Milan, 1941);
Attraverso lo Zibaldone (selections from *Zibaldone*),
ed. Valentino Piccoli (Turin, 1944); *Opere,* containing
*Canti, Paralipomeni alla Batracomiomachia, Operette
Morali, Pensieri,* ed. Sergio Solmi (Milan-Naples,
1956); *Operette Morali,* ed. G. Gentile (Bologna,
1918); *Operette Morali,* ed. M. Porena (Milan, 1921);
Operette Morali, ed. V. Piccoli (Turin, 1924); *Operette
Morali,* ed. M. Fubini (1933); *Lettere,* ed. M. Capucci
(1958); *Canti,* ed. F. Flora (Milan, 1937).

Studies and Articles on
Leopardi's Theory of Poetry and Criticism

Among the earliest studies of *Zibaldone,* that is soon
after its publication in 1898-1900, the most considerable and analytic interpretation is by Bonaventura
Zumbini (see especially vol. II, chapter 4) in *Studi
sul Leopardi,* 2 vols. (1902-1904), who calls *Zibaldone*
"an immense repertoire of scientific material in the
largest sense of the term." Emilio Bertana's 90-page
article "La mente di Giacomo Leopardi in alcuni suoi
pensieri di bella letteratura italiana e di estetica," in
Giornale storico della letteratura italiana, XLIV (1904),
193-283, deals, with analytical thoroughness, with the
various aspects of Leopardi's poetic, literary, aesthetic,
and linguistic theory, considering him as a "convinced
modernist and liberal," endowed with "an indomitable
energy of critical temperament." Romualdo Giani's
L'Estetica nei "Pensieri" di Giacomo Leopardi (Turin,
1904; 2nd ed., revised and corrected, 1929), elaborately

discusses, on the basis of extensive quotations from *Zibaldone,* Leopardi's thought in its multifold aspects —aesthetic, moral and philosophical—together with its source and the nature of its inspiration and implications. The only weak point of this book is that it tends to overstress the links—wherever there are links —between one thought or chain of thoughts and another or to create them where there are none, so as to give one the impression that Leopardi was systematically developing an organic theory. The corrective to this rather misleading tendency is to be found, among other things, in Mario Fubini's review of Giani's book (*Leonardo,* 1928) and in Clemente Rebora's article "Per un Leopardi mal noto," in *Rivista d'Italia,* September, 1910, pp. 373-439, where, while discussing Leopardi's love of music, the writer points out the advantages of Leopardi's having "suffered" rather than "systematized" his thought and philosophy. In his scathing, though not always justifiable, criticism of Carducci, Pascoli, and D'Annunzio, Enrico Thovez in his *Il Pastore, il gregge e la zampogna* (Naples, 1916) exalts Leopardi as being, together with Dante, over and above every other writer in Latin and Italian literature from Horace to Carducci, chiefly because of his "verbal nudity which dazzles one into tears." Thovez's rather exaggerated enthusiasm for Leopardi was nonetheless an important signal that set into motion a healthy reaction against D'Annunzio and indirectly heralded the new poetic idiom. See also Thovez's article "Giacomo Leopardi avvenirista," in *Il Corriere della Sera,* 22 November 1903, pp. 1-2, which is a review of R. Giani's *L'Estetica nei "Pensieri" di Giacomo Leopardi* and Umberto Bosco's article "Leopardi, Thovez e i Crepuscolari," in *Convivium*, May-June, 1936, pp. 263-72, reprinted in *Realismo Romantico* (Rome, 1959), for Leopardi's influence on modern Italian poetry.

Giuseppe Antonio Borgese's *Storia della critica romantica in Italia* (Milan, 1949; originally published in Naples, 1905) questions the authenticity of Leopardi's classicism, both in his poetry and poetic theory, and contrasts it with the essentially and uniformly romantic nature of his creative inspiration and temperament. Borgese's criticism is to be taken with a grain of salt and to be evaluated in the light of other, more balanced approaches and views regarding Leopardi's classicism-romanticism. For instance, in his monumental study *Leopardi* (Munich, 1923; Italian trans. Tomasco Gnoli, Naples, 1925) the German scholar-critic Karl Vossler attributes to Leopardi (in the chapter entitled "L'Estetica del Leopardi") in spite of the latter's numerous contradictions, "a pregnant truth, something like a new aesthetic in which the classic-romantic contrasts are overcome or eliminated." Vossler's is a very lucid and illuminating comment on the nature and importance of Leopardi's aesthetic thought, to be compared—and in certain respects, contrasted—with Fubini's essay "L'Estetica e la critica letteraria nei "Pensieri" di Giacomo Leopardi," in *Giornale storico della letteratura italiana*, XCVII (1931), 241-81. Fubini's article is, on the whole, one of the key evaluations of the critical, literary, historical, and aesthetic merit of Leopardi's poetics as found in *Zibaldone*. While denying, along more or less Crocean lines, that there is in *Zibaldone* any "original coherent aesthetic thought" or a "systematic critique" of those ideas and concepts of others like Aristotle or Madame de Staël, which Leopardi, with a rather superior quality of insight, perception, and breadth as well as depth of vision made his own, Fubini finds in *Zibaldone* "some motives of thought and sentiment which contributed to the dissolution of the old taste and criticism and to the formation of the new" as well as the lofty consciousness of the nature of poetry conceived "not as a delightful art, but as an exaltation of what is noblest and . . . divinest in us." In Fubini's *Romanticismo italiano* (Bari, 1953) the cultural milieu of Leopardi's early and late life is aptly described. Another distinguished Leopardian critic, Walter Binni, in his *La Poetica del Decadentismo* (1936), sets Leopardi's merit as a poet and as the father of modern poetry against that of Pascoli and D'Annunzio. Leopardi's vital pessimism is contrasted with Pascoli's morbid pessimism and the reason for the difference is justly supposed to lie in the different poetic theories expounded by Leopardi and Pascoli. For a comparison and relation as well as contrast between Leopardi and Pascoli with regard to their attitudes to poetry and to what they considered to be the best method of achieving poetic effects, see Vittorio Sereni's interesting article "Pascoli e Leopardi," in *Il Verri*, II (1958). See also Binni's *La nuova poetica leopardiana* (1947; 2nd ed., 1962) in which he relates, with a subtle and convincing power, the development of Leopardi's lyric poetry (from its early idyllic stage to its later and maturer philosophical stage) to the thought processes as described in *Zibaldone*—thought processes that specially concern the theory and nature of poetry. He recognizes, together with De Sanctis, that "the heroic ethics is the most poetic part of the Leopardian thought" which is just another way of asserting the Arnoldian truth that poetry as art and poetry as the criticism of life are, if not one and the same thing, then certainly inseparable.

In his University lectures *La Poesia e la poetica del Leopardi* (Milan, 1949) the late Francesco Flora deals in the first part with the nature, origin, and implications of Leopardi's theory of poetry, describing with remarkable lucidity and penetration what Leopardi's ideal of poetry was and how he consummately succeeded in realizing it. Flora evaluates this achievement in its direct relation with Leopardi's poetics and sees both poetry and poetics in their proper historical perspective and relevance. In his *Saggi di poetica moderna (dal Tasso al surrealismo)* (Messina, 1949), Flora attributes to Leopardi the poetic theorist the Baudelairean faculty—a faculty which is clearly seen in its full operation in *Zibaldone*—of discovering "what we would call today the analogy of things," and yet Leopardi is considered to be more lucid and more openminded than a Mallarmé or a Rimbaud or any hermetic poet, who has been virtually anticipated by Leopardi, in so far as certain fundamental aspects of poetic theory are concerned. Flora's *Leopardi e la letteratura francese* (Milan, 1947) may be consulted for a lucid and balanced discussion of the French source of Leopardian thought as well as of the degree of independence and originality in that thought itself in spite of its largely derivative character.

In his *Saggio sul Leopardi* (Milan-Rome, 1937; 4th ed., Florence, 1960), Giuseppe De Robertis analytically expounds as well as interprets the various channels—aesthetic, moral, philosophical, and linguistic—into which Leopardi's thought runs and relates them with his achievement as a poet. In *Studi* (1944), in the chapter devoted to "*Lo Zibaldone*," De Robertis talks of "the faithful mirror" which *Zibaldone* is and wherein Leopardi "loved best to talk of and with himself." See also the chapter "Leopardi romanziere" which describes the influence of Ugo Foscolo's *Le Ultime Lettere di Jacopo Ortis* on *Zibaldone*. In *Viaggio col Leopardi nell'Italia letteraria* (Milan, 1943), Giulio Natali discusses Leopardi's claim to critical originality made by De Robertis (see above) and by Vitaliano Brancati in his introduction to selections from *Zibaldone* published in *Società, lingua e letteratura* (Milan, 1941) and finds himself less inclined to admit that Leopardi's thought and criticism were really so original. In *Divagazioni leopardiane* (vols. V and VI, Pavia, 1894-1899) by Giovanni Negri, too, there is an elaborate attempt to evaluate and criticize Leopardi's pronouncements on Italian literary epochs and authors from Dante and *il Trecento*, to Foscolo and *l'Ottocento*. Fernando Figurelli, in his long analytical and evaluative essay on "*Il Discorso intorno alla poesia romantica* e la prima formulazione dell'estetica e della poetica del Leopardi," in *Giornale storico della letteratura italiana,* CXXVII (1950), 381-433, traces the historical and the literary circumstances in which Leopardi composed this essay and the relation it bears to *Zibaldone.* While lacking in "clarity and logical order of thought" or in "precise formulation of concepts" the *Discorso,* together with *Zibaldone,* attests to Leopardi's "acutest poetic sensibility" coupled with his "almost infallible taste in poetry." In his *Studio sul Leopardi* (1952) Francesco Biondolillo devotes a 34-page essay to Leopardi's poetics, in which he points out that Leopardi's criticism did not have "large perspectives" because his view of poetry was determined and even biased by the idyllic poetry he himself wrote. Biondolillo's own view of Leopardi's poetry is patently limited in so far as he takes account merely of the idyllic poetry in Leopardi, which is not all and which leaves out the philosophical poetry of "La Ginestra" and other poems.

It is, however, in Vincenzo Cardarelli's critical work and articles more than anywhere else that one finds an exalted and at the same time an authoritative affirmation of Leopardi's critical and philosophical as well as poetic and scholarly greatness and originality. One of the coeditors of *La Ronda,* Cardarelli published in its third number a very copious selection of passages from *Zibaldone* entitled "Il testamento letterario di Giacomo Leopardi" with a brilliantly frank and acute introduction. "No poetry after that of Dante has been so intensely lived" as that of Leopardi and consequently his poetic and critical thought merits more attention and respect than has been paid to it by Croce and his followers. Cardarelli justly points out that there is "an intrinsic order and apparent disorder in *Zibaldone*" and that it is the *Zibaldone* that has finally "liberated Italy from the too long and too acid an interference of Crocianism." All the important articles by Cardarelli are included in *Opere Complete*, ed. Giuseppe Raimondi (Milan, 1962).

Though not a literary critic in the professional sense of the term, Vladimiro Arangio-Ruiz too defends Leopardi, in *Grandezza di Leopardi* (originally published in *Civiltà Moderna*, July-October, 1938, pp. 229-60; 2nd rev. ed., Florence, 1947, in "Collana critici" series), against Croce's charge that because his life was something "suffocated" (strozzata), Leopardi was not really qualified to meditate on and arrive at sound conclusions about the nature of life as well as of poetry. "Everything in the world is nothing (nulla) including my own despair," said Leopardi; it is, says Arangio-Ruiz, "for one who understands it, the highest word"; for Leopardi "lived truly, lived as only very few really succeeded in living." Though not a philosopher in the Crocean sense of the term, Leopardi has a philosophy which is equivalent to "highest meditation . . . miraculously transformed and modulated into song," so that even though Croce mistakes "that creative and evocative force" for "delicacy and grace," from no poet, not even from Dante, has Italy "received a greater gift than the one she has received from her most unhappy and, at the same time, her happiest poet."

Croce replied to Arangio-Ruiz in "Polemica con Vladimiro Arangio-Ruiz," *La Critica,* XXX (1932), and in his essay on Leopardi in *Poesia e non Poesia* (4th rev. ed., Bari, 1946), he speaks of Leopardi's "pseudo-filosofia"—"Leopardi does not offer any but scattered observations, which are not deeply searched into or systematized; for he was lacking in the speculative disposition and preparation, and not even in the theory of poetry or art, on which he was so often led to meditate, did he achieve anything new or important." Croce's condemnation of the philosophical value of Leopardi's observations in the *Zibaldone,* including those on the art and nature of poetry, may be contrasted with, as in part at least it was a reaction against, the exaltation of the same by the Rondists and by others such as Giuseppe Rensi, whose article "Lo scetticismo estetico del Leopardi," in *Rivista d'Italia,* XXIII (1919), 318-29, considers Leopardi as being not only "our great poet, but also . . . our great philosopher." See also the same author's *Lineamenti di filosofia scettica* (Bologna, 1918), *La scepsi estetica* (Bologna, 1919), and *L'orma di Protagora* (Milan, 1920), especially the preface to the latter.

Luciano Anceschi's *Le poetiche del Novecento in Italia* (Milan, 1962) is a fundamentally useful book in considering the degree and forms of impact Leopardi's theory of poetry made on modern theories of poetry. In Anceschi's book he quotes very important and very relevant observations from other critics in order to bring out the true validity and significance of his thesis. For instance, he quotes De Robertis as saying, what might have also been said in precisely the same terms by the English critic F. R. Leavis and what is so relevant to any discussion of the value of Leopardi's *Zibaldone,* especially in the light of Croce's criticism, that "in order to create new criticism one does not need diverse aesthetic theories so much as sensibility" and that "only *Zibaldone* bears witness to the presence of an engagement ready to recognize in the problem of style a problem of high morality." Thus Felice Momigliano too in his article "Giacomo Leopardi e l'anima moderna," in *Emporium,* VII (1898), recognized quite early, even before the publication of *Zibaldone,* that "Leopardi is undoubtedly the profoundest psychological poet of our time."

The pioneering character of Leopardi's poetic theory is also brought out by the following works: Natalino Sapegno, *Compendio della letteratura italiana,* 3 vols. (1942); Pietro Bava, "Leopardi e la poesia europea," *Comune di Torino,* November, 1937, pp. 46-49; Francesco Biondolillo, "Attualità di Leopardi," *Quadrivio,* 22 August 1937, p. 8; Arnoldo Bocelli, "Giacomo Leopardi e il suo mito," *La Stampa,* 22 February 1939, pp. 3-4, "Leopardi e i moderni," *Lavoro nuovo,* 13 June 1951, "Leopardi e la letteratura del '900," *Risorgimento liberale,* 9 May 1948, p. 3, and "Fortuna di Leopardi," *Il Mondo,* 8 January 1957, p. 8; Emilio Cecchi, "Attualità de Leopardi," *Corriere della sera,* 30 May 1937, p. 3, and "Leopardi e noi,"

Il Marzocco, 13 August 1911; and Adriano Tilgher, "Leopardi e il nostro tempo," *Il Secolo la sera,* 28 June 1937, p. 3.

In the "Storia della critica" series edited by Giuseppe Petronio (Palermo, 1961), volume 21 is devoted to Leopardi. Edited by Cesare Goffis, it contains a critical-cum-historical review of criticism written on Leopardi from the earliest times to our own day, a very usefully selected bibliography, and an anthology of the critical essays and notes on Leopardi by thirty eminent Leopardian scholars and critics, including Francesco De Sanctis, Bonaventura Zumbini, Giovanni Gentile, Karl Vossler, Mario Fubini, Giuseppe De Robertis, Francesco Flora, Walter Binni, and Umberto Bosco. See also P. Mazzamento's *Rassegna bibliografico-critica della letteratura italiana* (2nd ed., 1953), which contains a long critical outline of Leopardian criticism and interpretation.

Valentino Piccoli's introduction to his selections from *Zibaldone, Attraverso lo Zibaldone,* 2 vols. (Turin, 1944), is a stimulating account of the essential nature of the kind of thought found in *Zibaldone,* which is regarded as a "vast spiritual autobiography" —"no writing" being "more important for the purpose of making us know Leopardi"—in which every thought is an integral whole by itself, "a small organic monad of the Leopardian thought that cannot by any means be broken."

In the second volume *Galileo a D'Annunzio* of *I Classici italiani nella nostra storia della critica* (1955), edited by Walter Binni, Emilio Bigi traces the critical fortune of Leopardi in Italy, undertaking a critical examination of what has so far been written on the various aspects of his work. Carmine Jannaco in his book *Filologia e critica nella letteratura italiana* (1953) discusses the grounds and the significance of Leopardi's antiromanticism and aesthetic naturalism and shows how they both culminated in a new kind of romanticism at once more profound and more human, more sincere and more universal, so that in whatever he wrote or meditated on there is an unfailing implicit or explicit sense of "the universality, the eternal contemporaneity of poetry." In *Poetica e cultura del romanticismo* (Rome, 1962), Mario Puppo compares Leopardi's poetics with that of Foscolo and traces the development of Leopardi's views on poetry from the *Discorso di un italiano intorno alla poesia romantica* to *Zibaldone*. Leopardi's poetics is regarded as the poetics of "an irrationalist impregnated with rationality." In his *La poetica dell'ermetismo italiano* (Turin, 1955), Mario Petrucciani studies and analyzes the nature of "the contacts between Leopardi and hermetism" and warns against exaggerating their importance. G. I. Lopriore, on the other hand, in his *Storia della letteratura italiana* (Lucca, 1958) finds in Leopardi's treatment of the question of "the origins of the vernacular languages and literatures" "the undeniable merit of having so decisively and clearly formulated a historiographic concept which we moderns even today . . . consider to be legitimately and solidly our own."

Among the moderns one of the most sensitive critics of Leopardi's art, Piero Bigongiari, in his *Leo-*

pardi (1962), containing his earlier criticism on Leopardi, such as *L'Elaborazione della lirica leopardiana* (1937), correlates the development of the Leopardian lyric in its external as well as internal forms with the development of Leopardi's poetic philosophy as found, above all, in *Zibaldone*. Relevant passages from *Zibaldone* are quoted, as well as references to it made by others, with a view to illustrating, interpreting, and corroborating the inner character of the motives and inspiration that went to the making of particular Leopardian lyrics. *Zibaldone* is thus seen to embody an "analytic experience of facts attested to by thought in action." Sergio Solmi, on the other hand, in his penetrating, well-balanced, and solid preface to his edition of Leopardi's *Opere* (Milan-Naples, 1956), establishes the connection between Leopardi's thought, studies, meditation, and even translations on the one hand, and the concrete essence in which all this transforms and embodies itself in Leopardi's poetry on the other. Solmi justly calls Leopardi "one of our most concrete moralists and investigators of men."

In this context of the interrelationship between Leopardi's thought and poetry, life and literature, Giovanni Gentile's *Poesia e filosofia di Giacomo Leopardi* (1939) may also be consulted as well as his review of Francesco Flora's edition of *Zibaldone* "*Lo Zibaldone* di Giacomo Leopardi," in *Giornale critico della filosofia italiana*, March-April, 1938. Other notable works on the same subject are: Giulio Augusto Levi, *Storia del pensiero di Giacomo Leopardi* (Turin, 1911); Giovanni Bertacchi, *Un maestro di vita* (Bologna, 1917); Pasquale Gatti, *Esposizione del sistema filosofico di Giacomo Leopardi*, 2 vols. (1906); Manfredi Porena, *Il Pessimismo di Giacomo Leopardi* (Genoa-Naples, 1923); Angelandrea Zoltoli, *Leopardi: Storia di un'anima* (Bari, 1927); Cesare Luparini, *Filosofi vecchi e nuovi* (1947); Alberto Frattini, *Il Problema dell'esistenza in Leopardi* (Milan, 1950); Riccardo Bacchelli, "L'illuminismo in Leopardi e Manzoni," *La cultura illuministica in Italia* (Turin, 1957); Lorenzo Giusso, *Leopardi e le sue ideologie* (1935); Adriano Tilgher, *La filosofia di Leopardi* (Rome, 1940); Giuseppe Citanna, "Giacomo Leopardi," *Il romanticismo e la poesia italiana* (Bari, 1935; 2nd ed., 1949).

A selection from other miscellaneous books, monographs, and articles that may be indirectly useful in the study of this particular aspect of Leopardi's work —namely his theory of poetry—and that are both useful and important in considering Leopardi's work as a whole would be: Walter Binni (ed.), *Giacomo Leopardi*, vol. III of Francesco De Sanctis, *La letteratura italiana nel secolo XIX* (Bari, 1953); G. Calogero, *Estetica, Semantica, Istorica* (Turin, 1947); Attilio Momigliano, "Il Carteggio di Leopardi," *Cinque Saggi* (1945); Ginafranco Contini, "Implicazioni leopardiane," *Letteratura*, n. 33 (1947); Emilio Bigi, "Tono e tecnica delle *Operette Morali*," in *Belfagor* (1950); J. H. Whitfield, *Giacomo Leopardi* (Oxford, 1954); René Wellek, *A History of Modern Criticism*, 4 vols. (New Haven, 1955); Giacomo Barzellotti, "Giacomo

Leopardi fu classico o romantico?" *Nuova Antologia*
(Rome, 1917); Geoffrey L. Bickersteth, *Leopardi and
Wordsworth* (London, 1927); Vittore Branca, "Dallo
Zibaldone ai *Canti*," *L'Osservatore Romano*, 9 August
1941; V. Bucci, "Leopardi e la critica," *Il Corriere
della sera*, 6 January 1924; A. Crispo d'Asdia, *Il pen-
siero estetico di Giacomo Leopardi* (Palermo, 1925);
G. Pulleni, *Le poetiche dell'Ottocento* (Padua, 1959);
Giuseppe Ungaretti, "'L'Angelo Mai' del Leopardi,"
La Fiera letteraria, 11 April 1946, "Immagini del Leo-
pardi e nostre," *Nuova Antologia*, 16 February 1943,
"Secondo discorso su Leopardi," *Paragone*, October,
1950; Enrico Bevilacqua, "Leopardi e la critica," *Nuova
Antologia*, 16 September 1930; Libero Bigiaretti, "Lo
Zibaldone di Leopardi," *Augustea*, August, 1937;
Martino Capucci, "*I Paralipomeni* e la poetica leo-
pardiana, "*Convivium*, September-October,1954; Fran-
co Ciarlantini, "Modernità di Leopardi," *Augustea*,
August, 1937; Riccardo Dusi, "Recensione a A. Crispo
d'Asdia, Il pensiero estetico di Giacomo Leopardi," in
Giornale storico della letteratura italiana, LXXXVI
(1925); "Recensione a R. Giani, L'estetica nei *Pensieri*
di Giacomo Leopardi," in *Giornale storico della letteratura italiana*, XCIII (1929); Alberto Frattini, "Il
più moderno dei nostri classici," *Il Messaggero*, 22
November 1956; Remy de Gourmont, *Promenades
philosophiques* (Paris, 1905-1908); Ferdinando Neri,
"Il pensiero del Rousseau nelle prime chiose dello
Zibaldone," *Giornale storico della letteratura italiana*,
LXX (1917).

Index

Index

Sartre, Jean Paul, 275
Sbarbaro, Camillo, 254, 255
Scalvini, G., 236
Schopenhauer, Arthur, 273
Science, and poetry, 35, 36, 44, 45
Sensations, 93
Sensibility, 3, 4, 7, 15, 17, 32, 33, 34, 41, 69, 112, 114
Sentiment, 51, 52, 66, 67, 74, 82, 83, 108
Sévigné, Madame de, 195
Shakespeare, William, 4, 60, 85, 149
Shapiro, Karl, 143
Shelley, Percy Bysshe, 6, 7, 9, 21, 69, 71, 78, 79, 123, 161; *Adonais*, 7; *Defense of Poetry*, 7, 21, 69; *Prometheus Unbound*, 7
Sinisgalli, Leonardo, 257
Smith, James, 244
Solmi, Sergio, 255
Sophocles, 4
Southey, Robert, 24, 29
Spettatore, 21
Stoabeus, 16
Style, 1, 13, 14, 20, 26
Sublimity, 82
Suffering, and poetry, 58, 59, 60, 61, 62, 70, 71, 72, 73
Synonyms, 213, 214

Tasso, Torquato, 8, 102, 105, 118, 233, 234, 271; *Discorso dell'Arte Poetica*, 8, 233; *Gerusalemme Liberata*, 233
Tennyson, Alfred, 60, 161
Theocritus, 17, 288
Thompson, Francis, 161
Thoreau, Henry David, 245
Thovez, Enrico, 250

Tillotson, Geoffrey, 6, 72, 198, 201, 208, 213
Tommaseo, Niccolò, 236
Tradition, 4
Tragic sense, 61, 62
Truth, and poetry, 36, 86, 98

Unamuno, A., 275
Ungaretti, Giuseppe, 236, 250, 253, 256

Vedantic philosophy, 120
Vico, Giambattista, 42, 44, 107, 129, 185
Virgil, 4, 24, 66, 67, 82, 105, 147, 160, 168, 173, 176, 224, 228, 238; *Aeneid*, 66, 67, 82
Voltaire, 24, 48, 190, 290; *La Henriade*, 190
Vossler, K., 97, 122, 156

Wellek, René, 168
Whitman, Walt, 55; *Leaves of Grass*, 55
Wilde, Oscar, 1, 70
Winters, Yvor, 252
Wordsworth, William, 1, 6, 9, 10, 28, 29, 31, 47, 48, 49, 52, 73, 87, 88, 89, 115, 123, 128, 152, 161, 163, 165, 166, 196, 203, 205, 208, 216, 221, 224, 252; *Lines Written a Few Miles above Tintern Abbey*, 115; *The Prelude*, 203

Xenophon, 216

Yates, William Butler, 43

Zanchini, Orazio, 141
Zumbini, Bonaventura, 241

G. SINGH, the author of this book, is Reader in English at the Università Commerciale Luigi Bocconi in Milan. He has received undergraduate and graduate training in his native India and has since taken a Ph.D. from the University of London and Dott. Lett. degrees from the Universities of Bologna and Milan. His earlier studies of Leopardi have appeared in Italy, Sweden, and Finland.

LEOPARDI AND THE THEORY OF POETRY was composed and printed in the Division of Printing at the University of Kentucky. It was set in Linotype Caledonia and printed on Warren Old Style antique wove paper. It was bound by the C. J. Krehbiel Company in Interlaken Arco Linen bookcloth.